THE FOUR TRIALS OF HENRY FORD

Gregory R. Piché

Published by Open Books

Interior design by Siva Ram Maganti

Cover images Henry Ford driving the 1896 Quadricycle, Courtesy: The Henry Ford Museum and Court Room No. 1, Wayne County Building, Detroit, Courtesy: Detroit Photographic Co.

ISBN-13: 978-1948598248

Contents

Introduction

THERE ONCE WAS AN upcoming election year for the Presidency of the United States. Among the candidates jockeying for position was a billionaire businessman. He was largely financing his own campaign and relying on his ability to master public media in unconventional ways to build up public support with a focus primarily in the rural areas of America. He planned to run an unorthodox campaign, on the cheap, by relying in large part on free media exposure. This candidate was known for outlandish statements to the media that were frequently and demonstrably false and appealed to the darker instincts of the rural population. He was prone to exaggeration and hyperbole.

He embraced overt appeals to bigotry and a strictly Nativist, "America First" doctrine championing isolationism and his ability to create jobs. The candidate, a teetotaler, was renowned for his sharp elbows in the business world. He was a well-known, thin-skinned, full-on narcissist, obsessed with his own image and success. He lacked personal empathy, except when there was something in it for himself.

This candidate had business interests in many countries and had a particular fondness for regimes run by strong, authoritarian men. He gratefully accepted accolades from totalitarian dictators. He used his great wealth to bully those who provided goods and services to his enterprises. While initially using the American legal system to advance his business and personal objectives, he was eventually consumed by it over a period of fifteen years.

The candidate was Henry Ford. "Every detached observer who

has studied the career of Henry Ford and knows the requirements of the greatest of offices at this juncture in the affairs of humanity must shudder at the thought of this man being in control of our national destinies... He is the victim of great gusts of passion as sudden and terrible as those which break over the tropics. What havoc will such storms wreck in the executive mansion?"—Oswald Garrison Villard.[1]

The question on many people's minds, then, was whether a wealthy but ignorant narcissist could competently and effectively serve as the President of the United States. The safe bet answer was "no."

---

1. *The Nation*, May 30, 1923

Preface

ON OCTOBER 21, 1929, just days before the start of the Great Depression, President Herbert Hoover stepped off a train traveling from Washington, D.C. to Detroit, Michigan, where he and his wife were met by Henry Ford and Thomas Edison. President Hoover arrived to attend a celebration in Dearborn, Michigan, recognizing the Fiftieth Anniversary of Edison's invention of the first commercially-successful incandescent electric light bulb. The day was dark and foreboding, with a torrential rain falling like a tropical monsoon.

The Hoovers first drove to downtown Detroit in an open car shielded from the elements only by raincoats, hats and a covering wool blanket across their laps. At the Detroit City Hall, the President made a public radio address while standing in the deluge. They then returned to Dearborn where Ford's Greenfield Village was still under construction, gleaming rows of newly transferred and reconstructed historic buildings, with visitors gingerly wandering from exhibit to exhibit with open umbrellas poised as they negotiated through the mud.

Later that evening, the Hoovers attended a gala dinner at the Henry Ford Museum, a model representing Independence Hall in Philadelphia, still partially under construction. There were many luminaries in attendance to help mark the event including Madam Marie Curie, Walter Chrysler, George Eastman, Andrew Mellon, Adolph Ochs, John D. Rockefeller, Jr., Charles Schwab, and even Orville Wright. Will Rogers, one of the speakers at the dinner, took the occasion to address Henry Ford: "It will take us a hundred years to tell whether you have helped or hurt us. But you certainly didn't leave us where you found us."

While a hundred years have not quite passed, we are getting close. And Henry Ford certainly did not leave us where he found us. Whether you believe Mr. Ford was a genius, an oracle, a hero, a visionary, or a self-absorbed autocrat, there can be little question that he has had an enormous impact on the industrial development of the twentieth and the twenty-first centuries that continues to play out. Henry Ford, the man, had many different traits, not all of them helpful or laudatory. Prior to 1929, he was personally and directly involved in a number of major lawsuits, each of which underscored the perplexing duality of the man and his character.

By examining those trials, we may unshroud the maddeningly mysterious personality and character of Henry Ford. He was a narcissist, marked by extremes of selfishness and grandiosity and a constant craving for recognition and admiration. He was constitutionally unable to acknowledge and credit talent and success among men who performed great services and generated transforming ideas for the benefit of the Ford Motor Company. Those who dared to rise at all from beneath his shadow found themselves either roughly dispatched by one of Ford's lieutenants, or constructively discharged and forced to quit because of Ford's dismissive treatment.

Ford was deftly non-confrontational, but he delighted in the manipulation and instigation of strife among subordinates. He studiously avoided titles in the company, so as to limit the authority of his executives and promote himself as the fount of all power in the organization. He loved to see if he could "break" a man. He had a life-long affection and fascination for inanimate and mechanical objects and living, flying birds,[2] but was largely unable to sustain meaningful personal friendships and relations with other human beings. He espoused humane polices for his workers but

---

2. Ford imported over four hundred birds from Britain and had five hundred bird houses stationed around his estate.

imposed an autocratic, fear-driven work environment in his factories. He once vowed to destroy his own company, brick by brick, rather than submit to labor union interference in the operation of his plants. He liked to present himself as humble and benign, when in fact he was mean and vindictive.

Henry Ford could be generous with his money, but rarely parted from it without attaching a string. He intensely loved his only son, Edsel, but constantly undercut his authority as President of the Ford Motor Company. He engineered the departure from the company of any man who gained Edsel's confidence and friendship. He wanted Edsel to be strong, forceful and independent, while at the same time demanding Edsel's subservience and submission. Ford was consumed with the preservation of the past, but hell bent on disrupting the present and future. Henry held great nostalgia for the rural life of the farmer, but hated farming and encouraged millions to move to the cities by putting America on wheels. He was a confusing paradox. Ford's unexpected industrial and financial success paralleled a destructive, blind self-assurance that nearly destroyed his extraordinary achievements.

Henry Ford was born in 1863 and raised on his father's farm in Dearborn, Michigan. Although he maintained a farmer's rural perspective throughout his life, he hated the actual drudgery of farm work. He was a natural born tinkerer who could visualize the way mechanical objects worked, and he loved the sensual touch and complex design of interlocking mechanical parts. He stated in his autobiography, *My Life and Work*, "My toys were tools—they still are. Every fragment of machinery was a treasure." He carried a desire to improve and ease the burden of farm work through mechanical means, which spurred his interest in the possibilities of the internal combustion engine.

Ford stopped his formal schooling at the age of fourteen and was always self-conscious over his limited ability to read, refusing several times to read aloud documents presented to him in a courtroom, claiming to have left his reading glasses at home. He first left home at the age of sixteen to find mechanical work and experience in Detroit. He blunted his own academic education with his departure into the world of mechanical production, gas engines, and electrical devices. He thought of himself as a creative thinker, unencumbered by the limiting weight of academic schooling. He could not draw and could not read blue prints, but he could formulate concepts in his mind that others could implement. He had a remarkable ability to identify and attract mechanical, administrative, and design talent and to delegate core executive and manufacturing functions to them, but he could never build a close and supportive relationship with them. Early emotional issues with his father may have contributed to the development of an introverted, aggressive, and narcissistic bent to his personality and his absence of personal empathy. Henry was always a thin man, with unusual diet peculiarities. He once advised a group of heart patients to ignore their doctors' advice and "get on the floor twice a day for half an hour and eat celery, corn and carrots until you feel all right again." He was five feet, ten inches in height and he never weighed more than one hundred forty-five pounds. He prided himself on his conditioning and his athleticism, often performing cartwheels in his youth to entertain his wife, Clara.

Clara Bryant Ford married Henry Ford in April, 1888. She was a devoted wife and mother and the "great believer" in Henry Ford's many ventures. She chose to occupy herself with the routine of the Ford family existence and avoided injecting herself in the operations of the Ford enterprise. She presented a matronly figure next to Henry Ford's skeletal frame. On those rare occasions when she chose to assert herself against her husband's course of action, such as his promise to destroy the Ford Motor Company, rather than to submit to union demands, Ford meekly conceded. Within the realm of her ordinary province, she was in complete control. She was not an early fan of the crank-driven model T internal combustion engine, preferring to drive about town in her Detroit Electric vehicle.

Henry Ford's first two ventures into manufacturing automobiles, using other people's money, failed. One, the Detroit Automobile

Company, organized in 1900, closed abruptly, and the other, The Henry Ford Company, became the Cadillac Motor Car Company, after he left. While he pretended to work on early models for those companies, he was really working intently on the development of racing cars, which he hoped to drive to personal public notice and acclaim. He sought fame and notoriety and he achieved it in his racing successes, reported in the local and national press.

Ford was consumed with preservation of the past and fixated on disruption of the present and the future. His nostalgia for the rural life fed his farmer's interest in the practicality of the automobile, not its comfort or design. This led him to vociferously resist any significant change to his beloved Model T, long after a shift in public taste for more refined vehicles.

Samuel Marquis, a minister friend of Henry Ford, wrote that Ford "would rather be a maker of public opinion than the manufacturer of a million cars a year, which only goes to show that in spite of the fact that he sticks out his tongue at history, he would nevertheless not object to making a little of it himself."[3] Marquis continued, "There rages in him an endless conflict between ideas, emotions and impulses as unlike as day and night—a conflict that makes me feel that two personalities are striving in him for mastery."[4] He described Ford as having "a complex mind of strength and weakness, of wisdom and foolishness, in which the shadows are more pronounced because of the depths which lie between."[5]

Ford was a voracious consumer of media coverage about himself. He regularly monitored and clipped flattering newspaper coverage during his litigation. Although an admirer of the *McGuffey Reader*, the early grade school composite of stories for children, he rarely read books, which he claimed "messed up my mind." He religiously followed the comic exploits of Little Orphan Annie.

---

3. Samuel S. Marquis, *Henry Ford – An Interpretation*, Wayne State University Press, Detroit 2007, pp. 9-10.

4. *Ibid.* p.69

5. *Ibid.* p.49.

According to Marquis, Ford's "chief ambition" was to be known as a "thinker of an original kind." His thinking was intuitive, not logical. It was also scattered. William Cameron, one of his lieutenants, wrote, "I always knew that he had a 25-track mind."

Ford gladly accepted the laurels for confronting the automobile industry trust,[6] for implementing the unprecedented five-dollar-per-day wage for his factory workers, and for developing mass production via the moving assembly line. Ford never shared credit for Ford Motor Company successes. He discredited the Dodge brothers, who extended credit to build the initial company and who invested heavily in equipment in their own machine shop to build everything in the original Ford cars except the body and tires. He ignored the contribution of James Couzens, who ran the entire business side of the Ford Motor Company, including finance, purchasing, and sales, keeping the company afloat while Ford tinkered in the shop.[7] He disregarded the design genius of H.C. Wills, a world-renowned metallurgist whose skills were key to introducing to a light and strong vanadium steel Model T auto.[8] He neglected the gifts of Walter E. Flanders, the engineer whose knowledge of electric tools and design of mechanical machinery led, with the assistance of Clarence Avery, to the development of the moving assembly line. He zealously donned the public mantel of a humanitarian industrialist. Yet he insisted on driving his workers to the point of exhaustion on the assembly line and employing spies and thugs to maintain order in his factories and promote resistance to labor organizers. He was a

---

6. The corporate or business *trust* was "[a] group of companies, industries, etc., organized to reduce or eliminate competition, or to control production and distribution for their common advantage." *Oxford English Dictionary*, Oxford University Press (3rd Ed. 2005).

7. Couzens was the real mover behind the five-dollars-a-day wage innovation. "In actual service to humanity and in unselfish use of his wealth his old running mate, Couzens, had done so far more that will live."—Samuel Marquis.

8. Wills also designed the famous Ford corporate logo.

confusing paradox, with an early positive public image at odds with his actual persona.

In the beginning, Henry Ford embraced litigation and the ensuing press coverage to develop a personal brand as a new kind of industrialist, a progressive Midas who cared deeply about the welfare of his workers and his customers to sell his cars. He employed courts of law and equity to advance his interests and his image, to build his brand. He used trials to explore important legal and social issues, and he welcomed playing them out in both the courtroom and the public media. He attempted to use the law and the media as both swords and shields, burnishing his own image. Initially, he was extraordinarily successful in both arenas. Personally, he was woefully inarticulate and incapable of giving a public speech. He hired staff to interpret and translate his incoherent homilies into oracular feed to an early adoring press. According to his longtime personal secretary, Ernest G. Liebold, "He didn't seem to have the facility of being able to go into much detail to explain his ideas. We had to feel our way and interpret Ford's views to the press." Ford believed in the value of free publicity over paid advertisements and frequently uttered rash but newsworthy comments to stimulate coverage. Fred L. Black, another of Ford's "interpreters" and the manager of Ford's own newspaper, *The Dearborn Independent*, stated,

> Henry Ford was the top guy for creating top stories. Nobody made Henry Ford from the publicity standpoint, except himself. Any Ford legend would start with himself. This idea that Ford was an ignoramus, and had his smartness due to his public relations men who engineered all of his stuff is absolutely untrue. It was a strange combination. He was a very shy man with an amazing sense of public value. Henry Ford was the most complex man I have ever known.[9]

Malcom W. Bingay, a journalist who knew Ford well, recorded

---

9. Black, Fred L., *Reminisences* at p. 158, Benson Ford Research Center, Dearborn, Michigan.

James Couzens' description of him in his book *Detroit is My Hometown.*[10]

> Ford is a bundle of contradictions. Or at least he seems so to the ordinary mind. The mistake everybody makes in trying to figure Ford out is that they depend on the usual, normal thought process to understand him. But Ford does not think along ordinary lines. He has thought processes all his own. How his mind works is more than I can understand.

Over time, Ford's public pronouncements and the press gained from his courtroom confrontations led to his humiliation and retreat into self-imposed isolation releasing the darker side of his complex nature.

This is the story of the four major lawsuits in which Henry Ford participated in the first quarter of the twentieth century. Each of these four lawsuits provides a window on the dualistic nature of Henry Ford's personality and his early rise and later fall in esteem in the public's consciousness during his lifetime. The suits include arguably the most singular patent infringement case of the twentieth century and a defining shareholder rights case, in both of which Ford was a defendant. These landmark cases were followed by two libel actions, one which he initiated and the other which he defended. All of the cases were closely monitored in the national press, which Henry Ford tried to manipulate to his own advantage. The first courtroom confrontation was both the gateway to and the propellant of the Ford Motor Company into the most spectacularly successful industrial manufacturing company in the twentieth century.

---

10. Bobbs – Merrill Co., Indianapolis & N.Y. (1946), p.125.

Part I

Columbia Motor Car Company And George B. Selden vs. C.A. Dverr, Ford Motor Company, ET AL.

Chapter 1

A Gauntlet Down

On a hot and humid noon hour in the early summer of 1903, a group of men from the newly formed Ford Motor Company met for lunch in the barroom of the Russell House Hotel. This august bar lay just off the Campus Martius of downtown Detroit and right across the street from the Civil War Monument to Michigan Soldiers and Sailors, dedicated in 1873. The clomp of horses and the wheels and bells of electric trolleys could be heard in the streets outside. The men included John S. Gray,[11] the newly installed President of the Company. Gray, a former candy tycoon, was then President of the German American Bank of Detroit and ostensibly in charge of the meeting. James J. Couzens, a hard charging, take no prisoners, wagon master on the business side of the Company and its Secretary/Treasurer. Henry Ford, fidgeting as always, twisting his hands, sat with his chair tilted back against the side wall of the room, his feet caught on the rung, his knees as high as his face. He may have looked like a gangly schoolboy but that he was not. Ford was congenitally unable to sit still for long periods of time.

The men met to discuss the Ford Motor Company becoming a member of the newly minted automobile manufacturer's trade Association of Licensed Automobile Manufacturers ("ALAM").

11. Mr. Gray, formerly an owner of a large candy company, was actively involved in opposition to the sugar trust in the late 1890s.

The invited guest, Frederick L. Smith, served as both the President of ALAM and officer of the Olds Motor Works, the company indirectly competing with the Ford Motor Company at the low end of the automobile sales market. The "curved dash" Olds Runabout retailed at about six hundred fifty dollars. Ford was manufacturing its vehicle at seven hundred fifty dollars with the intent aggressively to lower the cost further to expand its market.

ALAM was essentially a naked trust seeking to control membership in the early automobile industry in the United States for the financial benefit of its members, who had a big stake in maintaining exclusive membership, limiting production and maintaining high prices for automobiles. ALAM argued in public advertisements that it was really formed to protect the public from fly–by-night and unethical operators and that otherwise put purchasers of non-member automobile products at risk of liability for patent violations.

ALAM ruled the roost in the newly developing auto industry. It came into existence during a four-day closed meeting at the Manhattan Hotel in New York that commenced on March 3, 1903. In May, 1903, forty-three automobile producers stood ready to join ALAM As of July 1903, only fourteen manufacturers were selected. With the exception of Olds, the members were concentrated at the high end of the cost spectrum and hoped to dominate and control the market.

It planned to control the production and import of every automobile in America and to maintain high prices by limiting production and competition solely to benefit members. Attorney John Wendel Anderson called the meeting to order, to get Ford Motor Company into ALAM. Anderson had just invested five thousand dollars, borrowed from his father, to become a Ford shareholder. Anderson, a balding, stubby pencil of a man with sharp ambitions encountered Smith weeks prior and caught wind of ALAM's scheme. Smith bragged about "stabilizing the industry and barring marginal operators and *mere* assemblers from the organization. This rang alarm bells in Anderson's investment plans. Ford was an "assembler" at the time. But, truthfully, so were most of the members of ALAM. Eighty percent of automobiles "manufactured" in 1909 were actually "assembled" from parts produced by others. When Anderson asked how ALAM proposed to deal with "assemblers," Smith replied, "We are disposed to be fair. We take an inventory of their stocks, machinery, and equipment, whatever they may have, give them fair value and then they quit the business."

ALAM appointed Smith as its committee of one to rule on Ford's request for admission to its membership. He held, as his cudgel of choice, ALAM's acquired interest in a patent on the automobile, that had been issued by the U.S. Patent Office. ALAM brandished its righteous patent sword to limit production and extract royalties for the manufacture and/or import of every automobile in America.

WHO FATHERED THE AUTOMOBILE?

Popular American myth aside, Henry Ford was not the father of the automobile. He was no closer to the procreative event than a professional wet nurse, though handsomely compensated for being at the right place at the right time. George B. Selden, a patent attorney from Rochester, New York, claimed to be the legal father of the automobile. Selden had worked for years to obtain a United States Patent on the combination of a four-wheel vehicle with "[a]ny form of liquid hydrocarbon engine of the compression type." Selden filed his patent application in 1879, and successively amended it at two-year intervals thereafter, until 1895, when the U.S. Patent Office awarded him a "pioneer" patent No. 549160, on the automobile, which broadly encompassed all automobiles in America.

A patent is a limited monopoly in favor of a creative person to benefit from his or her unique invention or product that advances a state of art for the ultimate benefit for all. The *United States Constitution* grants to Congress the power to "promote the

Progress of Science and useful Arts, by securing for limited times to Authors and Inventors the exclusive Right to their respective Writings and Discoveries." Between 1860 and 1890, the number of patents issued in the U.S. climbed to five hundred thousand, ten times the prior number of patents issued during the seventy years combined. Strain on the resources of the Patent Office may account in part for the questionable grant of the incredibly broad Selden patent.

Selden claimed the basic elements of the carriage of an automobile in combination with the novelty of his *improved engine design* for internal compression combustion engine using liquid hydrocarbon fuel. These elements represent the seed of all the automobiles then being manufactured in the United States.

The Ford representatives, squirming agitatedly, told Smith no one man could claim ownership of creation of the automobile. Many fathers had developed the automobile and the automobile industry. Selden himself never produced an operating vehicle and made only a limited contribution to the advancement of the product and the industry, which adopted a totally different kind of internal combustion engine than pictured in Selden's patent application. Selden was an early, clever, "patent troll," skilled at manipulating broad, vague, descriptive language and the procedures of the patent office to maximize the reach of his limited accomplishment. He parlayed an early but weak patent application into a nebulous, but broad U.S. Patent through repeated biennial amendments to his application over sixteen years, quietly appropriating the technological developments of others in doing so.

The discussion at the Russell House in Detroit was genial and earnest at first. The Ford people sought agreement from Smith to let Ford into the club. Given the awkward nature of the discussion, Smith was evasive and refused to be drawn into accepting or refusing the Ford application. He suggested that the Company pay ALAM, which had exclusive rights in the patent, appropriate royalties for permission to use the patent for each of its cars manufactured. He suggested further that Ford limit its production and apply for membership to ALAM later when the Company was more solidly established. There was a stunned silence around the table. Flushed with anger, the crusty and intense James Couzens peering coldly at Smith through his pince-nez told Smith that Selden could take his patent and "go to hell." Smith, surprised, turned expectantly to Ford. Ford said, "Couzens has answered you." Smith gathered himself, pushed back from the table and quickly left the bar without the usual niceties. The patent challenge of the century was on.

If Henry Ford had qualms about the coming confrontation, he was not in any position to voice them. Although his name was on the company door, he had a history of failure in his prior two ventures, which collapsed largely due to his inattention and procrastination in getting product to market. In March, 1903 he was a minority shareholder in the Ford Motor Company, with his role limited to engineering and production. His reach and influence was limited by the powerful, aggressive personalities of James Couzens, a shareholder who ran the complete business side of the concern and John Dodge, another shareholder, whose company actually produced the lion's share of the parts for Ford automobiles. Couzens and Dodge forced a hesitating Ford to overcome his perfectionalist fear of failing, insisting that Ford cars be shipped and any flaws remedied after delivery. Whether he liked it or not, Henry Ford was along for the ride.

HENRY FORD: POPULIST TRUST BUSTER

The Ford Motor Company's legal challenge to the Selden patent directly confronted the automotive trust with the potential to liberate the competitive opportunities in the automotive industry and propel its figurehead, Henry Ford, into the national limelight as a populist and progressive trust buster in the mode of Theodore Roosevelt. Roosevelt's breakup of the railroad syndicate in the

Northern Securities Co case,[12] was the hallmark of governmental enforcement against trust-dominated industries in the United States. Congress had passed the *Sherman Antitrust Act* in 1890 which rendered illegal combinations that restrained trade. This landmark law came in response to popular demand for corporate accountability. It destroyed monopolies and curbed industrial combinations which limited competition and manipulated supply and price structuring. Presidents Harrison and Cleveland considered the Act weak and vague and for a while primarily used it against organizing labor unions.

Roosevelt did not stop with railroads. In 1895, the Sugar Trust controlled about ninety-eight percent of the sugar product in the country. Roosevelt enjoyed large and warm public approval for his "trust busting" activities, but he was careful to make distinctions between "good trusts" and "bad trusts" that were harmful to the economy and to consumers. President Taft, who succeeded Roosevelt, actually filed more antitrust suits—over ninety suits altogether in four years. Trust busting was one of the salient characteristics of what is now seen as the Progressive Era, a period of popular economic and social reform in the early twentieth century. The tides had turned away from the so-called "robber barons" and the late nineteenth century excesses of business and financial consolidation.

While a patent can be a socially useful "limited monopoly," that gives due credit to inventors, it can also be used for purely anticompetitive reasons. The Ford Motor Company fought against the Selden patent with all its fury and might. Even today, so-called "patent trolls" bring frivolous enforcement actions against alleged infringers asserting claims far beyond the patent's value or contribution to the prior art. The time and resources of the combatants was the only limit to these complex and heated trials and those resources expanded exponentially with spectacular growth and sales as the contest lumbered on.

The company's diligence and determination to resist anticom-

---

12. *Northern Securities Co. v. U.S.*, 193 U.S. 197 (1904).

petitive forces in the automobile industry propelled Henry Ford forward in the national consciousness, as a man of courage and principle. Resistance to the automotive trust placed Henry Ford squarely in the Progressive populist camp. What benefited one benefited all; Ford's self-interest served the public interest. James Couzens continually honed Ford's public image in advertisements to drive surging Ford sales.

> Early in the history of the automobile industry Henry Ford took the position that there should be no restriction in the price of an automobile. The automobile was a great institution, of stupendous possibilities, and so necessary that nothing should hinder its development, restrict its output, or hold up a fictious value.
>
> So, he refused to become a member of the automotive Trust. On the contrary, single-handed and alone his Company fought the so-called Selden patents for years and the Ford Motor Company has elected to make its own price on its products.[13]

In challenging Selden's patent and his claim to be the father of the automobile, the Company didn't assert that Ford, himself, held that distinction. It allowed that there were many contributors who advanced important designs, concepts, and inventions toward the ultimate development of a commercial automobile. The *Selden* case was the first and most successful of Henry Ford's legal contests. The public battle brought Henry Ford great acclaim, much to his taste; he found it exhilarating, difficult to live without, and impossible to share with others.

Patent infringement cases were an anomoly at the time, functioning largely without the governing hand of a trial judge on the rudder limiting the scope of evidence and interdicting the arguments and diversions of competing lawyers. The lawyers took their evidence by outside of a courtroom depositions and then dumped the mass on the bench of a judge to read the transcripts, examine the exhibits and render a decision, following wildly divergent ar-

---

13. Ford ad appearing in *Cycle* and *Automotive Trade Journal*, January 1, 1906.

guments of counsel. The process was messy, gruelling, expensive and unsatisfying. This single case led to a total revamping of patent procedure in the United States. More importantly it triggered the release of an emergent new industry that would revolutionize and dominate the twentieth century from the thrall of prototypical nineteenth century type robber barons who were intent on asseting control of the industry for tribute in royalties and profit.

Chapter 2

A Rich History: The DNA of the Automobile

ON THE WARM STEAMY Detroit evening of July 16, 1891, thousands of cyclists wheeled gleefully down the newly laid asphalt of Jefferson Avenue. Male and female, young and old, astride big wheel velocipedes and the modern chain and sprocket "safety" bikes, riders paralleled the Detroit River under the draping canopy of elm, buckeye, maple and horse chestnut trees. The "Garden City" crowds gathered. Fifty-thousand observers cheered their way across a bridge to Belle Isle, a leafy island in the river, where another twenty thousand onlookers eagerly gathered to await their arrival. An unending chain of bicycle-borne lanterns lit the way for the riders. Belle Isle became the cycling center of Detroit, with its miles of well-maintained trails along the river's edge, and its weekend race tracks.

The bicycle craze reached its apogee in 1896, rapidly fading, not so much from the appearance of the automobile as from the ubiquitous urban development of horse-pulled and electric-powered trolleys, providing easy, regular, and inexpensive transportation throughout and between cities. Horses and electricity had their day. Meanwhile, in the early '90s, a strange new animal hit the pavement: motorcycles.

Popular interest in cycling brought the advent of good reliable roads, which opened the way for new improved forms of transport. Hiram Percy Maxim, one of the officers of the Pope Manufacturing Company, initially built bicycles, then invented a gas-powered tricycle in 1895. The bicycle had many admirers. Maxim described the ascendance of the mechanical road vehicle:

> The reason why we did not build mechanical road vehicles before this, in my opinion, was because the bicycle had yet not come in numbers and had not yet directed men's minds to the possibilities of independent, long-distance travel over the ordinary highways. We thought the railroad was good enough. The bicycle created a new demand which was beyond the abilities of the railroads to supply.[14]

Henry Ford, working as a mechanical engineer in Detroit, fiddled in his spare time with four-cycle internal combustion engines. Ford wanted to find a way to reduce the weight and increase the power of engines and apply them to practical use on the farm and elsewhere. He longed to develop an internal combustion engine-driven motorcycle that would make travel affordable and available to the masses. Despite repeated efforts, he was unable to make a sufficiently lightweight engine that could drive a bicycle frame, so he turned his attention to a lightweight quad mobile made largely of wood with steel tubing parts, a steering lever, and a larger engine.

Ford was not the first or even the second American to succeed at producing an automobile. On September 20, 1893, Frank and Charles Duryea of Springfield, Massachusetts, built the first successful American automobile powered by an internal combustion engine. But this new street behemoth did not make instant waves. On March 6, 1896, when Charles B. King ventured on the streets of Detroit with the first gasoline-powered vehicle made in the city, he too generated little interest in the community. But one person was watching. A single, wiry and wily thirty-two year-old engineer and tinkerer shadowed King's automobile around town, envious of his success—Henry Ford. The

---

14. Hiram Percy Maxim. *Horseless Carriage Days*, N.Y. 1937 4 to 5.

era of the everyman internal combustion engine was dawning.

THE HORSE HATER

They call it the "lake effect." Cold arctic air whips across Lake Ontario to the south, absorbing the warmer lake water, resulting in heavy clouds of precipitation that pummel Rochester, New York with snow. On January 19, 1922, the Selden family interred their husband and father, George Bailey Selden, in the snow-covered Mt. Hope Cemetery alongside the Genesee River, southwest of downtown Rochester. The cemetery lies nestled between hills of glacial moraine deposited by the reluctantly withdrawing claws of ice age glaciers. Mr. Selden rests among the remains of such Rochester notables as Frederick Douglass, Susan B. Anthony, George Eastman, as well as his father, Judge Henry Rogers Selden and his uncle, Judge Samuel Lee Selden—all a part of his personal and family history. Inscribed proudly on George B. Selden's headstone is the appellation "Father of the Gasoline Automobile."

Although raised in a family with a history of making and writing the law, George B. Selden's real interest was in the world of machines and inventions. A very good mechanical engineer, Selden was a much less regarded "hands on" mechanic. His drawings and concepts bested his mechanical models. Selden briefly attended the University of Rochester before joining the 6th New York Cavalry during the Civil War. An unpleasant relationship with his horse cemented his preference for alternative forms of transportation. Following a frantic and inelegant dismount by the rider, Selden's horse ran into a tree and died. At the close of the war, Selden attended Yale to study the classics of literature, but his heart remained in the realm of the mechanical. Foregoing a liberal education, he transferred to Yale's Sheffield Scientific School, where he spent the last two enjoyable years of his formal education. Thereafter, he reluctantly acquiesced to his father's insistence that he return to Rochester and "read law" as an apprentice. In 1871, he joined the New York Bar as a patent lawyer.

Throughout his life, Selden maintained an avid interest in the prospects and designs for the gasoline-powered engine, both in the literature passing through the U.S. Patent Office in Washington, D.C. and in the emerging scientific and technical magazines shadowing the new mechanical features of automotive developments of the time. He attended the Philadelphia Centennial Exhibition in 1876, which fanned his interest in the Brayton gasoline-powered engine[15] and the potential for its adaptation to power a mechanical vehicle. Said vehicle, Selden knew, would not startle and die after a bad dismount. The Otto & Langen engine[16] was also on display in Philadelphia, but its bone-rattling noise and vibrations impressed him less.

Selden demonstrated a certain facility for mechanical design, obtaining and marketing a number of personal patents for such inventions as barrel hoop manufacturing machinery and an early typewriter. He later turned his focus to developing a reduced-sized, expanded-efficiency model of the Brayton gasoline engine. In 1878, he created a three-cylinder engine block with only one of the cylinders bored out. It weighed 370 pounds and generated two horse power of energy, but was disappointingly feeble in actual operation. It did represent a technical advance in that it vastly improved the power output per weight unit. He also enclosed Brayton's open crankcase, which he integrated with the engine block. Without actually constructing a model vehicle on which to mount his modified Brayton engine, Selden filed his patent application for "an improved road engine"—the patent claiming automobile paternity—with the U.S. Patent Office on May 8, 1879.

---

15. A constant-pressure gas engine without internal explosions, with an external compression chamber, operating much like a steam engine. It was invented by George Bailey Brayton in Boston, Massachusetts, and patented in 1874.

16. A four-stroke engine with internal pistons moved by internal, electrically-incited explosions, designed by Nicholas August Otto, displayed at the Paris Exhibition in 1867, and continually modified and improved over time.

Selden had a draftsman make drawings and a Rochester machinist, William Gamm, construct a non-working model of the vehicle and engine, which he submitted to the Patent Office with the application. Two witnesses also signed his patent application, W. M. Rebasz, a patent draftsman, and George Eastman, a young clerk working in Selden's Rochester office building. Eastman had an all-consuming interest in the technical development of photographic means and processes. Selden, a well-known amateur photographer working in Rochester at the time, served as a mentor and advisor to Eastman, encouraging Eastman in his efforts to move the technology of photography beyond treated glass plating. Selden prepared and filed Eastman's early patent applications with the Patent Office.

Through a careful and systematic process of biennial review and the amendment of his patent application, Selden both maintained his priority and incorporated subsequent surging technical advances in the industrial race for predominance in the new gas-powered vehicle manufacturing industry, upgrades all made by others. Selden never appealed any technical rejection of his application by a patent examiner but quietly and routinely submitted amendments, almost always just before the close of the two-year window for the approval of the application, which then had the effect of reopening the window for a subsequent two years. In an analysis of the "*Selden* Case" published in the *Journal of the Patent Office Society* in 1940, J. Harold Byers revealed that the total time spent by the Patent Office in the direct consideration of the Selden patent was only about seven months of the sixteen-and-one-half years that it was pending. Selden himself spent fifteen years and eleven months to make eighty replies to patent office actions and to pay the final fee.

On June 6, 1889, ten years into his patent quest, Selden broadened his written "description of the scope of his engine invention" to cover "any form of liquid-hydrogen engine of the compression type" to be used in his "improved road locomotive." He later tried unsuccessfully to delete the reference to "compression" type of engine to further broaden the scope of his patent, but his initial drawings and specifications could not be altered. They clearly showed an external compression feature on the engine. (Compression in the Otto-style engine occurred internally within the cylinder chamber itself.) In total, Selden made over one hundred separate changes to his application with nineteen original claims cancelled and replaced with strategic, technical revisions over the sixteen years that his application was pending.

Selden finally engaged the clutch on his application in 1895, following efforts by the U.S. Patent Office to clean out long-pending submittals. He received the grant of U.S. Patent No. 549,160 on November 5, 1895, viable for seventeen years from that date. He asserted that the novelty of his patent was a combination of the basic mechanical drive train of the automobile with the compression internal combustion engine using liquid hydrocarbon fuel. He had his patent, but not the wherewithal to make use of it. For a variety of reasons, Selden's efforts to find funding for the creation of his "invention" and to enforce it against alleged infringers failed. His laconic and acerbic personality seems to have played a part in his lack of success.

Selden generally projected a grim visage. His inability to articulately engage an audience became a real impediment to him as a lawyer and a promoter. He was very lean, with a thin-lipped frown below a close-cropped mustache. His dour courtroom presence, fluctuating moods and lack of litigation finesse ultimately resulted in Kodak entrepreneur George Eastman terminating him as counsel. Eastman said, "Selden was there but would not open his mouth . . . we want a fighter." Unfortunately, Selden had entered a profession for which he was ill suited, and his continued disappointment with the automobile filled him with a "barely suppressed impatience that sharpened a tongue already direct enough." Many years later, one of Ford's men, Rollo C. Carpenter, said of him, "Selden is quite the same man that he was during the famous trial, and I think he is just as erratic as he was then." Recognition as the automotive pioneer, long awaited, was in the end blunt and snatched from his grasp.

THE TRUE FATHER

If there is one single person with legitimate claim as the father of the automobile, it would probably be Siegfried Liepmann Marcus. Other inventors in Europe and America—Lenoir, Beau de Rochas, Otto, Langen, Brayton, Benz, Daimler, Rings and Schumms among them[17]—made significant contributions, but this polymath German Jewish inventor living and working in Vienna has the widest claim. As an inventor, he obtained one hundred thirty-one patents in sixteen countries on various inventions ranging from the T-handled plunger (a magneto-powered igniter of explosive such as dynamite), and improved stethoscopes to electric lights, and Morse code cable conductors. He never applied for a patent on the automobile, only on the components which he improved. He performed a number of early experiments with gunpowder-powered engines losing three fingers on his right hand as a result.

Marcus invented the internal combustion engine, built and ran his own primitive cart automobile in 1864, and ran it several hundred yards on the Mariahilferstrasse in Vienna. The Mariahlferstrasse has long been the upscale shopping street of central Vienna. There is a record that he drove his car on April 9, 1865, the same day that General Lee surrendered at the Appomattox Courthouse. Marcus frequently claimed that he was stopped by the police on the Mariahhilferstrasse for "driving without a horse." He agreed with the local constabulary to drive his vehicle only at night, to avoid disturbing the peace. He made trips up to twelve miles in his car. This vehicle had no clutch to disengage the power train, so a powerfully-built man had to lift the end of the cart off the ground until the vehicle started.

---

17. See Greenleaf, William, *Monopoly on Wheels: Henry Ford and the Selden Automobile Patent*, Wayne State University Press, Detroit, Michigan (2011) for complete history of the internal combustion driven automobile and the Selden patent dispute.

In 1865, Marcus applied for a patent on his "vaporisater, for the carbonization of atmospheric air." The patent was granted on June 1, 1866. He installed the first true carburetor on his second internal combustion-powered vehicle in 1870. Marcus also invented the electro-magnetic ignition. This "Viennese Igniter" permitted the acceleration and deceleration of the rate of ignition to the timing required for the gas explosions in the cylinder. Marcus successfully developed a four-stroke engine.

Why have so few recognized the untiring genius of this man?

Marcus' success and achievements were lamentably underappreciated, probably due to early anti-Semitism. A historical erasure of his accomplishments came during the Nazi era, where the rewriting of history and the destruction of inconvenient documents rose to an art form. The Nazis tended to favor the case of Karl Benz or Gottlieb Daimler as the father or fathers of the automobile. Marcus donated one of his early vehicles to the Techniques Museum fuer Industrie und Gewerke where it was on display until 1938, when the Nazis entered Vienna. A museum attendant hid it from the Nazis in a basement vault during the war.

This is not the only thread of anti-Semitism in the history of the automobile and Henry Ford's four trials, as we will see. Start to finish, the story circles in and through this terrain. In fact, Marcus' accomplishments as the father of the auto intertwined with the Selden trial due to competition with an earlier technology—the electric car. Nothing is simple when ambitious men clash for predominance.[18]

THE ELECTRIC HORSE SYNDICATE AND THE BIRTH OF ALAM

The years between 1900 and 1905 saw dramatic shifts in the structure of the new automobile industry. In 1900, approximately four thousand autos were manufactured in the United

18. The clash continues to day with Elon Musk and the surge in electric car technology.

States, one thousand six hundred eighty-one powered by steam, one thousand five hundred seventy-five powered by electric, and nine hundred twenty-six powered by gas. By 1905, the ratio had flipped decidedly. That year saw a total production of twenty-one thousand six hundred ninety-two vehicles; eighteen thousand six hundred ninety-nine or 82.6% ran on gas, one thousand five hundred sixty-eight or 9.2% ran on steam and one thousand four hundred twenty-five or 6.6% were electric.

The Selden patent litigation arose out of efforts of a New York investment syndicate to corner the market for manufacturing electric cabs in large cities. The syndicate welded together a conglomerate of electric vehicle and other manufacturing companies into the Electric Vehicle Company or E.V.C. It acquired an exclusive license to the benefits of the Selden patent from the inventor, himself, for a ten-thousand-dollar license fee, a royalty, and an ongoing royalty fee of fifteen dollars per vehicle, with a five-thousand-dollar annual minimum. The mercurial and brooding Selden was happy to finally reap economic benefit from his patent.

The Selden patent had no direct application to the production and use of electric vehicles, but it did provide an important and valuable hedge, providing the syndicate and E.V.C. with the opportunity to control, contain and limit competition from upstart gasoline-powered vehicles with its own electric vehicles. The syndicate soon realized, however, that it had backed the wrong competitor. Under growing allegations of fraud and mismanagement, the capitalization, stock price, and borrowing capacity of the E.V.C. began to implode, while the interest in gas-powered vehicles surged. Desperate for cash, the E.V.C. dusted off the Selden patent to help replenish its treasury. The syndicate, through E.V.C., chose to mount a high/low campaign against the swelling internal combustion automobile manufacturing field, a direct attack on the single most prominent car maker at the time, the Winton Motor Carriage Company. It also attempted several collateral assaults on marginal players, hoping to generate a storm of momentum that would sweep away all resistance to the Selden patent. In July 1900, the E.V.C. filed a patent infringement suit against the Winton Company and three other smaller companies shortly thereafter. The marginal companies had neither stomach nor resources for litigation. Their resistance collapsed immediately.

Alexander Winton, a naturalized Scot, was a force not to be trifled with. He migrated from bicycle manufacturing to automobile making in the last years of the nineteenth century. He organized the Winton Motor Carriage Company in 1897 and he actively promoted his products through car racing. He enjoyed an international reputation and briefly held the American land speed record of one minute and 14 ¼ seconds for a mile course in 1901. Henry Ford, seeking the fame and renown enjoyed by Winton, followed suit. Neglecting responsibilities in his early production ventures, Ford focused his attention on developing a race car. On October 10, 1901, Ford and Winton met head to head for a ten-mile race at the one-mile oval track owned by the Detroit Driver's Club in Grosse Pointe Township, outside of Detroit. The track was a flat, unbanked oval with wooden fencing set in marsh lands near the Detroit River.

Winton, who also produced gasoline driven cars, had much more skill and experience as a racer than Ford. Winton's "Bullet" car was by far the superior in power and performance. After leading for eight turns on the track, Winton developed engine trouble, and Ford surged to the lead to win in front of eight thousand cheering spectators. Ford's time was thirteen minutes and twenty-three and two-fifths seconds, or an average of about forty-five miles per hour, a blazing white-knuckle ride. Leaving the track, he stated, "Boy, I will never do that again."[19]

---

19. On October 25, 1902, at the Manufacturer's Challenge Cup on the same track, Ford sponsored another car named the 999, to again race Winton in a five-mile race, but this time he hired Barney Oldfield, a prominent bicycle racer, to man the car. Oldfield won setting a new American record of 5:28 after driving the vehicle "wildcat style" without reducing speed on the turns and lapping the field. Ford later drove his racer 999 to set a land speed record on the frozen ice of Lake St. Clair, but without racing competition.

The complex trial the syndicate brought against Winton was also a very bumpy ride. A number of Winton's expected allies turned on him and applied to E.V.C. for licenses in early 1903. Winton instructed his attorneys to seek a settlement which resulted in the creation of the Association of *Licensed* Automobile Manufacturers; thus, ALAM came into being.

In March, 1903, the designated "executive committee" of ALAM trundled up Fifth Avenue in New York to meet with the principals of E.V.C. and their lawyers. E.V.C. offered the Selden patent and all its licensing authority to ALAM in exchange for a modest royalty to E.V.C. and an even smaller royalty to their own cartel. ALAM said yes, becoming an exclusive trust syndicate sufficient to warm the cockles of a Rockefeller, a Vanderbilt, or a Gould.

ALAM designed a three-inch-wide brass plaque containing the stamped image of a never-produced Selden vehicle, in recognition of the tribute it paid on each unit, intending to rivet it onto every single car made or sold in America. One final note from this settlement: the E.V.C. lawyers demanded all of the documents prepared by Winton's lawyers for the defense of the suit against him. Included in those materials were papers provided by Siegfried Marcus' Austrian patent lawyer. These papers never surfaced again. Marcus' achievements as the progenitor of the automobile were suppressed. Sequestration of the Winton materials, particularly the Marcus papers, hampered all further challenges to the Selden Patent.

From the start, ALAM positioned itself as the only game in town.

James Couzens met the ALAM threats defiantly and clearly. "So far as our plan of action is concerned for the future it is extremely simple. We intend to manufacture and sell all of the gasoline automobiles of the type we are constructing that we can." The Ford Motor Company surged forward with the steely Couzens at the business helm, and Henry Ford orchestrating the creation of his greatest project, the Model T. In the press and in the courts, Ford and Couzens had one intention and one voice, fully aware that the Selden patent suit portended high risk and great opportunity. Opportunity lay in the apotheosis of Henry Ford as a hero of the common man, and parlaying that image to spectacular growth in sales and profits, to dwarf the expense of the litigation.

To that end, Couzens flooded daily and trade newspapers and magazines with letters and advertisements proclaiming the defiance of the tiny Ford Motor Company against the massive power of ALAM. He attributed all successes to the brilliant underdog, Henry Ford. Couzens, never interested in popularity for himself, watched as the "paladin of the people" he helped create became convinced of his own nobility and invincibility. Henry Ford would, in time, be seduced by the sirens of fame; Ford would harden and fall, wrapped in a counterfeit guise of humility in public.

Chapter 3

Knights, Bishops and Rooks

Patent infringement cases were an anomaly in the procedure of court trials at the turn of the twentieth century. They proceeded largely without the governing hand of a trial judge on the rudder to limit the scope of evidence and interdict the arguments and diversions of competing lawyers. The lawyers took their evidence outside of a courtroom in depositions, then dumped the transcripts on the bench of a judge forced to read them, examine the exhibits, and render a decision, synthesized from wildly divergent arguments of counsel. The process was messy, grueling, expensive and unsatisfying. In fact, this single case (*Columbia Motors/Selden vs. Ford Motor Company*) led to a total revamping of patent procedure in the United States. More importantly, it shaped an emergent new industry that would revolutionize personal travel, the titanic future of private transportation in the United States?

The players on the chess board of this famous trial deserve a closer look. Who were they and how were they motivated? What drew these fierce lawyers and engineers into this bughouse chess match? Meet Samuel Rossiter Betts, Frederick P. Fish, Ralzemond Allen Parker Esq., attorneys at law and the Coudert Brothers, the first truly major international law firm located in the United States; Jesse M. Smith, Rolla C. Carpenter, Charles E. Duryea three prominent American mechanical engineers; Sir. Dugald Clerk, a British engineer; and the patent they all fought over with such intensity.

THE DREAM TEAM

ALAM chose two principal patent lawyers to prosecute most of its patent cases.

Samuel Rossiter Betts of Betts, Betts, Sheffield and Betts, a cousin of William C. Whitney, one of the E.V.C. principals. Betts, cultured and sophisticated, was a dialed-in member of the Yale University elite. His family pedigree reached back to Elihu Yale himself. The second dream team lawyer, William A. Redding of Redding, Greeley and Austin, had been a longstanding veteran of the Pope bicycle patent infringement actions. Redding was a high energy, technically proficient member of the eastern establishment "silk stocking" patent bar. The Pope companies, through mergers and acquisitions, had acquired a large number of bicycle patents that enabled them to market the Columbia bicycle and to impose and sustain a ten percent royalty on most of the bicycles produced in the United States, anticipating ALAM's aims with the automobile industry. Both firms, located in New York City, were armed by intelligent, Ivy League-educated patent lawyers, who in dress, style, and manner, replicated lawyers appointed by the President of the United States to sit on the Federal Court bench in the State of New York.

The equally impressive Frederick P. Fish of the Boston firm Fish, Richardson, Herrick and Neave, was the formidable third attorney. Fish helped draft and organize briefs and presentations by counsel. Formerly the President of the American Telephone and Telegraph Company from 1901 to 1907, Fish was refined, articulate, and graceful. He steered AT&T through over six hundred patent cases in its first eleven years and represented patent holders in such inventions as the radio, the airplane and the air brake. He turned down the Presidency of the Massachusetts Institute of Technology, but served on its corporate board, as well as the Harvard Board of Overseers and the Radcliffe Board of

Directors. Fish was also the dean of the East Coast Patent Bar. The man held sway and used that sway with elegant force.

This patent enforcement "dream team" sought to divide and conquer Ford through a strategy of oppressive lawyering and intimidation. They filed three separate lawsuits: against Ford Motor Company; the O.J, Gude Company, a New York advertising firm that had purchased a Ford vehicle; and C.A. Duerr & Company, a New York Ford dealer (later replaced by John Wannamaker & Associates.) ALAM sought to set an example by suing a manufacturer, a distributor, and a purchaser of non-ALAM-approved automobiles. The three cases were later consolidated into one.

The Trust team also filed separate suits against Panhard & Levassor, and Henry and Albert C. Neubauer, two European firms who were importing vehicles into the United States. ALAM asserted that its patent prohibited foreign manufacturers from importing their vehicles into the United States, without payment of royalties as well. Counting on the power to overwhelm, ALAM refused to consolidate the evidence in the Ford and Panhard cases and objected to a consolidated record. This required Ford's legal team to produce and submit a complete duplication of depositions, affidavits, and exhibits for each case for the court's review, vastly expanding the time, volume, and expense involved in creating the final records. Ford's lawyers would of necessity be required to attend the depositions of the same witnesses in each of the cases, so as not to miss any important development that had not come to light in another case.

And the case flowed beyond court depositions and filings. Both ALAM and Ford sought to lift the sword of public opinion in defense of the parry and thrust of their litigation through a flurry of advertisements in newspapers and trade journals. ALAM warned Ford dealers and customers that in purchasing Ford products they would likely be the subjects of patent enforcement litigation and in danger of paying future damages. Ford responded by posting a bond to protect his customers and dealers. He gloried in billboard ads and published open letters that wrapped himself in the

Progressive Era mantle of free trade. The Ford Motor Company promised to protect purchasers of its automobiles and reminded customers that Selden's patent had never been enforced in a court of law. It stated, further,

> We are the pioneers of the GASOLINE AUTOMOBILE. Our Mr. Ford made the first gasoline Automobile in Detroit and the third in the United States. His machine made in 1893 is still in use. Our Mr. Ford also built the famous "999" Gasoline Automobile, which was driven by Barney Oldfield in New York on Saturday a mile in 55 4/5 seconds on a circular track, which is the world's record.
>
> Mr. Ford, driving his own machine, beat Mr. Winton at Grosse Pointe track in 1901. We have always been winners.[20]

The Ford publicity machine worked popular sentiment, fingering Henry Ford as the underdog, the purposeful entrepreneur, the man willing to oust the robber barons and truly serve the American public. His ringmaster, James Couzens, framed the whole case:

> In taking this position we cannot conscientiously feel that Mr. Selden never added anything to the art in which we are engaged. We believe the art would have been just as far advanced to-day if Mr. Selden had never been born. That he made no discovery and gave none to the world. If he did, it was a narrow and impractical one having no value, and that he and his assignees cannot monopolize the entire trade by forcing on it an unwarrantable construction of his claims by those interested in sustaining them.[21]

The ALAM team drafted several technical experts who were holdovers from the electric vehicle patent cases, including Edward M. Bentley, an electric and mechanical engineer, who served as an assistant patent examiner. Bentley's expertise, limited to electrical

---

20. The date was 1896, not 1893, and Charles King, not Henry Ford, made the first automobile in Detroit.

21. Quoted in Greenleaf, *supra* at 120.

machinery, gave him limited knowledge of the workings and history of the gasoline engine. In twenty-three days of depositions, Bentley impaled himself on his ignorance of the subject at hand. In the end, he even admitted that he had never actually driven a gasoline-powered vehicle. The stifled shout of hurrah from Ford's lawyers was not included in the court reporter's notes. ALAM's team, however, had more technological firepower. They called the acknowledged international master of the technology and history of the gasoline automobile, the Scot of all Scots, Sir Dugald Clerk, KBE, to the stand. The proclaimed viability and propriety of the Selden patent lay in his capable hands.

THE SAGE

The world recognized Sir Dugald Clerk, KBE,[22] a handsome, dashing and mustachioed Scot, as the mechanical engineer most identified with the technical aspects of the internal combustion engine. He had graduated from Anderson's University in Glasgow. He patented his own popular and successful two-stroke engine in 1881. This little powerhouse engine propelled countless large machines and boats and was later adapted to motorcycles, lawn mowers and small boats, until the Otto Patent on the four-stroke engine expired in 1890. Then, Clerk the innovator adapted the Otto-type compressor to his own two-stroke engine, with the ignition being carried by an external flame. He avoided infringement of the Otto Patent because his was only a two-stroke device. He, in effect, combined features of the Lenoir engine, which was inefficient and heavy, with those of the Otto, which was lighter and more efficient, thereby generating twice as many power strokes.

As a principal in the intellectual property firm of Marks and Clerk, Clerk served as a consulting engineer and international

22. Clerk earned his knighthood in 1914 – 1918, when he worked for the British Trench Warfare Committee and served as Director of Engineering Research for the British Admiralty (and Chairman of the Internal Combustion Engine Committee of the Air Ministry).

patent agent. He presented many important papers to the British Institution of Civil Engineers including "The Theory of the Gas Engine" (1882); "On the Explosion of Homogeneous Gas Mixtures" (1886); "Recent Developments in Gas Engines" (1886); and "On the Limits of Thermal Efficiency in Internal Combustion Motors" (1907). His papers twice received the Telford Medal, the highest prize awarded by the British Institution of Civil Engineers. He was a member of the Institution Committee on Standards of Efficiency of Internal Combustion Engines and Joint Secretary of the British Association Committee on Gaseous Explosions. Add to that Clerk's honorary Doctorate degrees from the University of Manchester, Leeds University, the University of Liverpool, the University of Glasgow, and St. Andrews University. Then consider his admission to the British Royal Society, the oldest scientific society in Britain (1660), which serves as the scientific advisor to the British Government,[23] and you have one tall expert witness. Clerk also authored a number of early books on the history and mechanics of the gasoline engine that were adopted as standard texts on the subject in Britain and the United States.[24]

What the sage wrote became gospel. What the sage said determined matters of international law.

Clerk reviewed the Selden Patent and deemed it valid and controlling in the art. Being a reasonable man, and an impeccable man, he admitted in his deposition testimony that his knowledge of American patent law was limited. He had based his opinion, in part, on his understanding that the Selden patent was not restricted by the type of engine (Brayton) shown in the specifications. Two foundational pillars upheld Clerk's opinion. First, that the Brayton and Otto engines were essentially the same under American patent law, both being a variant of a compression-cycle

23. The Royal Society's motto is Nullea in verba (Take nobody's word).

24. *The Theory of the Gas Engine (*1882); *The Gas Engine* (1886); *The Gas and Oil Engine* (1896) and *The Gas, Petrol and Oil Engine,* Rev.d. (2 vol. 1909-1913).

engine; and second, that Selden's concept had been an innovative and revolutionary development in quality and range of the automobile for the year 1879, the year to which Selden's patent priority related back.[25]

Clerk received a whopping twenty-thousand-dollar retainer from E.V.C. plus expenses for his opinion and testimony. Despite the size of his fee, Clerk was an engineer of high integrity and although supportive of the Selden patent, would reasonably qualify and limit his remarks when pressed by the defense, including the concession that his knowledge of American patent law might have been imperfect.

THE OLD LION

The Ford Motor Company came into existence when Alexander M. Malcomson joined forces with Henry Ford in 1902. Malcomson, thirty-six, a Scot, developed a coal supply business from scratch, serving households, businesses, steamships and train engines. He brought decades of business savvy to Ford Motors. He sported a long nose protruding from his mutton chop whiskers. Ford met Malcomson when Ford was purchasing coal on behalf of his employer, the Edison Illuminating Company. They also shared an Episcopal church connection. Malcomson's trucks could be seen all over Detroit roads with their distinctive "Hotter than sunshine" signage. Ford convinced Malcomson, who drove a Winton vehicle, that he had a new design for a vehicle with a vertical engine that would be simpler, quieter, and stronger than the horizontal engine used by Olds at the time.

Malcomson ushered Ford into the law office of John A. Anderson, in August, 1902, and had Anderson draw up a partnership agreement between Ford and Malcomson, with Ford providing his drawings and models and Malcomson providing capital: a five-hundred-dollar start. He also drew up an employment agree-

25. Greenleaf, supra, at 146.

ment for C. Harold Wills, a mechanical and metallurgical genius who had drawn the Ford plans. Wills, a hot-blooded, impetuous Welshman with a passion for the high life, the ladies, and ostentatious living, was viewed as the greatest practical metallurgist in the United States, having developed critical new steel alloys used in manufacturing.[26] It was Wills who designed the iconic, script Ford logo that underscores the corporate identity even today.

When Malcomson overextended himself in the bank-funded expansion of his business and had to find others to contribute capital to the new auto firm, two of his lawyers stepped into play. John A. Anderson and Horace H. Rackham profited largely in chasing down delinquent accounts for Malcomson's coal company. Anderson and Rackham had personalities both diverse and compatible while in professional harness. Anderson, extroverted and verbose, meshed cleanly with Rackham, introverted and laconic. At the start of the ALAM contest, the Ford Board of Directors deputized both men to consult with Ralzemond Allen Parker Esq., the most eminent and successful patent lawyer in the State of Michigan, concerning the viability of the Selden patent.

Parker had graduated from the University of Michigan Law School. And Parker, it was said, had never lost a patent case. He was sixty years old and near the end of a successful and contentious career. While law was his main occupation, Parker also had a flair for business. He served as President of the Graphite Manufacturing Company and the Superior Graphite Company and as Secretary of the Detroit-Wyandotte Motor Truck Company. For a number of years, he was the President of the Associated Charities of Detroit.

Parker's grizzled and rough-hewn visage, his rumpled clothing, the broad Whitmanesque hat that covered his truant hairline, his unkempt and unruly beard, all these projected a wild and leonine presence. Ivy League sleek, Parker was not. His features

---

26. Nevins, Allan *Ford: The Times, The Man, The Company*, Scribners, N.Y. 1954 at 227.

were at one with his personality. Although raised in the Midwest, Parker had descended from a prominent Connecticut family. His great-grandfather had served as a sergeant in the Revolutionary War, along with Benedict Arnold, in the Quebec Expedition in 1775. Parker, himself, had served with the 17th Regiment, Company E, Michigan Infantry from Ypsilanti during the Civil War. He mustered out after being wounded in the battle at Antietam, near Sharpsburg, Maryland, in September of 1862. Lead and the horrors of battle did not stop him. Parker served as Judge Advocate General of the Grand Army of the Republic in 1917. Mid to late-nineteenth century photos of Parker disclose more controlled personal grooming and tailoring than in his later years. His wife Sarah Electra Parker, beside him in later photographs, has severe features faintly reminiscent of Woodrow Wilson. One wonders why. Could it be her husband, Ralzemond A. Parker, with his wide-flashing eyes and relentless sense of engagement and tenacity in matters that interested him? He was not known for suffering fools gladly. Or suffering fools at all.

Assisting Parker in the technical aspects of the patent defense, attorney Elliott J. Stoddard had not only the schooling (Yale and Stanford), but was himself an inventor and writer who had patented two versions of a "hot air engine," one in 1919 and another in 1933, appropriately named the "Stoddard Engine." In 1903, Stoddard published a book entitled *Gas Engine Design*.

Parker took the Ford case with extreme prejudice. He had a preexisting knowledge and interest in the mechanics of automobiles, having himself owned three steam-driven vehicles, including a 1900 "Loco-mobile Steamer." "Motoring" was his passion and his favorite form of recreation. Parker owned the second automobile to be driven on the streets of Detroit and made the first automobile trip from Detroit to Flint, Michigan, over the Saginaw trail. He was known for his immersion in the technology of his cases, knowing as much about an invention as the patent holder. He was a student of the history of the automobile. No challenger dimmed his reign as the most celebrated patent lawyer in the State of Michigan. If Parker had a fault, it was his difficulty narrowing and focusing his arguments and marshaling a clear, succinct picture of the issues from mountains of evidence. His rough, rural manner and image would prove a challenge to the Ivy League graduates who populated the patent bar and bench in the Eastern cities.

Parker advised Ford, his main attorneys, his shareholders, and the two directors, Anderson and Rackham, that the Selden patent was over-broad and not enforceable. Parker under estimated the cost of the defense to run about forty thousand dollars, a daunting figure at the time for a company that had only twenty-eight thousand dollars in the bank. He negotiated a forty-dollar daily fee, plus expenses, an arrangement which was to provide him an ongoing source of headaches due to the intense flyspecking of his reimbursement requests by the ever-vigilant and proto-frugal James Couzens. Ford Motor Company rumors had it that when Couzens issued his annual smile in the spring of each year, there was a loud, resounding crack in the frozen ice of the Great Lakes waterways.[27]

THE THREE ENGINEERS

Parker lined up prominent technical witnesses. He enlisted the services of three distinguished mechanical engineers, Jesse M. Smith, Rolla C. Carpenter, and Charles E. Duryea. Smith, a president of the American Society of Mechanical Engineers (1909-1910) and a New Yorker, lectured on Patent Laws and the methods and procedures in patent cases. Carpenter was a professor of theoretical and experimental mechanical engineering at Cornell University in New York and a co-author of *The Internal Combustion Engines: Their Theory, Construction and Operation* (1909).

27. In a 1950 privately-printed biography of John Wendell Anderson, author Milo M. Qauif describes James Couzens as a man of iron will and unexpected financial acumen, and the principal cause of the early success of the Ford Motor Company. Charles E. Sorensen, in his memoir *My Forty Years at Ford*, agreed, calling Couzens the "field general."

Charles E. Duryea brought years of expertise, skill, and firsthand knowledge to the trial. He was in many ways the complete foil of George B. Selden.

Duryea had designed, manufactured, and raced an actual automobile. An early designer and manufacturer of bicycles, he and his brother Frank Duryea had run Duryea Manufacturing Company since 1888. Duryea had designed a bicycle with a smaller wheel for women, enabling the growth of female interest in cycling—no more high wheel cycles to trap long skirts. Most significantly, Charles Duryea and his brother designed and produced the first successful gasoline-powered automobile built in the United States, in 1892, which they road tested on September 20, 1893 in Springfield, Massachusetts. The original Duryea Motor Wagon was a former horse-drawn buggy with a four-horse power, single cylinder, gasoline engine. On Thanksgiving Day, November 28, 1895, Frank Duryea won the first automobile race in America, from Chicago to Evanston and back. The Duryeas formed the Duryea Motor Wagon Company in September, 1895, the first American automobile manufacturing company. With all these firsts, and an eloquent court demeanor, Duryea made a striking contribution to the team. Two years before the trial, in a letter to the editor that appeared in *Horseless Age* on February 6, 1901, Duryea had recorded his objections to the Selden patent.

> It is easily established that traction engines using disconnecting devices between the power shaft and the propelling wheel were built and operated in this country as early as 1870, and it has been further established by many court decisions that it is not invention to substitute one well-known power or device for another well-known equivalent in a combination.

All of Parker's expert witnesses, Smith, Carpenter and Duryea, in their testimonies, built brick by brick a solid wall of technical and historical evidence. They described the history of the state of the art of the internal combustion engine from its earliest days to the present. They underscored the divergence between Selden's

Brayton-style engine described in his patent and the far superior Otto engine adopted by Ford and other automobile manufacturers. They hammered home Ford's position that he and all other manufacturers were standing on the shoulders of many who had gone before—but Selden was not among them.

THE FRENCH CONNECTION

Panhard & Levassor and their Dutch import agents, the Neubauers, retained the services of the Coudert Brothers to defend them in the U.S. patent suits. Panhard automobiles with their Daimler engines produced the cream of early French automobiles with respect to quality and performance. They had constructed their first motor car in 1890 and their second in 1891. Panhard & Lavassor generally gets credit for having established the basic architecture of the modern automobile with an engine mounted in front, a rear wheel driver, and a clutch mounted between the engine and the gearbox.

The three Coudert Brothers lawyers were fervent Catholics operating in an environment of strong anti-Catholic sentiment in Protestant New York and New England. They all spoke fluent French. Charles Coudert, Sr., a Bonapartist, had escaped and fled a Bourbon prison in 1822. He founded the first truly major international law firm in the United States. At one time the firm had a monopoly on all Italian, German, and French estate practice in New York, and represented many European individuals and corporations. Frederick R. Coudert, Sr. enjoyed a long, fruitful career as an American delegate to the International Congress on the Law of Nations in Antwerp in 1877; as a member of the Venezuela Boundary Commission; and as an American delegate to the International Commission in Paris on the Bearing Sea in 1893 (which resolved a fishing dispute between the United States and Great Britain). He once refused an offer by President Cleveland to an appointment to the United States Supreme Court.

Frederick R. Coudert, Jr., his son, had gained renown as a

prominent international lawyer.[28] He was not, however, a patent lawyer. He and another partner, John P. Murray, stepped up to defend Panhard & Levassor and the Newbauers from the Selden Patent infringement. Murray took testimony, and Coudert prepared the briefing and arguments. Four years into the trial preparations, luck served Frederick, Jr. a steaming plate of evidence, and he was clever enough to take notice. Following a short walk from the Coudert offices to the Betts, Betts, Sheffield & Betts offices—at 120 Broadway, the Equitable Building,[29] the first skyscraper in New York—Coudert made an unexpected discovery in that law firm's lobby. It stopped him short. It made him smile. It raised the stakes. Coudert's discovery would have a most profound impact on the result of the Selden litigation.

THE PATENT

In 1908, while the Selden Patent Case was pending, Edwin J. Prindle of the New York patent bar published a series of articles written for *The Engineering Magazine* and later published in a collection entitled *Patents as a Factor in Manufacturing*. Prindle's book provided the lay reader an understanding of the nature of a patent and its value to the patentee. Basically, "[a] patent is a public grant, in the nature of a contract between the Government and the inventor." Further,

> The inventor on his part is required to disclose fully a new and useful invention or discovery which he has made himself. If the invention is not new to the public at the time the inventor makes his invention, then the inventor has given nothing to the public

---

28. A prominent internationalist opposed to bigotry and hyper-nationalism, Courdert spent most of his life opposing the forces of ignorance and prejudice. See Veenswijk, Virginia Kays, *Courdert Brothers: A Legacy in Law*, Truman Taaley Books/Dutton, NY, 1994.

29. The Equitable, with seven stories, featured the first public elevators in the city and contained the offices of most of the "well-established" law firms of the Gilded Age.

> which it did not already have. . . . if the invention is not operable, or is injurious to the public morals, it is not useful; if the patentee did not invent or discover the invention but learned it from others . . . the patent is invalid.

A patent may be obtained in the United States from the United States Patent Office by submitting a written description of the patent along with drawings and/or models of the invention. The Patent Office reviews all prior art with respect to the patent and makes an assessment as to whether the "new" invention is patentable. If it determines that the invention is patentable, it will issue a patent. The patent, thus issued, is not the final determination of invention, as patents can be and frequently are challenged as to scope and novelty in the Federal Court System with the United States Supreme Court being the final arbiter of enforceability.

A patent gives the owner an exclusive right to the use and manufacture of the invention for a period of years (seventeen years in 1908). The use of the patent by another, during the patent period, without authorization from the owner, is an infringement giving the owner the right to a claim of damages and the potential of a court injunction against its further use. As Prindle wrote,

> A new combination of old elements may be patentable, if it produces a new or improved result, or an old result in a new way. . . . A new use of an old device or machine or process may be patentable, if the new use is so different from the old use as not to be obvious to an ordinary skilled workman in the art.

Drafting a patent claim requires great skill and the parameters of an effectively drawn claim can be counterintuitive. Prindle claimed that "[t]here is no piece of English composition more universally misunderstood than the written claim of a patent." And the Supreme Court has said that a patent claim is one of the most difficult pieces of English composition to write. Generally, and wrongly, it's thought that the more complete a description a claim gives of the embodiment of the invention, the better and more enforceable it is. But over-particularization of the claim has a narrowing effect, requiring a patent enforcer to prove all of the described elements of an invention in the infringement action, where a more generalized claim is broader in scope and hence more easily enforced. As an analogy, Prindle offers this:

> A claim is like giving one a title to everything that will fit into a box. Now if no particular type of box were specified, the grantee would have a very valuable monopoly. Everything that would go into a square, or a round box, or an oval box or a star-shaped box would be his. But, if the box were stated to be a round box having a pin set up in the center of its bottom and extending up to a level with the top of the box, it is evident that nothing could be put into the box but round things having a hole in the middle, and the grantee would have a very much less desirable monopoly.

George B. Selden was a master at drawing and negotiating the broadest type of patent with the Patent Office. The Selden Patent raised a specter to all who considered it. The claim could reasonably be read as covering the entire construction of gas-driven automobiles—which was certainly Selden's intent—by combining the mechanical features of the modern automobile with a "liquid hydrocarbon gas engine of the compressed type." Or the claim might only really apply to the combination of mechanical features with the Brayton-style engine identified in the Selden drawings. He had not specified this engine type in the writings that he submitted to the patent office. Hence, Selden argued that his patent related to all compression-type internal combustion engines, in spite of the fact that his drawings specifically show a Brayton-style engine with external compression and the lack of an in-cylinder explosion driving the engine pistons.

The focus of the Ford defense aimed to demonstrate that the Selden patent was not a new invention in terms of the prior art, either singularly, the motor, or in combination with the vehicle; and, alternatively, this patent was limited to an automobile incorporating the Brayton-type of internal combustion engine. Ford Motor Company had adopted the Otto four-cycle engine for their vehicles. They'd never produced a vehicle powered in the manner of Selden's drawings. The defense would also raise a broader, emotional and political claim: that Selden himself contributed nothing to the public knowledge or advancement of automobiles, but merely catalogued developments happening around him, and he did this to enrich himself and help restrain trade and competition by a group of greedy corporate interests, who had bought rights to his patent.

The Ford lawyers knew that the anti-monopoly plea could strike a major cord among the public at large. The Progressive Era fancied itself just that, and the attorneys intended to capitalize on it. But public support meant nothing to Prindle; the patent author was unmoved by the monopoly issue.

> Within his domain, the patentee is czar. The people must take the invention on the terms he dictates or let it alone for seventeen years. This is a necessity from the nature of the grant. Cries of restraint of trade and impairment of the freedom of sales are unavailing, because for the promotion of the useful arts, the constitution and statutes authorize this very monopoly.

Prindle and many other commentators of the day perceived the monopoly in the grant of a patent as a profoundly important property right and a critical driver of economic and technological expansion. Others viewed the patent system as a restraint on economic development and technological advance, artificially raising prices to the consumer and on occasion adversely affecting the security of the country. Only in a courtroom could these arguments achieve their full heads of steam.

But even in the courtroom, that steam tended to fly in any number of directions. Patent appeals are very specialized, based on confusing and subjective principles, and they are docket-consuming. Most federal judges abhorred them. The basic concepts of patentability were vague and illusive. Some districts were known to be more patent friendly than others and the United States Supreme Court could not itself correct every aberrant patent opinion. Up until 1982, when Congress created the United States Court of Appeals for the Federal Circuit, patent appeals were taken to the Court of Appeals for each federal district, resulting in a wide variety of concepts and opinions frequently written by judges who had no particular experience in the world of patents. Even the Supreme Court found it frustrating to maintain competence, consistency and rationality in its opinions. One of the great intellectual patent judges of all time, Judge Learned Hand of the U.S. Second Circuit Court of Appeals, recoiled from a suggestion by the Supreme Court that patent cases be determined first by validity, not infringement.

> There are good reasons for allowing some latitude of choice. A decision resting upon non-infringement is generally much more secure than one on validity, at least when the question is whether there is a patentable invention. That issue is as fugitive, impalpable, wayward, and vague a phantom as exists in the whole paraphernalia of legal concepts. It involves, or it should involve, as complete a reconstruction of the art that preceded it as is possible. The test of invention is the originality of the discovery, and discovery depends upon the mental act of conceiving the new combination, for substantially every invention is only a combination.[30]

Thus, on May 14, in the august halls of the Federal District Court for the District of New York, in the year 1909, Judge Charles Merrill Hough, a known expert in the law of Admiralty, assumed the bench in the Selden case. The records before him constituted fourteen thousand pages, containing five million words of testimony embedded in six years' worth of lawyerly tactical maneuvering in depositions taken in New York, Providence, Boston, Lansing, Ithaca, Rochester, Detroit, Pittsburgh, and Philadelphia. Hough's experience with patents was limited, and the assignment he inherited was daunting.

---

30. *Harries v. Air King Products*, 183 F. 2d 158, 162 (2nd Cir. 1952).

Chapter 4

Rubber and the Road

THE ROLLING RECORD

"Mullett's Monstrosity" was the name applied by many New Yorkers to the United States Post Office erected in the lower triangle of City Hall Park in Manhattan in the late 1870s. The Victorian building adopted the Second French Empire aesthetic of Napoleon III's Paris. It contained four stories of elaborately colonnaded granite with a plethora of porches and iron cresting below a bulbous mansard roof that capped a fifth story.

The *New York Sun* called Alfred Mullett, the building's architect, the "most arrogant pretentious little humbug in the United States." Mullet ultimately fled with his aesthetic to Washington, D.C., where his Old Executive Office Building still functions as an occasional hideout for the President of the United States. Mullet's signature style never caught on in New York where the New York Historical Society and the Sons of the Revolution, both determinably preservationist in orientation, actively campaigned for its destruction.

The Post Office Building, in 1909, was a hive of constant activity. The three sides of the building arose from rough cobblestone streets interlaced with steel trolley rails. Hundreds of horse-drawn drays containing thousands of bags of mail drew up to the building's many loading docks to offload and reload the exuberant correspondence of the day. The Third Avenue Trolley, which started at the Post Office, ran every four minutes during the day, transporting 65,000 passengers a day.

The third floor of the Post Office building contained the chambers and courtrooms of the newly created United States District Court for the Southern District of New York. In the courtroom of the Hon. Charles Merrill Hough, Henry Ford, George B. Selden, an assortment of ALAM officials and lawyers on both sides of the Selden patent dispute eyed each other up close for the first time. The men steeled themselves for the start of a six-day oral argument on the meaning of the massive court record gathered by the attorneys over six years of prosecution. The record contained fourteen thousand pages of testimony, with over five million words. More than one hundred printed pages of inter-lawyer squabbles, spouting personal rancor and dismissive insults concerning scheduling and adjournments, spiced the record and the air.

The exhibits included patent publications, motorcar catalogues, advertisements, newspaper and magazine articles, contracts, account books, journals, diagrams, drawings and photographs. In addition, three actual functioning automobiles had been entered into evidence, two created by the Selden interests and one by Ford. Selden had never produced an actual automobile pursuant to his patent, so the Selden side decided to demonstrate that the Selden patent design could support the construction of an actual, practical vehicle. George Selden's sons, Henry R. Selden and George B. Selden, Jr., supervised the construction of Exhibit 89, the "1877" Selden, in Rochester, New York. Exhibit 89 contained a number of modifications in technology not extant in 1877, including timed electric ignition, a modern carburetor and recently-designed cylinder heads, oil pumps and other features. The "Selden" vehicles were never made directly available to the Defendants for testing and their functionality was highly contested by the Defendants even with the enhancements. During the trial, several demonstrations of the vehicles occurred with fits, sputtering, starts and stops, and no evidence of sustained performance.

By 1905, gasoline-engine driven vehicles clearly dominated

the field over steam and electric engines. The United States produced twenty-one thousand six hundred ninety-two vehicles in 1905, 86.2% of which were gas powered. Steam vehicles followed with 7.2% and electric vehicles with 6.6%. George H. Day, then president of the Electric Vehicle Company, realized the value of the Selden patent to the Whitney Syndicate: the potential to recover royalties that were tied to the growth and dominance of internal combustion engine products.

Ford attorneys were bound to attack the value of the Selden design, so Day ordered a separate Selden vehicle, Exhibit 157, which was manufactured in his Electric Vehicle manufacturing facilities in Hartford, Connecticut. Henry Cave, a very capable Electric Vehicle engineer, spent five years supervising its construction. The Hartford vehicle, like its Selden counterpart, had features unavailable in 1879, including a water jacket, speed-changing gears and pneumatic tires. The Hartford vehicle ultimately tested out at 15 horsepower compared to the 2 horsepower generated by the Rochester effort. The generous and recent technical advances incorporated into the vehicle led attorney Frederick R. Coudert to exclaim, "Much Hartford, little Selden," in his impeccably French English accent.

Mr. Parker, with skepticism, expressed much interest and desire to inspect and test the Selden vehicles, both before and during the trial. The claimants fended off any close examination of the vehicles by the defense lawyers and their experts, for years. The Claimant's lawyers repeatedly ignored requests by Parker that they submit the vehicles to specific written test criteria. Neither of the Selden vehicles performed with grace or efficiency on the streets and tracks of New York, or anywhere else, despite their post-patent technical enhancements. In clouds of gasoline, steam and oil, they spluttered, lurched, jumped and halted, rarely able to sustain either continuity in operation or distance in transport.

Judge Hough kept his thoughts to himself, but seemed more interested in whether they could run at all.

The Selden interests relied on the argument that even modest movement was a success; more time and effort, applied in 1879, would have produced a more competent product.

The Ford Motor Company, for its part, decided to produce a workable automobile exhibit of its own to establish that a practical and workable internal combustion engine existed in the art prior to the 1879 Selden patent application. They sought to prove the workability of the engine designed by Jean Joseph Etienne Lenoir, a Belgian, living and working in France in the 1860s. The Lenoir non-compression engine was admittedly heavy for the weight of the vehicle and required impracticable volumes of water coolant to prevent overheating. During many days of deposition questioning, Dugald Clerk repeatedly testified in his deposition that the Lenoir engine was too heavy for practical use as a driver for an automobile. Clerk further admitted that if in fact the Lenoir engine could be shown to be reasonably capable of driving a light mechanical vehicle, the scope of the Selden patent as a "pioneer," transformative patent would have to be "reconsidered."

Snapping to the challenge, Ford technicians produced a workable Lenoir engine, which they installed in the chassis of a 1903 Ford Model A. The Ford lawyers, focusing on the performance of the engine rather than the vehicle that contained it, argued that the engine technology of the 1860s fully anticipated the developments of 1879, subscribed by Selden. The Ford idea was to discredit the Clerk testimony that the Lenoir engine could never work in an automobile, but was it enough to overcome Clerk's impressive stature as a witness?

HENRY FORD

Henry Ford testified twice. Keenly aware of the enormous stakes involved in the case and the potential impact on the growth and development in this wildcat, burgeoning industry, he chose brevity and clarity. It served him well. The record in the Selden case was, indeed, massive as the attorneys were determined to leave no stone unturned, no witness undeposed, no exhibit unexplored, no insight unplumbed. Most of the testimony presented for Judge

Hough's review was either numbingly historical or solemnly technical in nature. Among the first to give his evidence, Ford testified by deposition on November 25, 1905, and December 5, 1905, without pedantry or pomp.

Ford's testimony was, in fact, among the briefest of any of the leading witnesses in the case. The Selden crowd tried to paint him as a mere assembler and arranger of automobile parts, saying he contributed little to the art or the development of the gasoline-engine driven vehicle. They presented Ford as a simple craftsman who successfully borrowed from those who had preceded him. Ford took their accusations and spun the meanings. He insisted that his success as a manufacturer resulted directly from standing upon the shoulders of those innumerable contributors to the art who had preceded him. And while he gave them credit and praise, Ford allowed that no contribution or borrowing whatsoever had come from George B. Selden. Ford, simply, in monosyllabic language, unadorned by elaboration or fanfare, described his history and involvement in the development of the present-day automobile. That development, he told an interviewer years later, involved history, timing and achievement:

> I invented nothing new. I simply assembled into a car the discoveries of other men behind whom there were centuries of work, and the discoveries of still other men who preceded them. Had I worked fifty or ten or even five years before, I would have failed. So, it is with every new thing. Progress happens when all the factors that make for it are ready, then it is inevitable. To teach that comparatively few men are responsible for the great forward leap of mankind is the worst form of nonsense.[31]

In his testimony, Ford described his motives. First, it was the potential of helping farmers with threshing and sawing wood that drove his interest in the gasoline engine. "My people say that I

31. Quoted in Greenleaf, supra, at 138, from article in *New Outlook*, September, 1934, entitled, "The Schoolmaster of Dearborn."

was trying to build an automobile when I was ten years old." This drew a hearsay objection from ALAM attorney Betts, which was one of thousands of objections in the deposition transcripts never actually ruled upon by a judge.

The early motors that Ford experimented with in the 1890s were of the 4-cycle "Otto" type, which he first learned about in "English scientific books." Those heavy, stationary engines suited large industrial applications. As a young man, Ford developed experience repairing Otto-type engines while he was employed at the Eagle Iron Works in Detroit.

Ford's first attempt to construct a motor vehicle involved attaching a small Otto engine to a bicycle; he found the motor much too powerful for the vehicle. Ford was thirty-three years old. The American Otto-type engines were normally smaller and weighed less than their European counterparts but still were too hefty for a bike. Ford followed developments and refinements in the Otto engine in technical magazines such as *American Machinist* and *The Horseless Age.* He first became aware of a gasoline engine powering a mechanical vehicle with a disengaging clutch when Charles E Duryea presented the first gasoline drive automobile in America in 1892. Ford personally observed the first trial run of Charles H. King's vehicle in Detroit on March 6, 1896. Ford clearly and unequivocally admitted borrowing technology developed by others, only not from Mr. Selden.

ALAM's attorney, Betts, asked Ford whether it would hurt his business if the Selden patent was sustained. Ford replied, "It would not affect us, as we do not infringe the Selden patent, in my mind." Asked further whether the suit was a boon to his business, Ford stated, "Yes, through the publicity we obtained through fighting it." Given the growing increase in Ford production, it was actually cheaper for Ford defend the lawsuit than to pay the royalty payments demanded by ALAM. Following Ford's testimony, the gathering of out of court testimony for the court relentlessly ground on, unencumbered by the constraints of a judicial ruling as to the materiality or admissibility of the evidence being developed.

GEORGE B. SELDEN

There is a strange chemistry of personality that allows for the fusion of opposites and the bonding of the incongruent. Not so with George B. Selden and Ralzemond A. Parker. They disliked each other with blinding intensity both because of their differences and their similarities. Both were accomplished patent lawyers and Civil War veterans. Both had a deep and abiding interest and knowledge in the early technology of the automobile and the internal combustion engine. Selden was cold, hard and dismissive. Parker was hot, active and aggressive. Selden cut a tight figure, being thin and a bit of a dandy. Parker was overweight and disheveled. Their similarities clashed. Their dissimilarities collided.

Selden saw Parker as a bumpkin interloper, driven to deprive him of due recognition as the "father of the automobile," and the financial remuneration to which he felt he was entitled after successfully shepherding his sixteen-year patent application through the U.S. Patent Office. The number of years Selden had spent unsuccessfully pursuing financial backing to monetize his patent left him edgy, impatient and deeply embittered. Parker viewed Selden as a canny fraud, who cleverly manipulated the patent regulations to worm his application through, and overwhelm the application-saturated patent office to obtain a patent for an "invention" for which he never produced a contribution to the art or the technology.

Parker called George B. Selden for a contentious cross-examination concerning the integrity of his patent. Selden was characteristically caustic and defensive. It was patent lawyer vs. patent lawyer, "mano a mano." Parker worked his opponent up into a fine steam.[32] Then, Selden boldly asserted, "None of the so-called prior

---

32. The Selden cross examination by Parker took place two years after his direct examination through his lawyers between July 6, 1908 and August 17, 1908 in New York. See Volume 6 of the *Transcript on Appeal* of The *Columbia Motor Car Company et al. vs. C.A. Duerr and the Ford Motor Company et al.*, pp. 2855-3201, at Benson Ford Research Center, Dearborn, Michigan., Accession 1704.

inventors had arrived at my fundamental principal of a lightweight engine, and as this principal is absolutely essential, they could not succeed, nor could anyone succeed, at this late day, by assuming and conglomeration of any of their so-called inventions."

That is to say, Selden dismissed the import of all of the prior contributors to the technology of the automobile.

Further, Selden testified that Exhibit 89, constructed by his sons for the infringement case, established the bona fides of his patent. He stated that the purpose of Exhibit 89 was

> [T]o demonstrate to the court that a self-propelling road engine built exactly in according to the drawings and specifications of my drawings and application, filed May 8, 1879, Patent No 549,160, November 5, 1895, was a practically operating and useful machine, which the said Exhibit has now fully proved by repeated trials during the last four months.

Parker complained that the Selden brothers had added to the construction of the Exhibit. Selden dismissed these upgrades as "slight mechanical differences."

> Exhibit 89 is built to a scale and almost a Chinese copy of the drawings of my application and patent and it contains nothing whatever which was not shown or described in by application and patent.

Parker picked and probed at his adversary's every sensitive flaw. Selden adopted a campaign of grumpy avoidance, responding to Parker's thrusts with long-winded refusals to answer pointed and dangerous questions. In response to Selden's claims about the performance of his car, Parker stated, "I think you stretched the truth woefully." Frustrated at Selden's refusal to respond to specific technical inquiries, Parker summed things up: "In fact, taken all in all, you don't know very much about this case, do you?"

Selden grew cooler and even more rigid. "I am again obliged to you for the insinuation, but it is my opinion that I know enough about these cases to show up the utter futility of the defense proposed in them."

When Parker highlighted Selden's non-contribution to the technical art of the automobile, Selden took a shot at Henry Ford and Parker. "So far as I know, Mr. Ford made no invention which is in practical use today."

Selden, while disparaging what he described as Henry Ford's lack of personal invention in the development of the automobile, compared to what he asserted as his own, could not help but acknowledge Ford's relative success in the market. Even then, Selden couldn't avoid expressing his small-minded peeve that some Ford advertising may have led some readers to the impression that Ford was being represented by another, more widely known and admired Parker.

> I may add that personally, I am on good terms with Mr. Ford and that I rather admire his business skill with which he managed his enterprise, even if sometimes it did invoke advertising of which seems to me to be rather illegitimate character, such for instance as the advertising which has led some of the public to infer that the defense in this case is being conducted by Judge Alton B. Parker.[33]

Selden repeatedly referred in his patent application to a "liquid hydrocarbon engine of the compression type." "I am not aware that provisions to the date of my invention any attempt was made to reduce the weight of a road locomotive by the production of a liquid hydrocarbon engine capable of locomotion or that there was described or constructed a compression hydrocarbon engine of such a design that it was capable of propelling a road locomotive . . ."

Parker then tried to attack Selden's view of the scope of his patent. And received more gobbledegook in reply.

> **Parker:** If I understand you, it is now your understanding that so long as an operative combination is produced, the mounting of your engine on a road carriage anywhere and anyway for the

33. Judge Alton Brooks Parker was a conservative Democrat who lost the 1904 presidential election in a landslide to Theodore Roosevelt.

> purpose of driving the same and with any sort of connection between your engine and the propelling wheels would be within your original invention?
>
> **Selden:** I am not aware of that there is in them any construction in such regards and as my invention is the pioneer in the act, my understanding on it under existing decisions is to be liberally construed.

Insisting that the "compression" wording broadly described all modern internal combustion engines, Selden surprised the assembled by smiling and pushing forward across the table toward Parker, with clipped modesty, unsuited to his broad claim, and with a higher pitch to his voice, he asserted that his patent covered both the Brayton-type engine and the Otto-type engine in combination with the mechanical features of the vehicle.

Parker went temporarily silent. Selden's drawings clearly showed only a Brayton-type engine which operated more closely to the steam engine technology (a constant flame and an external compression cylinder) and was a forerunner of the diesel engine. The Otto-type engine occupied a different world (relying on a compressed petroleum gas and air mixture ignited by a series of electrical sparks to create mini-explosions within the cylinder to drive the operating pistons). In this case, silence seemed the best way to drive Selden's grandiose message home.

Without the presence of a judge, who could require a witness to answer a question directly, Selden never stopped dancing around the questions put to him, gladly leading Parker on a fractious chase into irrelevant rabbit holes of obfuscation, while adamantly refusing to address specific technical ambiguities in his patent application. What was the exact ratio of turning speeds of the crank shaft to the drive wheels of his vehicle? Selden refused to answer even "yes or no" questions put to him. He challenged Parker: "You have tried several times to dictate my answer to me, and as far as I know, you have not yet succeeded, and I doubt whether you will . . ."

Parker, at a point of extreme frustration, exploded: "Mr. Selden I will cross examine you all summer if you don't answer that question. That is as sure as you are sitting in that chair."

Selden sat firmly on his principles. Since he had obtained a patent on a "pioneer invention," as opposed to an incremental development patent, his patent was to be broadly and liberally construed regardless of certain vagueness in the detail. He underscored that

> [T]he examiner did recognize clearly that I had done something which Brayton had not done and in that respect, we have the later endorsement by the Commissioner of Patents himself in his Report to Congress of 1895 of my invention as the pioneer in the art, and still further the endorsement by the highest practical authority in the world, Mr. Dugald Clerk, of my invention as the pioneer, and Mr. Clerk showed that he was fully acquainted with the Brayton engine in all its details.

He groused that circumstances led to Ford's construction of a car before him.

> According to the record it is clear that long before Mr. Ford went into the field at all, I had built a liquid hydrocarbon engine, which I believe was the first that was ever built, capable of road locomotion, but for various reasons detailed at large in my direct examination, principally poverty and my inability to get anybody with money to engage in my enterprise, Mr. Ford preceded me in the actual application of my invention to a car.

Poor Selden grumbled that poverty had kept him from realizing his dream. Parker felt no sympathy. He argued that Selden's vehicle did not apply some absolutely new way of combining a certain motor with a certain road carriage; and that a motor carriage capable of being driven by any number of several motors was not patentable. He argued that the use of any motor, even if new in design, would be an old use predating the Selden patent, because the Selden patent wrongly claimed the first practical use of any engine with a carriage.

Parker, in the end, stressed Selden's changeable and inconsistent claims. He honed in on Selden's biannual changes, noting particularly his application changes to broaden the scope of his patent claim, after the Benz Otto patents were taken in this country in 1888, so as to benefit from the technical experiments of others. Many, if not most, of Parker's thrusts at Selden were buried in a mountain of blurred and technical discussions that would numb the mind of any lay reader disposed to read them. Any judge unschooled in and uninterested in technical detail would likely grab at the simplest, most direct avenue to a reasonable resolution. How much the judge in the case actually read of this testimony is unknown, but there were some who suggested, not much. Complexity, even with accuracy, was working against Parker.

DUGALD CLERK

The lawyers in the Selden patent case called forty-two witnesses for the complainant and forty witnesses for the defense. The most important and pivotal witness in the case was Dugald Clerk, called by the Selden side, whose unassailable reputation and expertise with respect to internal combustion engines rendered him a most formidable opponent. Parker made his cross-examination of Clerk both earnest and respectful, devoid of the rancor of his confrontation with George Selden.

The examination harkened to George Bernard Shaw's observation that "England and America are two countries separated by a common language." Clerk's responses to Parker's questions were careful, measured, nuanced and precise, which made it very difficult for Parker to pin him down on a subject—without the entanglement of a web of qualifications and caveats.[34]

> **Parker:** If the running gear of Selden's structure, including the propelling wheel and the steering gear, would operate as such,

34. Parker's examination of Dugald Clerk on August 20-23, 1906, is available at The Benson Ford Research Library, Dearborn, Michigan. Accession 1, Box 173, File 13, pp. 1-774.

regardless of the kind of motor which drove it, and if the motor which drove the carriage operated as a motor the same as it would in any other relation where it was used as a motor, and if the carriage body was adapt to carry persons and goods, the same as any other carriage would be, even in a horse drawn vehicle, can you say that the complete operation of the vehicle is anything more than the sum of the functions performed by these elements?

Clerk: In the abstract sense in which you appear to put your question, your conclusion may be true, but nevertheless the combination made by Selden, including the elements you mention, has produced an entirely new technical result, that result being, as I have repeatedly explained, a road vehicle propelled by a motor and controlled by gear, the weight and bulk of which is practically negligible, and consequently Selden produced the new technological effect of a self-propelled motor vehicle practically free from the usual bulky obstructions. In the abstract sense in which you put the question, I think that on the whole I may agree with you. That is assuming abstractly all these things, then no doubt each acts as you suggest it would act separately. It by no means follows, however, in my view, that there is no invention in making the combination, which seems in your mind to follow from your proposition.

Parker sought to move Clerk to focus on Selden's "selection" of a Brayton-style engine as being the true core of his invention.

Parker: Selden's improvement in this sense is due to simply to the selection of a motor which possesses the qualities which enables him to get rid of the obstructions, and if he has built a better road vehicle than others, that better road vehicle is due to the fact that he has employed a better motor. Isn't that true?

Clerk: In using the word "selection" you would appear to imply the existence previous to Selden's application for a patent of a motor in a form ready for application to Selden's purpose. In this use of the word "selection" I disagree with you. I agree with you, however, if "selection" means the selection of a thermodynamic cycle and the production of a suitable engine using that thermodynamic cycle. Selden's invention no doubt consists partly in the selection

> of a "suitable" thermodynamic cycle, but this selection would not constitute invention in my view unless he showed some adequate means of reducing his selection to practice. That Selden, in my view, has done, as I have repeatedly explained. The better road vehicle produced is undoubtedly produced because Selden has chosen a better motor, but as I understand it, Selden was the first to apply a motor of this type in a form in which it could operate successfully in a road vehicle, and accordingly, it seems to me that it is hardly accurate to use the term "selection" except in the limited meaning which I have given it. Selden's invention is, as I have stated, in answer given in my direct examination, an invention of application, and the invention resides in the selection, if you like, of a suitable type (thermodynamic true) of motor, and in the application of that type by such practical alternations as are necessary to produce an engine such as I have repeatedly described.

Parker tried to obtain an admission from Clerk that the "selection" of a different type of engine, producing much better results, would also result in an invention. Clerk resisted. "If the application be once made, then no subsequent application of the same type, although perhaps in a better manner, could be subject for a broad claim. It might of course supply subject matter for limited claims dealing with any special modifications, but only the first application could in my view be held to be fit subject matter for a broad claim."

Parker used the patent language describing the engine to try to narrow the scope of the Selden patent to the Brayton-style engine.

> **Parker:** I ask you, if you do not understand the claim to mean that all of the impulses given by the number of cylinders, whether two or more, must be given during a single rotation of the power shaft, and I ask this because the language is "during the rotation," only one rotation is mentioned.
>
> **Clerk:** Doubtless Selden's intention here is to get continuous impulses around his crank cycle. There I agree with you, but where we differ appears to be more upon the legal effect of the matters, which I have pointed out, and perhaps on such legal point I should not express any opinion.

The discussion continued to parse the differences and similarities between the Brayton – and Otto-type engines. Clerk further testified that as of 1879, the date of Selden's patent application, there were four commercially successful gasoline engines on the market: the Lenoir, the Brayton, the Otto and Langen, and the "Silent Otto." Parker sought to move Clerk to admit that Selden's original concept of attaching a gasoline engine to the front wheel drive gear had been expanded and broadened by him over the sixteen-year life of the patent application, but he prompted only an evasive reply.

> **Clerk:** It in one sense may be considered broader, so far as that particular statement is concerned, that is, obviously he does not now limit himself to applying the engine directly to the driving wheel, but referring to other parts of the specifications as originally filed, I find he actually shows his engine connected to the driving wheel through gearing, so that even assuming your contention to be right, that the later statement is broader, it is not broader than the mechanism actually described from the first.

Parker suggested to Clerk that the early Lenoir engine might reasonably have been applied to a mechanical carriage before the Selden Application, which drew firm denials from Clerk.

> **Clerk:** On your assumption at the date of the original application, it might, as you say, be an engine which could be mounted on the driving axel, but I have already discussed the Lenoir and other engines, and it flows quite clearly from my previous discussion that no Lenoir engine, for example, could be got in such a form as to operate on any driving axel.... The obtainable pressures in a Lenoir engine are less than half of the available pressures easily obtained by Brayton, and the mechanical arrangements of the Lenoir are such that no Lenoir engine was ever made which was capable of the speeds of rotation of the Brayton or constant-pressure-type engine. Accordingly, no Lenoir engine was ever built which gave results as to the power for weight which could be compared to an engine of the Brayton type.

Clerk also rejected the feasibility of adapting the Otto and Langen engine to Selden's vehicle.

> **Clerk:** You are quite correct; the Otto and Langen engine could not possibly be adapted to operate in the position shown by Selden, nor could it be adapted to operate in any carriage at all.

Clerk admitted that the silent Otto engine was more economical and reliable than the Brayton, but he cleaved to Selden's argument that the scope of his patent covered all internal compression engines regardless of time or quality.

Parker, having led the courtroom on a long tour of all the engines of the year in question, 1879, then challenged the notion that the "selection" of the Brayton engine was an act of invention.

> **Parker:** If we assume that graphically that he [Selden] had those four engines laid out before him to choose from, aside from adapting an engine to a special purpose in making the choice, could you say that he had any more than exercised the skill of a constructive engineer?

> **Clerk:** I have already stated that, in my view it was an act of invention to take the operative cycle of either of those engines and adopt that cycle in a form which would carry out the purpose. . . . although at the present time, it is difficult in view of the numerous applications to automobiles of engines of this type to see the subject matter point, yet as I have already said. . . . Selden has done and accordingly performed, as I understand the question, an act of invention.

Parker directed Clerk back to the "engineer" component of his question.

> **Parker:** I think you misunderstand my question, I excluded any adaptation of the engine, but merely referred to the selection of the engine to be adapted. Would you consider that any more than the action of a skilled engineer?

> **Clerk:** Even that act, in my view, might very well be invention,

> because at the date of Selden's application, as far as I know the subject, merely every engineer engaged in the construction and design of gas engines would have scouted the very idea of applying either the Brayton engine or the Otto silent engine to the purposes of a road vehicle.

The assured, wise, unflappable Scot continued:

> I understand from the record that the evidence shows that Mr. Brayton himself had the idea of adapting his engine to the purpose of, first, street locomotion and, second, road 'bus" locomotion, and I also understand from the evidence that he failed to carry his idea into practice. That is why I have said in my previous answers that it is not sufficient to constitute invention to have an idea. It is necessary in addition to give such discrimination and drawings as will enable that idea to be carried into effect. I quite agree with you that the mere idea itself, unless carried successfully into effect, does not supply subject matter for an invention.

Clerk's testimony added some three hundred thousand words to the Selden case trial record. He, at the end, quietly admitted, "If Mr. Parker is right as to American patent law, I fear that I have broken down the case of my side." But, the validity of Parker's views as to the law, were still very much in play.

HIS HONOR

Charles Merrill Hough, a former partner in the New York City law firm of Robinson, Biddle and Ward, had, like his firm, specialized in maritime and bankruptcy cases. This expert in maritime law had also served, as his principal client, the Pennsylvania Railroad. President Theodore Roosevelt, when considering Hough's appointment to the bench, feared that Hough would appear to favor railroad, corporate and trust interests. Roosevelt's advisors and political agents sold him on the idea that there would be a value in having a judge on the court who understood how corporations operated.

Judge Hough had a reputation for feeble health and a harsh exterior persona. Some lawyers had objected to his appointment to the Federal bench on the basis of his lack of judicial temperament—an inability to project evenhandedness and dispassionate fairness in his treatment of litigants and their lawyers. This particular infection still afflicts many judges to this day.

Those who knew him considered Hough to be bright and energetic, if lacking in patience, and deep consideration of the implications of factual scenarios brought before him. His basic intelligence and quickness of mind, on occasion, led him to incomplete and inadequate consideration of the issues before him. Lawyers appearing before him noted that the "high initial velocity of his mind was conspicuously effective in mastering facts, analyzing evidence, and applying general principles to concrete cases." Hough was "impatient of irrelevance, incompetence, and prolixity." The Judge struck terror in many legal hearts. Felix Frankfurter, who later became a justice of the United States Supreme Court, reported walking around the United States Post Office building in New York twice before appearing before Judge Hough in order to quiet his own anxiety. But the very qualities that made him a quick study of the cases before him could also lead to inflexibility and incomplete consideration of a litigant's case.

Judge Hough graduated from Dartmouth College in 1879—the same year Selden took out his contended patent—and became a member of the New York bar in 1883 after "reading law" as a law firm's legal apprentice. His colleagues marked him as "gruff, conservative, witty and warm," anticipating the personality, intellect and distinctive demeanor of recently departed United States Supreme Court Justice Antonin Scalia. He was described as "easily the most learned American admiralty judge of his generation." He was the author of *Reports of Cases in the Vice-Admiralty of the Provence of New York and of the Court of Admiralty of the State of New York*, (1715-1758).

Hough befriended and frequently critiqued the Hon. Learned Hand, an admiralty and patent expert on the United States Second Circuit Court of Appeals (the appeals court to which Hough, himself, later ascended as a judge appointed by President Woodrow Wilson).

Hough was not above assailing judges above or below him in the judicial hierarchy when he disagreed with their decisions. In an article published in the *Harvard Law Review,* he directly challenged Justice Oliver Wendell Holmes' admiralty decisions as having "not increased certainty of maritime law and . . . [having] impaired the tradition of enforceable customs of the sea." He attacked Holmes as "bagging an epigram" as usual in his phrase hunting. Holmes said that Hough had a "spicy tongue."

Hough didn't think much of the legal profession as a whole either. In his memoirs, he wrote,

> There are some practicing lawyers, possibly a hundred in the whole United States, who are not parasites, whose services to clients are regarded by the laity as a favor, and there are plenty of men who have studied law and know quite as much as the practitioner, who have no clients and do not want them. But the first class is too small, and last to detached from life of the bar to count. Nor do the judges make any difference, for they are overwhelmingly taken by popular election from the ranks of practitioners and are neither better nor worse than the ruck; the most active-minded of them often expect to return to practice after a judicial bath and rest, and even when they remain on the bench the practitioner's attitude has become second nature – they are too old to change when they cross the bar.[35]

If James Couzens' annual smile could crack the ice in the great lakes, Judge Hough's glare could freeze the lakes in July. With his wire-rimmed glasses mounting a moustache, he had a demeanor not un-

35. Part of Hough's personal memoir, was published posthumously in article "Concerning Lawyers," 5 *The Ohio State University Law Journal* 1, 6-7 (December, 1938).

like his benefactor, Theodore Roosevelt,[36] but without the humor and charm. More than one lawyer was caught speechless with terror while mesmerized by Hough's diamond stickpin and tie protruding from the black depths of his robes and the terror of his wrath.

During the Selden side's opening argument, Hough interrupted with a disturbing declaration. "Someone will have to explain to me what the liquid hydrocarbon engine is." This troubled ALAM's lawyers not at all. Mr. Parker, aware that he had a long slough ahead of him, struggled vainly to guide Judge Hough through the complicated and twisting corridors of the history and technology of the internal combustion engine. His explanation as to why the Selden design was not a "pioneering invention" relied on this fundamental understanding. Hough, who had a penchant for a quick strike to find the heart of any legal issue, appeared more receptive to the easy simplicity of the Selden claimants, that the Selden patent, having been endorsed under the imprimatur of the United States Patent Office, represented a basic fundamental patent.

The Judge interrupted oral arguments briefly, at 3:00 p.m. on June 1, 1909, to permit the Judge and the lawyers to adjourn to one of the many outdoor balconies of the Post Office Building to watch the start of an auto race. This New York to Seattle race commemorated the Alaska, Yukon, Pacific Exposition, and it held New Yorkers in thrall. President William Howard Taft touched the start button, and Mayor George B. McClellan, Jr. fired a gold-plated starter pistol. Only six of the anticipated thirty-five participants left the starting line; a cross-country tour proved challenging for cars at the time. On returning to the courtroom following the start of the race, Panhard & Levassor attorney, Frederick R. Courbert, commented wryly to those present. "Your honor, there is something that puzzles me, I don't see

36. Hough returned the favor to Roosevelt in 1910, when he dismissed for lack of jurisdiction a federal criminal libel action against the *New York World*, sponsored by Roosevelt, alleging the libel of the U.S. Government (and incidentally Roosevelt, Robert Taft and others) for asserting corruption with regard to the purchase of the Panama Canal.

a Selden car. I see a Ford car, two Ford cars, but I see no Selden car," to which the judge laughed briefly with the other lawyers. A Ford Model T arrived first in Seattle, but suffered disqualification for having replaced an axel, during a stop in Utah, an inauspicious omen for the Ford team in the courtroom.

The sides undertook very different approaches to the briefs submitted to the Court and in their arguments. The Selden side opted for simplicity and broad strokes, dismissing the claims that Selden himself lacked contribution to the art of the invention of the automobile and had manipulated the patent system to achieve his patent. The team asserted that he did nothing that he wasn't legally entitled to do and that the patent office, with its technical expertise, declared that he had achieved a pioneer patent which clearly entitled him to broad application as a precedent. They risked all, relying on Judge Hough's quick, clean intellect to honor their quick, clean claims.

The Defendants relied on highly technical, at times cumbersome explanations, detailing prior patents that they deemed applicable, attacking the lack of "invention," decrying the lack of "operability" of either of the Selden vehicles, challenging Selden's methods in his application process and, finally, disparaging the value of Selden's contribution to the industry.

Six days of sweltering testimony and summer heat left everyone exhausted. Following the closing arguments, Judge Hough, grumbling about the size of the record, decamped to his summer home in Rhode Island to review the record and the briefs and to search for the logical key to this controversy and to craft his opinion.

Chapter 5

Verdict, Victory and Vindication

THE DECISION

Judge Hough released his decision on September 15, 1909. Given the technical complexity of the case and the monstrous scope of the record, his relatively quick decision suggested an incomplete and simplistic review of the record, which would inherently favor of the Selden interests. The decision which came as little surprise to the east coast legal establishment, rocked the public media. ALAM's lawyers had pled a simple, coherent case that recognized the broad application of a "pioneer patent;" the Ford defendants had asserted that Selden's patent was technically unpatentable because of the existence of prior art and, if patentable, should be narrowly construed. A Ford Motor Company dealer in New York, after reading the opinion, voiced his dismay to Henry Ford.

> I don't believe for a minute that he [Hough] ever went through any of the testimony for certainly he has not had time to do it, as I understand that he sat in court way in July on different cases, and with his vacation, would not give him time to read over any of the testimony and consider the facts which he should have done. He has practically given them a broad claim on everything that they asked for, and a judge of the United States to get up and render a decision on this sort on a fake piece of junk, which

> Selden had, seems to me to be ridiculous.[37]

This "fake piece of junk," in Hough's detailed finding, was Selden's valid and "eminently patentable" claim. In his opinion, the presumption of validity attending the grant of a patent by the Patent Office and the description of the Selden patent were subject to broad application and interpretation. He concluded further that the Defendants had infringed the patent. The judge noted that he was looking for "one lack" of materials for a good road wagon existing in 1879, which was provided by Selden, which Selden claimed to be his modification of the Brayton engine. In evaluating prior engine art, Judge Hough relied heavily on the testimony and publications of Dugald Clerk.

> [T]he court is fortunate in having in evidence a book entitled *The Gas Engine* published in 1895 by Mr. Dugald Clerk, who has also testified with admirable clearness as an expert for complainants. It appears that the materials for this book were gathered during the very period of Selden's experiments, while so completely has Clerk furnished a classic on the gas engine art that even counsel, who sharply criticize his evidence, support their arguments from his book to such an extent that it is not too much to say that many chapters thereof could be reconstructed from their briefs.[38]

Judge Hough alighted upon Selden's adaptation of a lighter Brayton engine to road carriages as filling the "lack" he was looking for, giving force to Selden's patent as of 1879, while dismissing the differences between the Brayton and Otto engines as immaterial based upon Selden's broad patent application description of a "liquid hydrocarbon gas engine of the compression type."

> It therefore seems clear that the phrase "compression type" as applied to internal combustion engines, is reasonably indicative of a class, and appropriately describes an unmistakable and in-

---

37. Gaston Plantiff letter to Henry Ford, September 16, 1909, Accession 1, Box 142, at the BFRC.

38. Hough opinion at 172 F 923 (September 19, 1909).

> variable species of the genus gas engine.
>
> *
>
> They [variations] occur, or may occur in all compression engines, and are no more significant of specific or generic differences than are variations and rapidity of health in different men, or the same men at different times.

Hough's attempt to obscure and minimize the differences between the Brayton and Otto engines shifts from biology to grammar, apparently in pursuit of "bagging an epigram" himself.

> These terms [constant pressure and constant volume] appear to have been devised by Mr. Clerk, and first used in his book, before alluded to, as convenient phrases useful in studying the operation of engines and classifying their phenomena. The terms are instructive, as in the separation of nouns into declinations and verbs into conjugations; but much of the argument about the words attaches an undeserved importance to them.

The judge went on to make specific factual findings regarding Selden's achievement.

> When he was ready to file his application, he had completed and experimentally operated one cylinder of a three-cylinder engine of the general type Brayton had patented in 1872 and 1874. He intentionally built a plurality of cylinders to obviate or minimize the necessity for a "fly wheel." He produced an enclosed crank case (which immediately reduced weight to an enormous extent) and used a small piston with a short stroke (which made possible the speed that would compensate for the loss of piston head area). This engine, with allowances for adjuncts Selden did not use, but (as experience has shown) should have used, weighed less than 200 pounds per brake horse power, as compared with over 800 pounds in the lightest form of Brayton's, and is capable of over 5000 revolutions per minute, as against less than 250 by any type of gas engine known built or suggested in 1879.

Hough went on to underscore the importance of Selden's modifications to the Brayton engine, as testified to by Clerk, finding that "[t]he adaptation of the engine alone was something never before attempted (so far as shown). Such adaptation might have involved an infringement on Brayton, but that didn't prevent Selden's combination from being strikingly new, useful if it would work, and eminently patentable." He specifically rejected the Defendant's arguments that Selden's placement of the Brayton-type engine in his patent drawings precluded application of his patent to the Otto engine used by them, and all other modern automobile manufacturers; because of the broad reach of a pioneer patent, Selden could claim a patent on a "broad range of equivalents" including the application of the Otto engine to an automobile.

The Judge specifically rejected the prior precedent advanced by the Defendants of Brayton's own application of his engine to an omnibus in Pittsburg, Pennsylvania, because of its failure of success for unclear reasons. He did acknowledge the unique nature of the case.

> No litigation closely resembling these cases has been shown to the court, and no instance is known to me of an idea being buried in the Patent Office until the world caught up and passed it, and then embodied in a patent only useful for tribute. But patents are granted for inventions. The inventor may use his discovery, or he may not, but no one can use it for 17 years. That 17 years begins whenever the United States so decrees by its patent grant. That the applicant for patent rights acquiesces in delay, or even desires delay, is immaterial to the courts, so long as the statute law is not violated.

Judge Hough agreed with the arguments by the Defendants that Selden did not contribute much to the art of the development of the 1909 automobile, and that he manipulated the patent rules for sixteen years to broaden the scope of his patent to encompass recent technical developments. He essentially agreed with those complaints, but discounted their effects. Hough held that Selden "did not overstep the law. He did delay . . . . If he did not delay unlawfully, what intervening rights did he permit to spring up?" In other words, Hough, finding that Selden had legally engineered his sixteen-year delay for the prosecution of his patent with the patent office, he found there could be no rights to infringers emanating from that delay. Even if Selden did contribute little or nothing to the technical advancement of the automobile, he obtained his patent by following the rules of the patent office and he was entitled to the benefits granted to him.

Finally, Judge Hough, fully embracing the patent office determination that Selden's patent was a pioneer patent, entitled to broad application against subsequent equivalent inventions, vented his esteemed spleen on the Ford team of lawyers, Parker in particular, for what he viewed as the unnecessary expansion of the issues in the case and the resulting size of the record. He chastised the Defendants for their objections to the "operativeness" of Selden's patent because of the technical changes to and deficient performance of the Selden exhibit vehicles, Exhibits 89 and 157. Hough inexplicably found the former to be a "Chinese copy" and the latter to be "within the range of equivalents" of the Selden Patent.

> The evidence on the subject of operativeness is the most flagrant example of unsupervised testifying I have ever seen or heard of .... They [defendants] raised a false issue over which months of time and volumes of print have been expended. The serious and I think only question was, and is, whether a machine made in substantial conformity to drawings and specifications, without going beyond the range of equivalents permitted, was operative, even though rudimentary.

The Judge appended an extended footnote to his opinion expressing his dissatisfaction with the court of equity procedure, that of gathering testimony and exhibits outside of a judge-monitored proceeding, because of the "cost, volume, squabbles and intemperance of the record." He noted, "[N]aturally tempers give way under such ill-arranged procedure and this record contains language uncalled for and unjustifiable from the tort discourtesies to the lie direct."

ALAM ASCENDENT

Of course, the decision shook the Ford Motor Company to its core but not its resolve. According to Ford shareholder and lawyer, John W. Anderson, "We thought we were in great jeopardy. We were feeling very blue indeed." But, Anderson went on "We resolved to die hard." The Company rejected an overture from ALAM to discuss settlement and started the ground work for an appeal to the federal Second Circuit Court of Appeals. James Couzens put on a bold face, "We were never afraid of the outcome."[39] Ford issued a telegram statement to its dealers and to editors. "Selden suit decision has no effect on Ford policy. We will fight to a finish."

On March 1, 1911, the *Detroit Free Press* published an editorial praising Henry Ford's resistance, entitled "Ford the fighter, salute." It described him as "equal to his weight in wildcats." The editorial continued, "Of the cause behind him, the lawyers are more able to talk, but as a human figure he presents a spectacle to win the applause of all men with red blood: for this world dearly loves the fighting man, and needs him too, if we are to go forward." Ford reprinted the editorial in the Ford house organ, the *Ford Times,* along with other adulatory comments, including one from a customer.

> When I purchase my Ford car, I don't want Mr. Ford or anyone else to give me an indemnifying bond to operate the same, as I feel that the Supreme Court of the United States will quickly see the injustice of your claim, and award to Mr. Ford such a verdict as will forever close the mouths of a lot of jealous minded manufacturers who are unable to compete with him on price and quality.

Parker, though physically and emotionally exhausted, continued to assert that the Hough opinion was wrong and would be overturned on appeal. Frederic Coudert, representing Panard and

39. Quoted in the *Detroit Journal,* January 11, 1911.

Levassor, faced a dispirited and disillusioned client, who wanted to quit. Coudert went to France and convinced them to stay by offering to prosecute the appeal free if he was not successful.

Following the Hough decision, ALAM consolidated its commanding position in the automobile industry by admitting a large number of new members, almost doubling its size, while continuing to reject applications from manufacturers it deemed unworthy. Most of the new members came from the upstart Association of Motor Car Manufacturers, of which Ford was a member. Ford Motor Company thus found itself essentially alone in its resistance to ALAM following the shock of the decision. The power and influence of ALAM cast shadows everywhere. Its members included eighty-seven percent of automobile manufacturers. In 1910, Buick, Winton, Cadillac, Hupmobile, Franklin, Hudson, Mack, Packard, Oldsmobile Studebaker, Dodge Brothers and many other manufacturers were paying royalties to it for licenses, amounting to over two million dollars in revenues annually. Selden personally pocketed about two hundred thousand dollars as his share of the royalties actually paid to ALAM.

Charles Clifton, then president, treasurer, and general manager of ALAM and head of the Pierce-Arrow Motor Car Company, warned the newcomers to the industry that "[s]ome patent attorneys, not appreciating the importance of the decision, or for other reasons, have evidently encouraged people to manufacture cars in the face of this decision, a procedure which may result in a heavy loss for those endeavoring to enter the field at this late date." Attempting to wrap ALAM in a soft PR mantle, Clifton continued, "[w]ith a view of protecting the public and thereby increasing the popularity of the automobile, it has not been the policy of those who controlled the patent to extend its protections to new and untried or doubtful products."[40]

Mr. Clifton then left for a month's cruise on the steamship Molke for the West Indies and the Spanish Main for a well-

40. *Automobile,* February 24, 1910.

earned Caribbean rest. Henry Ford said, in *The Automobile* journal, "We will have something to say, which will be the result of sufficient deliberation to make it sound attractive."[41]

ALAM published full-page ads in *Harper's Magazine* and many industry-related journals warning purchasers of Ford automobiles as to the hazards of using unlicensed automobiles.

> Both the basic Selden patent and all other patents owned as aforesaid will be enforced against all infringers.

The Ford Motor Company responded with ads of its own reminding Ford customers that Ford had purchased a bond to protect its customers from patent claims and urging them not to be frightened by the "Trust Scarecrow" and the Selden "Bogey Man." Ford inundated dealers and newspaper editors with telegrams reading, "We will fight to a finish."

In the summer of 1910, Judge Hough rejected the Selden team's proposed draft of an injunction against the Ford Motor Company from producing unlicensed cars in favor of a bond in the amount of three hundred fifty thousand dollars to cover damages and royalty obligations during the anticipated appeal. During his summer vacation, Judge Hough took time out to attend a number of patent litigation conferences as a speaker to discuss the reasoning and implications of his decision in which there was much public and professional interest.

PECULIARITY OF PATENTS

The grant of a patent can provide the holder with immense benefits at the public expense in exchange for the holder's contribution and advancement of the art. Edward J Prindle, in *Patents as a Factor in Manufacturing*, describes their potential impact on business.

> Patents are the best and most effective means of controlling competition. They occasionally give absolute control of the market,

---

41. Id.

> enabling their owner to name the price without regard to the cost of production, as for example where they cover all forms of devices for accomplishing a given purpose [pioneer patents]. There are a number of great companies whose position commercially is almost wholly due to the possession of controlling patents.[42]

Judge Hough's decision affirming validity of the Selden Patent was a triumph of form over substance. George Selden, despite his undisputed, canny manipulations of the rules and regulations in place at the time, did play by those rules and his invention did receive the imprimatur of the U.S. Patent Office, albeit at a time when the Patent Office vigilance and attention to detain was diluted by an unprecedented volume of patent applications. However, Judge Hough mechanically dismissed as irrelevant Selden's complete failure to provide that benefit which justifies the anomaly in the law allowing a temporary monopoly—the acknowledgement and reward to the patent holder for his or her contribution to and advancement the art. Hough essentially scrutinized the record for flaws in the Patent Office determination, and finding none, affirmed its actions. He chose to keep his assessment and review on the superficial level and to skip lightly over the substantive policy underpinnings that justified the social utility of patents in the first place.

Hough failed to focus on this fundamental issue even when it appeared in one of the very cases he cited in his opinion. In the United States Supreme Court case of *Seymour v. Osborne*,[43] an 1871 case cited by Judge Hough in his opinion, the court explained why patents are not regarded as monopolies in the law. The Court indicated that letters patent were not to be viewed as monopolies, but public franchises, and of benefit to the public "as tending to promote the progress of science and the useful arts and as a matter of compensation to the inventor for their labor, trial, and expense in making the invention, and reducing the same to

42. Prindle, supra at 84.

43. 78 U.S. 576 (1871).

practice for the public benefit, as contemplated by the Constitution and sanctioned by the laws of Congress."

Judge Hough's affirmation of the Selden Patent as a "pioneer patent," entitled to broad protection from infringement, was even more baffling to the Ford side, given Selden's lack of real contribution to the art. Pioneer patent designations were rare in invocation at the time and applied to invention of a primary character where the mechanical functions performed by the machine are, as a whole, entirely new. All subsequent machines which employ substantially the same means to accomplish the same result are infringers, even though a subsequent machine may contain improvements in the separate mechanisms, which go to make up the machine. Pioneer patents were meant to apply to inventions such as Howe's sewing machine, Morse' electrical telegraph, Bell's telephone, McCormick's reeper and the Wright Brother's airplane control system.

A pioneer patent can be easy to apply but difficult to justify, because of the subjective nature of the finding and because of the lack of guidelines as to where one man's inspiration ends and another man's begins. Even the United States Supreme Court has had difficulty in separating the wheat from the chaff when it comes to pioneer patents. In the Supreme Court case of *Westinghouse v. Boyden Brake Company*,[44] the Court in a five to four majority held that Boyden's novel automatic brake invention was not equivalent to the Westinghouse train air brake patent because even though it did reach the same result, it did so by substantially different means. On the other hand, the four dissenters in the case argued that it was a pioneer patent and "one of the highest values to the public. . . . which entitles the proprietor to a liberal protection from the courts in construing the claim described as a means of carrying the invention into practical operation."

When Hough affirmed the Selden patent dismissing the lack of "operability" of Selden's design as immaterial to his decision,

---

44. 170 U.S. 537 (1898).

and then criticized the Ford lawyers for even raising the issue, he sent Parker into a near apoplectic rage. Parker advised Henry Ford and the Company that Hough's decision would be overturned by a higher court and they must appeal.

THE APPEAL

The Ford Board approved Parker's filing of an appeal to the U.S. Court of Appeals for the Second Circuit, which had jurisdiction over all of the federal district courts in New York, Connecticut and Vermont. With all the national publicity, the Ford Motor Company was effectively printing buckets of cash in profits from exploding sales, but now it would have to file an appeal bond that could have devastating financial consequences if the Company were to loose the appeal. Parker himself, now sixty-eight, was near exhaustion and was emotionally stunned by the recent death of his daughter. He also decided that he and his colleague, C. Benton Crisp, were the wrong team for the face of the appeal. He recommended two prominent New York City patent lawyers, Edwin S. Wetmore and Livingston Gifford. Ford hired them with the understanding that they would be assisted by Parker and Crisp, behind the scenes.

Ralzemond A. Parker threw himself into honing and narrowing the appellate briefs for the appeal to the Court of Appeals. The wily old lawyer gladly and strategically took the backseat in the presentation of the appeal. He kept a low-profile role in the oral arguments, deferring to his younger and more "Eastern" colleagues. A Second Circuit panel of three judges, Emile H. Lacombe, Henry G. Ward and Walter C. Noyes, set the appeal for four days of argument commencing on November 22, 1910. Of the three judges, only Judge Noyes had significant patent experience. Just nine months after the contentious Hough hearing, both sides convened for the appellate arguments.

The unquestionable star among the participating lawyers was thirty-nine-year-old Frederic R. Coudert, counsel for the Panhard & Levassor defendant, who walked into the courtroom for oral arguments with a copy of Dugald Clerk's brand new, revised, two-volume magnum opus, *The Gas, Petrol and Oil Engine.* Just published by John Wiley, this expert tome had greeted him in the waiting room of one of the Selden law firms, months prior, proudly displayed like the legal hand grenade it now became.

During his argument, Coudert managed to contain his caustic wit. He asked the ALAM attorneys quite soberly to concede that their case was based largely upon Clerk's testimony. They agreed. He then asked whether they relied upon Clerk as a paid witness or as the author of the standard treatise on gasoline engines. Here, Coudert dramatically produced the two-volume set for all to see. The Selden lawyers jumped to their feet objecting to the book as not being in evidence. Judge Noyes responded: "I think we can judge well enough if what he has to say is applicable or not."

Coudert continued. "Let's see what Mr. Clerk has to say about it [the Selden engine]. Not Clerk with a retainer in his pocket but Clerk, the author." After waiting in silence for three beats to focus attention, the lawyer advanced. "This man who for six years was their retained expert has not a word in his book, not a single syllable, about Selden." Further, he went on,

> In no work upon gas engines or upon automobiles is the name Selden mentioned. If Selden made the invention which he requests the court to find, it seems incredible that not a single scientific writer has ever alluded to it. It is hardly possible that the whole scientific world, including Clerk, is wrong, when it describes the perfection of the automobile engine to Daimler, Benz and Panhard & Levassor.

Coudert then read Clerk's assessment of the Brayton engine saying, "No one has yet succeeded in carrying Brayton's engine further than he [Brayton] did." Coudert turned to the bench as asked the court,

> Will the court prefer the theories of Clerk the retained expert

> witness to those of Clerk the distinguished scientist, composing the "classic" on gas engines? If no one succeeded in carrying the Brayton type of engine further than Brayton himself, wherein did Selden make any improvement?

The answer was not long in arriving. On January 9, 1911, the appellate court affirmed the validity of the Selden patent as it related to the Brayton engine, but denied any infringement by the Defendants.[45] Judge Noyes, who wrote the opinion, underscored the vast differences between the Brayton engine and the Otto engine. Noyes wrote that Selden "made the wrong choice" and that "[t]he Defendants neither legally or morally owed him anything." The court noted that, "[w]hile he [Selden] withheld his patent, the public learned from independent inventors all that it could teach . . . for the monopoly granted by his patent had nothing to offer in return. The public gained absolutely nothing from his invention."

The court agreed with Judge Hough that Selden's technical compliance with the patent laws, "even if it may be only useful for tribute, must be viewed without prejudice and absolute judicial impartiality." It then proceeded to eviscerate its effect by acknowledging the patent's validity, while cramping its scope. The court—adopting the classification of "constant pressure" type and "constant volume" type engines as described in Clerk's earlier, 1887 volume, which had been admitted into evidence—undertook a point-by-point comparison of the differences between the Brayton two-stroke and the Otto four-stroke engines. This comparison further relied on Clerk's report that the Selden patent contemplated the use of the Brayton-type engine. The Selden patent provided no guidance as to how Selden's changes to the Brayton engine could be applied to the Otto engine.

> A patent is granted for solving a problem, not for starting one. Its description must explain the invention itself, the manner of making it, and the mode of putting it in practice. In the absence

45. 184 F 893(2nd Cir. 1911).

> of knowledge upon these points, the invention is not available to the public without further experiments and further exercise of inventive skill.

In other words, the court firmly rejected the idea that Selden's modifications to the Brayton engine solved the "problem," to the public benefit, that could be applied to the Otto engine. The court's finding declared, "[A]ny contention that a motor vehicle constructed by the patentee according to the teachings of the patent operated so successfully as to demonstrate that Selden had solved a great problem, and is entitled to the status of a pioneer inventor is, we think, without foundation."

The court noted that although Clerk had earlier testified that the differences between "constant pressure" and "constant volume" were immaterial, they were important enough that Clerk made them the basis of classification in his book, and that the court must regard the differences as "substantial." The court refused to extend the doctrine of equivalency from the Selden patent to the Otto engine.

> It is our opinion, for these reasons, that in this road locomotive combination embracing as its engine element an engine of constant pressure type, the substitution in place of such engine of an engine of the constant volume type, destroys the unit of the combination because the two engines do not perform the same functions in substantially the same way.

In adopting the Otto engine, the court ruled, the defendants did not infringe Selden's patent. Although the court only referred to Clerk's early edition of his classic work, it is clear that Coudert's argument regarding the later volumes resonated with the court. When Clerk's published insight and his court testimony diverged, the court felt free to use his published word. Judge Noyes later informally told Parker that Parker's exhaustive, compelling brief had made a major impact on the court's thinking. Parker told his colleagues that the judge said "the case was decided on Clerk's cross examination, his book, and my brief, that they did not take anything else practically into account."

The turnabout in the appellate court established Henry Ford as the image of a plain spoken, gutsy, champion of free enterprise—a plucky "David" successfully challenging a multi-headed "Goliath" trust bent on exacting tribute and licensing favorites to participate in the explosive growth of the American automobile industry. Ford was packing for a trip to New York to attend the Automobile Show at Madison Square Garden when he received the news. He and Edsel wanted to personally tell Parker the news and drove out to see him at his rural Royal Oak home. Parker was extremely emotional and cried, while he contemplated that he would now be able to fully retire after an eight-year battle.

Not to take anything away from Ford, the real "David" was Couzens. This short, serious, driven businessman directed Ford Motor Company from outside the spotlight. Couzens wouldn't back down from any challenge to Ford Motor's superiority. Colleagues described him as "not easily frightened." But as powerful as his influence was, Couzens' name was not on the door of the Company. Flush with success after the legal battle, Parker said, "I think on the whole that Couzens is about the smartest man I ever knew and he is one to take to the bottom of all of the trouble," because Couzens could descend to the bottom and still come up fighting.

Couzens' and Ford's united stance brought a surprising outcome. Although ALAM briefly toyed with the prospect of appeal to the United States Supreme Court, the company ran out of fight. Instead, its board chose to embrace Ford and James Couzens as valiant opponents. ALAM invited Ford and Couzens to their annual dinner in New York held at the Hotel Astor in the New York theater district. The ALAM gathering bejeweled the Madison Square Garden Automobile Show with a sumptuous evening event. Pushing through all the formal gowns and glitter, Henry Ford showed up in a grey business suit. Shouts of "Ford! Ford! Ford!" raised his entrance to that of royalty.

ALAM president Clifton invited Ford to share several puffs of a ceremonial Indian "peace pipe," to enthusiastic and deafening applause from the audience. Many attendees were financial beneficiaries of the Ford Motor Company victory in that their companies would no longer be subject to licensing fees. Clifton, saluting the "unification" of the warring elements of the industry said, "For the first time in all these years. . . we find victory in defeat." Ford nervously declined to speak. He simply offered the crowd a remark made by one of his lawyers, W. Benton Crisp: "You were all manly opponents. We are proud to greet you as friends."

The following evening, the Ford Motor Company held a victory celebration a block away at Rector's restaurant in Manhattan. Unlike the Astor, this newly constructed Second Empire hotel had a sense of the common man about it. The common man ascendant and unleashed. Parker, his adversary, William A. Redding and a number of ALAM's lawyers attended as well as many elated Ford guests. The restaurant, characteristically noisy and ostentatious, ruled as New York's "lobster palace." While elegantly appointed, the restaurant also hosted actresses, chorus girls and other females of similar repute, which ultimately led to its failure in polite society a few years later. Parker, obviously having a wonderful time, exclaimed to all, "Henry Ford is the greatest man in the automobile world . . . and the Ford organization is the greatest automotive organization in the world." Parker, still nursing a grievance like a slow martini, didn't mention Couzens, who had constantly fly-specked his expenses and attorney's fees.

COROLLARIES

The landmark Selden case cost nearly five hundred thousand dollars in legal fees, took five years from start to finish, and stood out as the most financially important patent case tried in the United States. ALAM counsel, William A. Redding, put it all into perspective: if the case had been tried in court like others, in front of a judge, it would have taken "sixty days, not five years." Parker agreed in the main about the deficiencies of patent litigation procedures, but he also attributed a great deal of the time and expense of the case to the "vast industrial interests" and "the complexity of automotive art." In 1912, the U.S. Supreme Court, heeding the complaints of Judge Hough and many patent lawyers, amended the procedure for patent disputes, effective on February 1, 1913. Patent trials entered into the normal procedural orbit of regular civil litigation, requiring the presentation of evidence before a judge in a trial.

The automobile industry, like the prosecuting and defense attorneys, prospered during the Selden case. Auto production increased from five million units in 1900 to two hundred fifty million units in 1910. ALAM dissolved in 1912, its reason for existing having imploded. With the evisceration of the Selden patent, competition reigned. The industry developed a *modus operandi* for the future by drafting an industry-wide cross-licensing agreement in 1914, effective in 1915, which permitted the easy and useful growth and sharing of automotive technology without patent restrictions. This dexterous streamlining boosted the growth of the industry even further. The ten-year cross licensing agreement has been renewed every five years since 1925.

One could argue that Ford Motor Company's determination to fight ALAM resulted in better court procedures nationally, and a strong, new collaborative spirit within the auto industry. And yet Ford Motors, for its part, did not join the cross-licensing arrangement, preferring to go it alone. Ford Motors did develop many "protective patents," and maintained an open source policy with respect to its innovations, consistent with Henry Ford's anathema toward patents.

In 1938, Edsel Ford appeared as a witness before a congressional committee investigating the impact of patents on concentration of economic power. The young Ford testified that Ford Motor Company had been threatened over three hundred eighty-six times and sued over sixty times for patent infringement to that date, and his company had collected no royalties on its patents. He declared that his father, Henry Ford, had regularly acquired patents on new devices to protect his company from patent claims by others.

Early on, Federal judges didn't understand and didn't like patent cases, but patent enforcement has rebounded since 1913 and gained favor among the Federal judiciary. In 1992, all patent appeals were directed to a new specialty court in Washington, D.C., the Federal Court of Appeals. The introduction of this new, technically savvy court led to significant improvement in the success of patent holders seeking damages for infringement. Now seventy-five percent of the court decisions favor patent holders, where in the past there was a seventy-five percent verdict record in favor of the alleged infringers. This may be in part due to the subjectivity and imprecision involved in applying complex, abstract terms and standards to highly technical and arcane evidence. In early cases, many non-patent federal judges admitted they felt adrift. The current prevalence of patent judges on the bench, formerly members of the patent bar, has revolutionized patent litigation. There are now very few patent cases that are accepted by the United States Supreme Court, which tends to rely on the technical expertise of the Federal Court of Appeals.

While the Selden case was pending, there was another famous pioneer patent case regarding the pioneer patent for the lateral control of aircraft owned by the Wright Brothers that demonstrates what might have happened to the automobile industry if ALAM had been successful. Frederick Fish appeared for the Wrights and W. Benton Crisp represented the infringer, Glenn Curtiss. The patent litigation substantially retarded the growth of aircraft technology and military air power in the United States until the government forced those in the industry to agree on "the sharing of technical patents following the commencement of World War I, through the development of the Aircraft Manufacturer's Association." In 1929, the patent combatants merged to create the Curtiss Wright Corporation.

Henry Ford continued to obsess over his personal self-promotion. From his racing days on the flat and dusty turf at the Grosse Pointe Race Track and on the slick and fractured ice of a frozen Lake St. Clair, he sought glory and personal fame and notoriety even at the risk of personal harm. In his foresight in the untapped market for quality, inexpensive automobiles he parlayed his intuition and tinkering into riches. Ford's challenge to ALAM mined a mother lode of public opinion and the politics of the Progressive Movement connecting with the deep antipathy to big business domination of the American economy, of which Ford later became an illustrious exemplar. A Girard, Kansas editorial supported his cause.

> SUCH A CAPITALIST REBEL – a traitor to his class, if you will – is Henry Ford, the automobile king who has an industrial domain that is pretty securely established. No man-not even the most impassioned toiler denouncing the system that oppresses him – has uttered more caustic condemnations of capitalism than has Henry Ford, the capitalist who figures his fortune in multiplied millions. The orthodox capitalists feel "sore" at Ford. They say nasty things about him. Editorial writers of the conservative and reactionary press take their cue and alternately denounce and ridicule the Detroit manufacturer. But Mr. Ford still goes serenely on his chosen way, telling tales out of school and smashing the dearest fetishes of the profit grabbing system – forcing the public to sit up and listen seriously because Henry Ford is a big man, a man who has attained success, who possesses prominence and power and above all knows what he is talking about.

Meanwhile the massive publicity surrounding the Selden case helped fuel near exponential growth in the company. The dividends paid by the Company to the shareholders were extraordinary. It paid out ninety-eight thousand dollars in 1904, two hundred thousand dollars in 1905, zero money in 1906, ten thousand dollars in 1907, five hundred thousand dollars in 1908, three million six hundred thousand dollars in 1909 and two million three hundred thousand dollars in 1910.

In the summer of 1914, Henry Ford, with his new-found prestige, found himself called upon to advise the President of the United States, Woodrow Wilson, on issues related to spurring a sluggish economy, whetting his own appetite for a broader role in American life. His advice to Wilson and to the press was determinedly anti-intellectual. "I would take all of the college professors in the world bar none, and put them out in that factory and then see what they would do with it." On a more helpful and realistic note, Ford suggested "Whether you think you can, or think you can't, you are probably right."

Pre-World War I, Detroit was a wide open, hard-drinking town with more brothels than churches.[46] Over seventy percent of the City's population was foreign born and only half of the town could speak English. It was known as a determinably open labor venue, where employers could almost get their own way. Ford adopted what appeared to be a benevolent "progressive," pro-labor and pro-consumer attitude toward Ford Motor employees, which rapidly eroded with the introduction of mind-bending mass production. The shift from an artisanal work force to repetitive unskilled labor left workers at the beck and call of the industrial giants, subject to arbitrary layoffs and terminations.

Prior to 1915, the presence of James Couzens and John F. Dodge along with Edsel Ford buffered Ford's autocratic temperament. The constant publicity of the Ford Motor Company and Henry Ford, as a result of the patent suit and the frequently dropping price of the Model T, led to a steady and increasing accumulation of cash in the Company. James Couzens, then treasurer, announced, "Our dividends paid to stockholders appears large when compared with those of other automobile companies because we have paid out of profits instead of putting them in the treasury. We do not ask our shareholders to accept paper dividends which are immediately put into new buildings, elaborate equipment and other extravagances." Couzens was in for a surprise.

Still Ford basked in his populist image as a paladin for the common man and factory worker. He had beat terrible odds in slaying Selden's claim to fatherhood of the automobile. He had

46. Detroit had one thousand six hundred licensed pubs, one thousand illegal "blind pigs," illegal, unlicensed pubs and over five hundred brothels, the number of "blind pigs" grew exponentially during prohibition.

sold record numbers of affordable cars during those same years. He had, likewise, gifted his shareholders generously for trusting him, for backing his strong if high-minded horse. Henry Ford's majority interest in Ford Motor Company stock, his instincts about his ability to influence public opinion, his ambition to create an unprecedented vertically integrated industrial enterprise capable of building automobiles from raw materials, and his contempt for the value and import of those contributing the capital to fund his enterprise led him to discount and ignore the interests of his shareholders in lieu of his broad vision of creating an industrial behemoth under his sole and complete control.

Part II

Dodge vs. Ford Motor Company

Chapter 6

A Minority Rebellion

On November 1, 1916, on a crisp fall day in Detroit, with the pungent but pleasing smell of burning leaves in the air, Edsel Ford married Eleanor Lowthian Clay. John F. Dodge and his brother Horace E. Dodge were ten percent shareholders of the Ford Motor Company, and John Dodge was a close friend of the Clays. The Dodges were glad to celebrate, with Henry Ford, the marriage of Ford's son to Eleanor Clay, despite ongoing tension between the Dodges and Henry Ford over shareholder's rights and dividends. The couple solemnized their vows, next door, at 121 East Boston once owned by Eleanor's late uncle, J. L. Hudson. Hudson had been a prominent Detroit department store operator, and one of the founders of the Hudson Motor Car Company. Thus, two lines of automobile heritage joined in matrimony that day. The three-story, clapboard house had a round central brick turret with a conical French-style roof and large veranda. The ten-thousand-square-foot home contained about fifty rooms. The interior boasted a wealth of carved oak woodwork and Pewabic tiles, from the nearby Detroit pottery. The bride and her maids wore simple dresses with Russian-style headdresses, adorned with pearls and rhinestones.

The short and simple ceremony, performed by Rev. H. Smith of Central M.E. Church, was followed by a prayer and an orchestra playing the "Wedding March" from Wagner's *Lohengren*. Thomas Edison and his wife, Mina, attended, among many distinguished guests. Ironically, the first owner of Hudson home had been Alexander Malcomson, Henry Ford's original partner in the Ford Motor Company, whom Ford had ruthlessly squeezed out. Days of joy and days of struggle. Ford and John Dodge spoke amiably after the newlyweds left. Dodge told Ford, "Henry, I don't envy you a damn thing, except that boy of yours."

Edsel Ford was everything that his father was not—open, friendly, cultured, and artistic. He was a man of vision and determination, of loyalty and compassion, but constitutionally, utterly unable to oppose or contradict the will of his father, even when convinced Henry was wrong or that his actions threatened the best interests of the Ford Motor Company. For years, Edsel did what he was told by Henry Ford, and Henry intentionally isolated his son from those in the Company who sought or appeared to have his friendship and attention. Though the elder Ford employed roundabout methods of retaliation, his aim usually resulted in the departure of his targets from the Company. Many who knew and loved Edsel Ford, including all of Edsel's family, believed that the internal conflict and pressure Henry Ford fixed on Edsel hastened his early demise from stomach cancer.

But that was years in the future. In 1916, Ford reveled in his son's wedding as well as the outlandish Ford Motor Company growth that had followed the Selden victory—economic growth unseen in any industrialized nation to date. Success and expansion beyond most men's wildest dreams. Yet even in victory, Ford ruled with a restless and treacherous hand. And the men closest and most devoted to him in business—James Couzens and the Dodge brothers—had recently fallen out with Ford. A fall both costly and dizzying.

COUZENS' EXIT

As Vice President, Treasurer and Business Manager of Ford Motor Company, James Couzens had masterminded and managed the company's vast economic growth since its inception.

Couzens put together an unparalleled dealer network across the country with over seven thousand licensed and authorized Ford agents. In 1911, Ford production rose from eighteen thousand six hundred forty-four units to thirty-four thousand five hundred twenty-eight, and it more than doubled its production by 1913. Ford beefed up its Highland Park plant as a start; by 1915, Ford owned and operated thirty-one regional manufacturing facilities. During this period of rapid expansion, three major events shook the Ford Motor Company that were to have a lasting imprint on Ford and the automobile industry.

First, Ford managers adopted use of the moving assembly line in 1913. Ford resisted this change, so they installed the first one in the Ford Highland Park plant while Henry Ford was out of town. David C. Nye in *America's Assembly Line*[47] writes: "It was the culmination of decades of laborsaving devices, new management ideas, improvement in metal alloys, increasing precision of machine tools, and experimentation with production." Ford became the "fortunate beneficiary of synergies among the exceptional, talented people he recruited."[48]

Ford's newly appointed plant, after a year of tweaks to the line, produced one thousand two hundred twelve chassis in a single eight-hour day, with one hour and thirty-three minutes of man time per vehicle, verses twelve hours and twenty-eight minutes of man time—the prior best time for stationery chassis assembly. Henry Ford became a rapid convert. In Europe, the dominance of the craftsman ethic and the aversion to novel power tools and machines kept production well below American standards. But in the United States, the factory line revolution had arrived.

Henry Ford took the Ford Motor Company shop methods and mechanical procedures to the San Francisco Exhibition in California, in 1915. He basked in the limelight of public amazement and fascination with the mechanical genius and possibilities of

---

47. *MIT Press*, (Cambridge, MA 2013), p.2.

48. Ibid. p. 11.

mass production. The names of those who actually stretched the limits of industrial organization and imagination, William E. Flanders, William C. Klann, Clarence Avery, and many others who contributed to the "genius," have long since faded from the ledger of history. Henry Ford happily accepted and promoted his personal fame as the founder of mass production.

Second, on January 5, 1914, the Ford Motor Company announced it would double its workers' wages, paying five dollars a day for an eight-hour day for unskilled labor. Henry Ford gladly took credit, but the inspiration really came from James Couzens. Couzens advanced this stunning wage increase, perceived as radical at the time, to help staunch the flow of employee turnover generated by the mindless repetition of the assembly line. Couzens also aimed to maximize plant manufacturing capacity by moving from two to three daily shifts, putting workers within financial reach of purchasing their own Ford vehicles. He knew the doubled wages would offer a third advantage: invaluable publicity for the company as a progressive organization. Indeed, flabbergasted competitors loudly denounced Ford's new policy, saying it would wreak havoc in the industry, lighting a starburst of national publicity and cries of acclaim from the general public. Couzens predicted that doubled pay would also spur employees to double their labor. Ford's foremen learned to yell "hurry up" in fourteen different languages.

The third event occurred on October 13, 1915, when James Couzens resigned.

His resignation came as the culmination of a long series of provocations by Henry Ford, some personal and some political. As always, Ford had avoided direct confrontation. Ford began his assault on Couzens by undermining his authority with employees and treating him with disrespect. Couzens vowed that he would always work with Ford but never work for him.

Ford's backhanded tactics had few taboos. He would silently speed up the assembly lines on his workers. He would announce the firing of loyal staff by removing their desks overnight or having the desks dismembered with an ax. When Couzens' dear young son Homer died in an automobile accident in California, Ford offered false rumors, not support. He accused Couzens of slacking on the job and sent that message flying through management.

When Couzens cautioned Ford about using the *Ford Times* magazine to pursue Ford's personal anti-war diatribes, Ford only increased his bilious attacks, Couzens' sense of propriety be damned. Couzens insisted the *Ford Times* was a valuable public relations tool, and Ford's anti-war expressions during the run-up to World War I were not generally popular. In response to Couzens' criticism, Ford had the *Times* print this personal gem: "To my mind the word 'murderer' should be embroidered in red letters across the breast of every soldier." Couzens exploded and handed Ford his resignation. According to Couzens, "I decided that I had had enough of his Goddamned persecution."

Couzens' resignation removed the last roadblock to the complete day-to-day control of the Ford Motor Company for Henry Ford. Though Couzens remained a board member and a shareholder, many of the board members, including the Dodges, were appalled and dismayed at the loss of Couzens' tight fiscal control of the Company. The Dodges had not always warmed to Couzens personally, but they greatly respected his talent and contribution to the Ford Motor Company's success. Charles E. Sorensen, one of Ford's men, wrote in *My Forty Years at Ford*,[49] "Couzens was the driving force during the early years, dominating sales, service, advertising, and dealer and branch territorial allotments. He was relentless in keeping after Ford." The economist, John Kenneth Galbraith, wrote in the *Liberal Hour*,[50] that after Couzens left, Henry Ford "took full command, and the company was never so successful again." Galbraith also noted the energy that Ford then devoted to his personal cult of myth. "In the years that followed, Ford was a relentless and avid self-advertiser. . . . Only the multitude remained unaware of

49. Sorensen and Williams, *My Forty Years at Ford*, (Collier books, N.Y. 1962.)

50. John Kenneth Galbraith, *The Liberal Hour*, (Houghton Mifflin, 1960), p.155.

the effort which Ford, both deliberately and instinctively, devoted to building the Ford myth. . . . He was the first and by far the most successful product of public relations in the industry."

A WEDDING OF OPPOSITES

In 1916, free of Couzens' managerial harping, Henry Ford fixed his enormous appetite for getting his own way on the Dodge brothers, the suppliers of the majority of Ford Motor Company's parts. Henry Ford relaxed and chatted with John and Horace Dodge after Edsel's wedding ceremony like the old comrades they were. Old comrades who were boiling up a lawsuit to rival anything the Detroit courts had ever seen.

The contentious summer months between Ford and the Dodge brothers had faded in no one's memory. Ford, seeking to expand his own parts plants and lower the cost of the Model T even farther, had threatened to cut the Dodges out of his parts supply pie. The Dodge brothers, in response, had given Ford one years' notice: they chose to protect their own considerable investment in plants and equipment by forming their own automobile company to compete with Ford; by terminating their supply relationship and all management and directorship duties at Ford; and by remaining Ford shareholders.

Ford expected their lawsuit to land on his desk any day.

John Dodge, due to the rancorous sparks flying in all directions, had been reluctant to attend Edsel's wedding. But the bride, Eleanor Clay, who fondly called him "Uncle John," prevailed upon him to attend. "Won't you please come for me," she pleaded. Ford himself abhorred personal confrontation, preferring to work around corners with company board members effecting his plans. So, this pleasant and memorable wedding day proceeded, gracing the social pages of Detroit's dailies with elegance and smiles—but it did not erase the approaching storm. Comrades be warned.

The Dodge brothers' longstanding relationship as the single largest major parts supplier to the Ford Motor Company had lasted a decade, from its inception in 1903. The brothers loved the auto industry and were passionate shareholders. They openly questioned Ford's constant pressure to drive down the price of parts and to lower the cost of Ford vehicles when there was already too much demand for the vehicles to be met by the Company at existing prices. They followed, with rising concern, Ford's plans to move all or most of the Ford Motor Company parts supply in house, into the new plants. When Henry Ford announced, earlier that summer, that he would withhold special dividend distributions in order to fund plant expansion, particularly the development of coke ovens and steel plants at the new River Rouge location in Dearborn, the Dodges swung into action. They pled with Ford, as major shareholders, to be heard. But Ford refused to answer John Dodge's letters, refused to meet with him or even to attend board meetings while the controversy persisted.

The brothers then tried to sell their Ford stock. Henry Ford refused to buy it back, saying that he already had enough stock and didn't need more. Ford insisted, with a righteous clip of his fist on the table, that the Company's shareholders had already been adequately rewarded for their investment. He needed the funds for expansion (and conveniently forgot his criticism of the other major automobile companies who also withheld dividends for expansion). Ford had been expecting a lawsuit in early October and even welcomed it, prepared to use the publicity from the suit to advance his personal image and interests, just as he had in the *Selden* suit. The Dodges, on the other hand, sought justice for their labors. They knew exactly how Ford had arrived at his successes: with Dodge ingenuity, savvy and tolerance of risk every step of the way, as well as the unheralded contribution of many others, which Ford usually declined to acknowledge.

ALL THINGS DODGE

Back In 1903, the Dodges had a prominent, precision machine shop in Detroit, second only in size and performance to Leland

and Faulconer Manufacturing Company. The Dodges were engaged in providing mechanical parts to the Olds Motor Works when Henry Ford talked them into rejecting their deal with Olds and contracting with the Ford Motor Company to provide the chassis, axels, drive trains and internal combustion engines for the Ford cars. Horace Dodge substantially redesigned some of the drive train parts for these cars. The Dodges ended up manufacturing about sixty-five percent of the Ford cars, everything except the carriage and wheels. Assembly began in a former ice-house, with a rail link located on Mack Avenue in Detroit, owned by another Ford shareholder, Albert Strelow.[51] In 1910, the Dodges' brand new Hamtramck Plant was the largest and best-equipped machine shop in Detroit, with large overhead cranes, electric generators, steam hammers, various jigs, annealing ovens and electric tools. They developed advanced material-handling systems even ahead of those implemented at Ford. In 1910, they employed over one thousand workers at their plant.

The early economics of Ford productivity brought a favorable margin to the Company and its shareholders. Early cars were sold for eight hundred fifty dollars including the fifty-dollar optional tonneau seating. The Company paid the Dodges two hundred fifty dollars for the engine and the drive train. It paid fifty-two dollars for each body. It bought seat cushions for sixteen dollars, and four wheels and four tires for forty dollars per set, respectively. All told, the cost of the parts for each vehicle was three hundred eighty-four dollars. The labor cost per vehicle was twenty dollars. Overhead, including salaries, rent, sales commissions and advertising, amounted to one hundred fifty dollars per vehicle. The total cost of the car then was six hundred four dollars, leaving a profit of two hundred forty-six dollars per car or a healthy per unit profit of about twenty-nine percent.

The change in contracts, to service Ford vs. Olds, required the

51. Strelow accepted an early buyout of thirty-five thousand dollars for his interests and lost all of his money in an ill – fated Alaskan venture. He later returned to Detroit to work in a Ford factory.

Dodges to personally invest sixty thousand dollars to retool their machinery and equipment. That is the equivalent of about sixteen million dollars today; no small investment in time, money, and faith. When the Ford Motor Company could not pay for its initial order of six hundred fifty units at two hundred fifty dollars a unit, the Dodges ended up with a ten percent interest in the stock of the Company. Ford paid in stock for their forbearance, and gave them the rights to assume ownership of all of Ford's assets were the Company to fail. The Dodges accepted this ten percent ownership at considerable financial risk to themselves. But the brothers didn't fear risk. They embraced it. They seared themselves into automotive history with their tenacious hard work and daring.

John F. Dodge and Horace E. Dodge were born four years apart in Niles, Michigan. Their personalities and skills varied widely: the brothers were different but complementary. John, wildly combatant, liked to shoot first and aim later. In the end, John would surrender passion to logic and become an effective big-picture manager. He had a volcanic temper, which quickly subsided when the situation called for it. He protected his reputation and that of his friends with vigor. On one occasion, John Dodge interrupted his dinner at the Detroit Athletic Club to drive to the home of a *Detroit Times* newspaper editor to thrash him, punching him several times, for printing disparaging remarks about Dodge and his friends. Following the interruption, John returned to his steak and finished his meal with a glass of beer. One of John's funeral eulogizers characterized him as a "great, lusty man, who with a ripping oath could back into a crowd and get his way." He was generous with his donations to charity and to friends in need. He even arranged for his company to provide annuities to the widows of "Buttons" and "Brown," two African American bar tenders at one of his favorite hangouts, Charlie Churchill's Saloon on Woodward and Jefferson Avenue. Despite his rough-hewn nature, one friend described John as having a "moral code as sincere as any churchman's."

Horace E. Dodge, the younger and quieter of the two brothers, loved to tinker with mechanical devices and to race his boats and yachts. He designed many mechanical products and tools, not a few of which ended up being used on the factory floor. He was a musician. He had an enormous pipe organ installed in his Grosse Pointe Farms home and he could play the violin. Friends described him as a "mechanic with the soul of a poet." Horace personally supported many Detroit charities and arts organizations including the Detroit Symphony Orchestra. The Orchestra's director at the time, Ossip Gabrilowitsch, had married one of Mark Twain's daughters, Clara Clemons, also a musician. The orchestra played the funeral march from Beethoven's *Eroica* Symphony to honor Horace after his premature death at the age of fifty-two, in 1920.

The Dodges, while alive, were inseparable. They took their meals together. They obtained matching suits from the same tailor. They worked hard together, spending eighteen-hour days or more in their machine shops, often staying overnight. A prominent Detroit businessman said of them, "No two men worked harder or more soberly toward their objectives." Their workers liked and respected them. Their factories kept a slower and more humanely reasonable pace of work. The brothers made special efforts to stay in touch with the factory floor. They avoided the heavy-handed intrusion into their worker's lives that Ford personnel managers and "spotters" pursued. Until the passage of Prohibition, the Dodges even offered ice-cold tin pails of a refreshing libation for the workers on hot days. They installed a fully-equipped medical clinic at their plant. They provided a machine shop for the use of their workers in their spare time called the "playpen," where men could tinker with and fix mechanical objects from home. Throughout their lives, John and Horace meant to be dealt with as a single unit. They would accept no mail at their plant not addressed to both of them as the Dodge Brothers.

All things mechanical fascinated the Dodge brothers: typewriters, bikes, cars, and boats. John Dodge constructed his own high-wheeler bicycle at the age of thirteen, and Horace Dodge invented and patented an important dirt-free ball bearing used in bicycles. They were aggressive devotees of the bicycle craze of the late 1900s. After selling their bicycle and patent interests, they aggressively pursued the close-tolerance mechanical trade in Detroit, moving from bicycles and typesetting machines to stoves and automobiles.

They played hard together, whether hunting, fishing, driving or boat racing, not infrequently raising hell in the wide-open saloons of Detroit. The two brothers shared ownership of a three-hundred-thousand-dollar steam-driven yacht, but they could not agree on where to take it. John preferred the Upper Great Lakes, while Horace favored the Thousand Islands. They flipped a coin for the ownership of the boat. Horace won, but out of respect, he took John to the Upper Lakes. All for one and one for all.

The Dodges, particularly John, liked to use his fists, and the two brothers frequently fought each other, although disagreements never lasted. They were known, on occasion, to meet the sunrise over the Detroit River together, following a weekend night on the town. Their weekends gained them notoriety. John might pull out a gun and demand a bar owner dance on a table while he threw whisky glasses at a mirror behind the bar, or pick a fight with a pesky lawyer encumbered with two wooden legs. Repentant on Monday morning, he would always make amends with a financial settlement.[52] John did not always get along with James Couzens. Early in the Dodges' involvement with Ford Motors, John requested Ford agree to a parts payment plan. When Couzens blurted, "I will not stand for that," Dodge turned to him and said, "Who the hell are you?"

The Dodge name still holds prominence in automobile lore, even after its absorption into the Chrysler Corporation. Recent television ads for Chrysler pay homage to the spirit of the Dodge brothers, showing a couple of young men in boaters swinging

52. The author's maternal grandfather, George W. Hergenroether, served as Vice-Treasurer of the Dodge Brothers and provided the compensating amends.

from chandeliers. And swing from chandeliers they did.

Although the Dodges both owned property in Grosse Pointe, they were never really fully accepted in the Grosse Pointe social circuit. Grosse Pointe existed for "old money." Money, that is, derived from extraction (lumbering and mining); transportation (railroads and ships); and money from early manufactures (paint, stoves and pharmaceuticals). The rowdy brothers were admitted to membership at the Detroit Athletic Club only after "deep misgivings." When the Grosse Pointe Country Club rejected Horace as a member, he vowed to build a house nearby that would make the club house look like a "shanty." Which he did. John received notice that his children would not continue to be welcome at the Grosse Pointe Liggett School, if more unflattering portraits of the brother's nocturnal exploits reached the local papers.

But the brothers were not all illicit fun and games. The fun and games only balanced their genius for business. That business, on July 9, 1914, included legally establishing their new automobile corporation—thanks to Henry Ford's stubbornness. The Dodge Brothers started Dodge Motors with five million dollars in capital stock. The Company issued fifty thousand shares at one hundred dollars per share. Each of the brothers subscribed to twenty-four thousand nine hundred ninety-five shares. The Dodge brothers quickly converted their Hamtramck plant into a full-production automobile plant. They moved remarkably quickly in the change-over because they had the luxury of making all major decisions themselves. They knew what they wanted and what they needed to accomplish the transition. John and Horace occupied separate offices at opposite ends on the main floor of the plant so as to maintain a constant connection with the needs of the company. By 1915—just one year into production—they rose to third place by volume of automobiles produced in the United States.

The Dodge brothers' plant hummed and throbbed with the mechanized pulse of mass production. The rhythmical beating of heavy steam hammers, electric tools and mechanical devices, the constant whirl of rubber belts and high overhead cranes moving across the ceilings, the ever-present hiss of heat-treating furnaces, and the gurgling of molten metal produced a steady symphony of highly-coordinated industrialization, producing the wonder of the American gasoline-powered automobile.

Henry Ford had rejected the Dodges' early suggestions for improvements to the Model T. They now introduced a sturdy all-steel body for their runabout, which they sold as a mid-priced vehicle, not in direct competition with Ford's low-priced Model T. They obtained their steel bodies from the Edward G. Budd Company of Philadelphia, Pennsylvania, despite the additional cost of transporting the parts to Detroit. Like Ford, the Dodges froze the exterior design of their cars in favor of regular improvements to the mechanics. Unlike the Model T, Dodge vehicles were equipped with an electric starter, not the arm-breaking crank typical of all Model Ts. The U.S. Army purchased a number of Dodge Brothers cars, known for their dependability, in the Mexican War campaign of 1916. George S. Patton, Jr. led the first motorized cavalry charge in Mexico against Francisco "Poncho" Villa in a Dodge vehicle. Many of their commercial vehicles served as ambulances and supply lorries during the First World War. John Dodge received the *Legion d'Honneur* award from the French government for the Dodge Brothers' rollout of precision recoil mechanisms for French field artillery pieces used in the War.

Henry Ford never felt comfortable with the Dodges. He disliked their bravado, their directness, and their behavior after hours. This self-contained, abstemious and indirect man did respect their diligence and efficiency. Ford's wife, Clara Ford, thought them crude and uncouth. Both brothers had red hair, and Henry Ford had a superstitious fear of people with red hair.[53] Red-haired people were rumored to be ill-tempered, untrustworthy, sexually aggressive, smart and eccentric. The Dodges, despite their occasionally eccentric behavior, were scrupulously honest and in-

---

53. Ford also objected to initially having a thirteenth shareholder funding the startup of Ford Motor Company, because it was an unlucky number.

tensely loyal to their friends. John Dodge once sent a check for fifteen thousand dollars to a dealer in New York to cover the cost of lost commissions when the Dodge Brothers couldn't deliver their product on time. Still, they often opted for high drama. The Dodges held a spectacular gala at the Book Cadillac Hotel in Detroit, celebrating the introduction of their new car in March, 1914. Henry Ford must have heard of the dramatic closing when John Dodge clambered onto each and every one of the while linen tablecloths and darkened the room by smashing each electric light in the chandeliers. Good night, all!

Generous of heart, the Dodges disdained Henry Ford's miserly approach to life and to business. As shareholders, early on, they enjoyed a "double dip," getting profits as major Ford parts suppliers and also their dividends as shareholders. But Ford disarranged that fortuitous dip quickly. He "loaded up" on parts from the Dodge brothers and then refused to accept further shipments unless and until they lowered their prices. He simultaneously undertook a campaign, never fully duplicated in the industry, to bring more and more parts production in-house, in pursuit of the ultimate goal of vertical integration of automobile production from raw materials to finished product. Ford loved control more than he loved anything in the world.

Early on, the Dodges had watched Henry Ford's high-handed squeeze out of Alexander Malcomson, his initial partner and equal co-shareholder in the Company. In November, 1905, Ford established a separate corporation, the Ford Manufacturing Company, to rake off the profits of the Ford Motor Company to the shareholders of his new company. Malcomson, a coal distributor who had secured all of the initial investors in the Ford Motor Company from his office, his legal staff, his friends and relatives, was not invited to participate in the new company. The Dodges, Ford's only early investors not brought in by Malcomson, held few illusions or expectations of loyalty or thankfulness from Ford. They relinquished their office and board seats at Ford Motor Company in the autumn of 1913 hoping that their stock shares and a bold new lawsuit could get Ford's attention.

SERVICE WITH A SMILE

Henry Ford had a lifetime love and fascination for birds. He had birds on his mind and stars in his eyes when he purchased two thousand acres of bottom land along the Rouge River[54] in Dearborn, Michigan, in 1915, to build his giant River Rouge Industrial Complex. He initially thought of the land as a bird sanctuary, but quickly moved to more practical uses. It made clear business sense to him to circumscribe shareholder dividends in order to fund the Rouge. He'd built and sold nearly a million cars at profits of over one hundred million dollars. He had paid regular shareholder dividends of five percent per month, or sixty percent yearly, on his declared capital stock of about two million dollars. Ford Motor Company's special dividends had also paid out bountifully: one million dollars in 1911, four million dollars in 1912, ten million dollars in 1913, eleven million dollars in 1914, and fifteen million dollars in 1915. The company had also accumulated a healthy surplus in excess of its capital stock in the amount of forty-nine million dollars in 1914, which leapt to a staggering one hundred eleven million dollars by 1916. Clearly, Ford Motor Company was a robust and thriving enterprise.

And Ford felt the need to innovate, to tinker on a grandiose scale with his business model. Since Ford Motor Company's inception, the goal had been to create affordable cars. He and his board had reached their current lofty financial status while steadily lowering the price of the vehicles they produced. Volume fueled their visions of an even brighter future. By 1914, Ford cars cost just four hundred forty dollars per vehicle. Ford sold five hundred thousand automobiles at that price. He proposed to reduce the price to three hundred sixty dollars per car even

54. The Rouge River was inappropriately named as it was never red. Until recently it was highly polluted and even caught fire in 1969.

though Ford Motors could not keep up with public demand at four hundred forty dollars. The Dodge brothers were not alone in objecting to this dangerous decision. The new price would likely cut the net profits of the Company by forty-eight million dollars.

Borrowing money was anathema to Henry Ford, who considered banks as instruments of world domination and oppression by Jews. In the decade prior to 1916, the Ford Motor Company regularly paid annual regular and special distributions of dividends in the amount of forty-five percent of earnings. Henry Ford had little difficulty convincing himself that his shareholders had been sufficiently compensated for their investments and chose to halt all special distributions to shareholders to divert funds to gratify his vision of a new, giant industrial compound with access to navigable water.

The plan confounded the Dodges who were watching their potential dividends and the value of their shares whittled away by a needless forty-eight million dollar cut in profit margins and expansion of plant capacity. Henry Ford could play maverick economics with his own money, but the Dodges' thought him unfair to play with theirs. They wanted out.

Ford had an answer for this. By expanding both his plants and equipment, including the construction of a state-of-the-art smelting plant, Ford Motors could drive down the cost of iron used in its cars by about fifty percent. It all made perfect sense to Henry. Shareholders be damned.

The law relating to shareholder rights in private corporations was relatively unformed in the early twentieth century. Courts generally provided wide latitude to corporate management decisions preferring not to get involved in internal corporate disputes. Henry Ford, however, repeatedly made the point to the public in the press that he was operating the company for the public benefit—"for humanity" (a species he rather liked better in general than in the particular).

He preached that every man, woman and child in the U.S. deserved the benefits of a reliable family car. Profits became an incidental by-product of his public megalomania. Profits only mattered insofar as they allowed him a greater industrial and public stage. Ford both championed the common man and repudiated the rights of his own shareholders, largely limiting them to a return of interest on their original contribution with no consideration of their proportional ownership interest in the growth of the capital of the organization.

John P. Davis, an early student in the history of the development of corporations, remarked, "[a] very conspicuous result of the industrial development of the Nineteenth Century has been the enlargement of the physical unit of greatest industrial efficiency beyond the capacity of the individual." The need to raise capital beyond the resources of the individual or the family enterprise expanded the corporate form, but what are the rights of shareholders in the industrial enterprise? Do shareholders own a percentage interest in the capital or the residual assets of a corporation, or are they relegated to the status of mere creditors of the corporation? These issues still resonate between shareholders and corporate management today. Management has by far the more compelling hand in large corporations because the best interests of the shareholders become increasingly nebulous with the growth of the size of the corporation. The hive takes on its own life far beyond the contributions of any of its individual bees. Courts find it extremely difficult to parse the interests of the shareholders, who bring diverse views and concerns, and they will generally refuse to intervene in the face of the "business judgment" rule; a longstanding rule which extends broad discretion to the management of corporations in implementing business policy and decisions. Discretion which Henry Ford loved to wield like a scepter and take to an extreme.

The morning after the Ford wedding, as Edsel Ford embarked on a two-month honeymoon to California and Hawaii, the Dodges caused a complaint in equity in the Wayne County Circuit Court to be served upon Henry Ford, and obtained a temporary injunction against further development on the River Rouge project. Family first, then business. The brothers had no love of scepters at all.

Henry Ford was, of course, furious at the Dodges' duplicity in serving him with legal process immediately after the wedding, where he and John Dodge had chatted amiably, without hint of rancor. No doubt it was a little too close to the type of around-the-corner confrontation that Henry Ford himself would have preferred to inflict.

The Dodges, in their lawsuit, sought an equitable order requiring the distribution of accumulated cash as dividends to shareholders and an injunction prohibiting the development of the River Rouge complex. The resultant final decision by the Michigan Supreme Court has never been overruled, but it remains a controversial benchmark in the history of corporate law relating to shareholder rights.

Chapter 7

In Chancery

In their lawsuit against the Ford Motor Company, the Dodge brothers sought to enjoin all of Ford's capital expansion projects and to force a dividend of fifty percent of the accumulated profits to be declared and paid to shareholders. The Dodges had a fourfold complaint. It contended that 1) a Michigan statute limiting the amount of capital stock with which a manufacturing company could be incorporated made it unlawful for a corporation to accumulate more than fifty million dollars in profits, so that the balance must be distributed to shareholders; 2) the anticipated further reduction of the price for Ford cars would make competition by others impossible, and thus, create a monopoly in violation of the *Sherman Antitrust Act*; 3) the building and operation of a smelter would be *ultra vires*, beyond the authority of the company; and 4) the failure to distribute a large part of the surplus as a dividend to shareholders, by the directors, was a breach of fiduciary duty on their part. Both brothers knew they were taking on not just Ford Motor Company, but a worldwide trend in the uncontested monopolization of capital into the hands of the very few, a trend which U. S. courts had up until then treated with avoidance and/or kid gloves.

Ford's initial response to the Dodge suit was to trundle over to the *Detroit News* editorial offices with the Ford Motor Company general counsel, Alfred Lucking, in tow, to meet with the news editor, Edwin Gustav Pipp. Pipp had been described, more than once, as Henry Ford's personal public relations firm. Pipp was a sure bet to provide a sympathetic portrait of Henry Ford and his motivations to an already admiring public—and to challenge the integrity, responsibility and greed of the Dodge brothers.

Pipp published his first article on the suit on November 4, 1916, entitled,

> "Ford Makes Reply to Suit Brought by Dodge brothers. Says Present Plans of Expansion Are Only In Line With Past History of the Company. Declares That on Investment of $10,000 Dodges Have Drawn Out $5,517,500 in Dividends and Still Have Holdings That They Value at $50,000,000. Attorney Alfred Lucking Says 'The Suit Against the Ford Company Has Political Motives'."

And those were just the headlines. The second sentence of the article misses no opportunity for Ford promotion:

> Mr. Ford discussed the suit, making his statements quietly, simply, dealing in sums that ran into the millions as modestly as the average manufacturer would deal in thousands, as the grocer would deal in hundreds, and as the toiler would deal in dollars, all the while his bearing and statements showing an earnestness, with an occasional note of sadness (with no note of fear) that made you think that he was wondering how anyone in the world could attempt to interfere with the great plans he has for extending the business of his organization and giving employment to more men, and much less how that interference could come from men with whom he had been associated in business for a long time, and who could profit by his efforts.

In this same Pipp article, Ford crushed the Dodge brothers' objections to lowering the price of Ford cars when the company could not meet existing demand for the product. "And let me say right here, that I do not believe that we should make such an awful profit on our cars. A reasonable profit is right but not too much. So, it has been my policy to force the price of the car down as fast as production would permit and give the benefits to users and laborers with resulting surprising enormous benefits to ourselves. The men associated with me have not always agreed with this policy."

Ford then stressed the value of the vertical integration of the company's products through making its own iron, steel, and resulting mechanical components.

> Why we used to buy many millions of dollars' worth of our parts from the Dodge Brothers themselves. It was on the profits of their sales to us that they built their enormous plants. We are now making the parts ourselves at an enormous saving and are giving our customers the benefit of that saving in the reduced price of the car. And will it be a bad business if we save still more money for our customers and our laborers and ourselves by making our own steel? To deny that is not making ordinary common sense.

Ford objected to borrowing money for expansion and wanted to fund future expansion entirely out of retained earnings.

> I have always wanted to have enough cash to spring our purchases without borrowing. I have always been opposed to going to Wall Street because I don't want them to get our hide. We are not afraid of them because we have the cash assets. They enable us to get all of our materials at the lowest price.

He dismissed the contribution of the Dodge brothers to the company by minimizing their funding and ignoring the debt that they had to undertake to finance their production of parts for sixty-five percent of the early Ford automobiles.

> "How much money did Dodge Brothers ever put into the business?" Mr. Ford was asked. [Presumably by Mr. Pipp.]
>
> Ten thousand dollars, but I don't think any of it was in cash. There may have been a check for some – the books will show that – but my recollection is that it was largely if not entirely put in work.

And without mentioning that he himself had never put a penny of his own at risk[55] in funding the startup of the Ford Motor Company, Ford dismissed the Dodge objections to his policy as "ungrateful."

> I don't think they can complain any on a policy of expansion when that expansion has enabled them to draw over five-and-one-half million on ten thousand and still have holdings worth $50,000,000 on their own valuation. [The price at which they offered to sell their interest to Ford.]

Ford stressed that there was no harm to shareholders in his policy and he would more acutely feel any harm as he was a fifty-eight percent owner and had more to lose. Ford then let his attorney, Lucking, drop a political bomb. Edwin Pipp quoted Alfred Lucking at the end of the article:

> One other thing, Mr. John F. Dodge is an intense partisan of Mr. Hughes,[56] actively engaged in politics at the present time, and I have received absolutely reliable information, which I believe to be true, that this suit was started by Mr. Dodge just at this particular juncture for political purposes.

Pipp would soon parlay his work at the *Detroit News* to become the editor of Ford's newly-acquired *Dearborn Independent* newspaper. He left the *Independent* in disgust soon thereafter, when Ford began a campaign of anti-Semitic publications. Pipp started his own publication, *Pipp's Weekly*, in 1922, with a series of unflattering articles under the title "The Real Henry Ford." Claiming to know "Henry Ford as no other writer does," he produced an entirely different and unflattering "inside" take on Ford's character.

---

55. All the initial shareholders put up either capital or provided parts, the Dodges did both. Henry Ford only put up his designs.

56. Charles Evans Hughes, the Republican nominee for President of the United States, barely lost to Woodrow Wilson in the 1916 presidential election. Ford supported Wilson in the election.

THE BUSINESS JUDGMENT RULE

The Dodges' case theory ran against the grain of American corporate law, in particular the "business judgment rule," which offered wide latitude to corporate executives in the management of their companies, both before and after the Michigan Supreme Court's final decision. In the years prior to the filing of the Dodge suit, the American Congress had made efforts to regulate and control the so-called "money trust"—the few powerful corporate managers and bankers who attempted to control the world's wealth and power. Senators and congressmen regaled its negative impact on the American economy. In 1913, a Louisiana lawyer and congressman, Arsene Pujo, led a congressional committee investigating the abuse of public trust by American financial institutions. The findings of the Pujo Committee led to public support for adding the 16th Amendment to the United States Constitution to impose the national income tax; to the creation of the Federal Reserve to regulate the economy; and to passage of the Clayton Anti-Trust Act of 1914—all to prohibit corporate excesses. In the Pujo Committee report, the Committee noted the near-unbridled power of corporate management in making decisions on behalf of corporations.

> None of the witnesses called was able to name an instance in the history of the country in which the stockholders had succeeded in overthrowing an existing management in any large corporation, nor does it appear that stockholders have ever succeeded in so far as to secure the investigation of the existing management of a corporation to ascertain whether it has been well managed . . . . [In] all great corporations with numerous and widely scattered stockholders . . . the management is virtually self-perpetuating and is able through the power of patronage, the indifference of stockholders and other influences, to control the majority of stock.[57]

---

57. Pujo, Arsene, *Report of the Committee Appointed Pursuant to House Resolutions* 429 and 504 to Investigate the Control of Money and Credit, Washington, D.C., Government Printing Office (February 28, 1913), at 146.

Little has changed since the findings of the Pujo Committee. Courts remain reluctant to interfere with corporate management decisions that are in any way tied, no matter how tenuously, to the long-term benefits of their corporations. Shareholders in large corporations are generally too widespread and diffuse to mount an effective challenge to management action. While the Ford Motor Company was a large, highly-capitalized corporation, it was unusually closely held, with relatively few shareholders, hence few who could espouse clearly diverse financial practices and interests. Henry Ford, the owner of fifty-eight percent of the stock, could not help himself, apparently, from ignoring his board members and pandering to public opinion as a champion of the people, opposing excessive corporate profits and underscoring his publicly espoused view that the industrial corporation was at heart some sort of charitable, eleemosynary institution organized for public good. It was these views that would be mined by the Dodge Brothers' counsel. Oh, Henry. Sometimes, saying less is more.

OF COUNSEL

Alfred Lucking, a former U.S. Congressman and a prominent Detroit lawyer in his mid-fifties, had a longstanding career in litigation and in Michigan Democratic politics. He lost his Congressional seat in 1904 and a later bid for the U.S. Senate in 1912. He served as General Counsel to the Ford Motor Company and Henry Ford's personal lawyer. He appeared on occasion before the United States Supreme Court. He was a round-faced jovial man, with bushy eyebrows and a monkish ring of hair around a glistening and protruding pate. Lucking was a highly skilled lawyer who served as counsel for the Ford Motor Company from 1914 to 1923. Born in Ontario, Lucking had moved to Michigan as a child and attended undergraduate and law school there. Lucking dressed in conservative dark blue suits with slightly old-fashioned winged collars. Flamboyant he was not, but a worthy adversary in the courtroom.

His adversary, Elliott Grassettle Stevenson, also born in Canada, approached trial work with flair. The Michigan bar admitted him to practice in 1877 and he was known for the adroit and aggressive examination of witnesses. Tall and elegant, with swept-back grey hair, a white moustache, and penetrating blue eyes, Stevenson exuded confidence. He started his practice in the days when Michigan lawyers moved from circuit to circuit in sleighs traveling over ice. A contemporary said that although Stevenson had been in near-constant battle for more than a quarter of a century, "it takes a vigorous man to outfight or to outthink him." Further, Stevenson "was ever unruffled by any statement of an opposing counsel and finds keen joy in detecting the vulnerability of an opponent."[58]

A number of additional lawyers worked on both sides of the case; two are of particular note. Lucking chose the elderly Horace Rackham to assist him. Rackham was a founding shareholder of The Ford Motor Company and a member of Ford's Board of Directors. Stevenson brought along Ernest Kanzler, a young lawyer in Stevenson's office who, ironically, had married Josephine Clay, Edsel Ford's sister-in-law. The lines were drawn and the legal parties assembled.

This was not the first clash between buttoned-down Lucking and Stevenson the gallant, nor would it be the last.

---

58. Burton et al., *The City of Detroit, Michigan 1701 to 1922,* (1922) Vol. 5, p 944.

Chapter 8

Eleemosynary Institution?

Henry Ford exuded immense confidence. Having successfully parried the attacks by the automobile royalty in the *Selden* case, challenging his very right to produce cars at all, he was sure that the Dodge brothers would be easy marks in court and provide him with yet another public forum to burnish his image as a new kind of revolutionary industrialist, one imbued with the judgment, ethics and sensibilities of the common man. The Dodges played by different rules. They were direct, physical and in your face—no working by indirection or manipulating conflict around corners. They knew how to take and deliver a punch. They had no respect for Ford's "pie in the sky" social engineering and "wacko" economics. They would fight hard, fight fair—but in the courtroom, not in the newspapers.

In addition to the Ford Motor Company, the Dodges named individual Ford directors Henry Ford, James Couzens, David H. Gray, Horace Rackham, and Frank L. Klingensmith in the suit. Couzens and Gray confessed to the allegations in the Dodge complaint. The Company and the others filed their answers on November 20, 1916. The answers asserted that the expansion projects were in the best interests of the Company and perfectly consistent with long-held policies of the Company to avoid borrowing for capital expenses at all costs. Ford claimed that his refusal to grant the Dodges an interview in September or October of 1916 had been animated by his supposition that the purpose of the interview was actually to press Ford to purchase the Dodges' stock. The Defendants asserted that it had been the Company's practice for the previous eight-to-ten years to cut product prices annually. They concluded that, indeed, the Company was currently unable to meet existing demand; but in the event of a falloff of the business, great sums of money would be needed to maintain operations and to avoid employee layoffs. Therefore, they chose to conserve and accumulate earnings and believed their approach to be both sound and practical.

Shortly thereafter, on November 29, 1916, a three-judge panel of the Circuit Court of Wayne County, Michigan, sitting in chancery (equity), heard the Dodges' Motion for an Injunction stopping work on the River Rouge complex. The judges filed their opinion on December 9, 1916. Two of the judges responded,

> We are of the opinion that the expansion of business, by the way of the establishment of a smelting plant, at the River Rouge, should be restrained pending an early hearing upon the question whether the diverting of accumulated cash profits to that end is an abuse of discretion on the part of the directors. This involves a mixed question of fact and law, and we feel that the allegations of the bill, and the showing in support thereof, makes this a question to be decided only on a hearing upon the merits and therefore matters should stand as they are, pending such hearing.

The third judge concurred in the issuance of the injunction but declined to rule as his colleagues had, that the Company could legally engage in the smelting business, because of a limiting provision in Michigan's *Corporations* statute. The Defendants appealed the injunction to the Michigan Supreme Court arguing that the injunction would create the potential for a substantial loss to the company because of existing contracts already let. The Supreme Court modified the injunction by permitting the Company to spend up to ten million dollars, providing the individual defendants posted a ten-million-dollar bond to reimburse the company should the Dodges prevail.

The Court remanded the case for a hearing on the merits, which began on May 21, 1917, in the Wayne County Courthouse in Detroit. Although eighteen witnesses gave testimony in the trial, the confrontation between Henry Ford and Elliott Stevenson took center stage in the proceedings. Ford assumed the role of a plain-spoken, unorthodox, well-meaning, common man, an entrepreneur with a passion for helping mankind. Stevenson prepared himself to extract damning evidence of Ford's autocratic and idiosyncratic behavior with obvious relish.

FAWNING COHORTS

Stevenson began his cross examination of Ford by asking about his refusal to meet with the Dodges, despite their concerns about the Company's anticipated major expenditures and the cancellation of dividends in order to pay for it. Stevenson read from an October 10, 1916, letter that Henry Ford had belatedly sent to the Dodges. Though he refused to meet with them, Ford did in fact respond. The letter confirmed Ford's decision to forego dividends. Stevenson wanted to confirm his intention.

Stevenson asked Ford to confirm the position he took in his letter to the Dodges, in particular the statement that "In view of all the conditions of business, and *other* extensions [doubling production capacity and adding a smelting plant], which have been determined upon for so long a time past, and to which we have been watching, that it would not be wise to increase the dividends at the present time." Stevenson wanted Ford to confirm the arbitrary and peremptory conduct of his actions.

"That was your position, wasn't it?" Stevenson asked Ford.[59]

"Yes."

"And when you sent this letter, you informed the Dodge broth-

59. The Transcripts of *Dodge vs. Ford* (1917) prepared for the Michigan Supreme Court, were provided by the Benson Ford Research Center in Dearborn, Michigan.

ers that according to your policy, it wasn't wise to pay any more dividends? Just answer so that the stenographer will get it."
Ford replied, "Yes sir, according to the letter."

"So that you made up your mind to not pay any more dividends for the present, at least, hadn't you?"
"For the present, yes sir."
"For how long? Had you fixed in your mind any time in the future, when you were going to pay?"
"No."

Stevenson then put it to Ford that the Board of Directors of the Ford Motor Company were dependent upon his direction and attuned to Ford's personal bidding. He believed that there was no record of the Ford Board of Directors ever rejecting a proposal initiated by Henry Ford. Stevenson, a man of great independence, placed little value on fawning cohorts. He examined Ford in detail about a recent, October 10th board meeting.

Q. And you had decided that you were going ahead and spend all the money that was available, for extensions?
A. Mr. Lucking: I object to that; it doesn't say that.

Q. What?
A. We had not spent any money.

Q. You hadn't spent any money?
A. No.

Q. On October 10th you had not spent any money?
A. Not very much.

Q. But you had decided on spending the money?
A. Decided to bring it up to the board.

Here, Stevenson huffed a little and screwed his mouth into a frown.

Q. You had decided on spending it, hadn't you?
A. As far as I was concerned, yes.

Q. So far as you were concerned; you were pretty nearly "it" in

the Ford Motor Company, weren't you?
A. No sir.

Mr. Lucking: "He ought to be; he owns 58 percent of the stock." Stevenson smiled obliquely. He said to the stenographer, "Take that down."

Q. I am very glad to have that; he has got a lot of dummies on this board of directors. You admit it. That is just what we have alleged.
Ford sat up straighter, his schoolboy slouch forgotten.
A. You will find out whether I have dummies or not, before we get done.

Q. We will see as to how much dummies the rest of them are, and when you pull the string, how quick they jump.

SMELTING PLANT EXPERIMENT

Stevenson questioned the wisdom of Ford's plan for the Company to produce its own iron and steel in light of pig iron prices being then below the current cost of production. Ford quietly outlined his plan to obtain a new, uniform mixture of iron that would lower costs by avoiding extra refining procedures.

With his white eyebrows raised in wonderment, Stevenson continued.

Q. Who is doing that sort of thing now?
A. Nobody.

Q. Nobody?
A. No.

Q. You are going to experiment with the Ford Motor Company's money, to do it, are you?
A. We are not going to experiment at all; we are going to do it.

Q. Nobody yet has ever done it?
A. That is all the more reason why it should be done.

Q. Therefore you are going to undertake to do something that nobody else has done, that nobody else have even tried to do?

A. Oh certainly. There wouldn't be any fun in it if we didn't.

Q. You are going to find some fun in it?

A. Yes, certainly.

Q. But at the expense of the Ford Motor Company.

A. That is all I am working for, at the present time, is to have a little fun, and to do the most good for the most people, and the stockholders.

Stevenson, his voice laced with sarcasm, used his examination to underscore the unprecedented and, in the Dodges' view, reckless underpinnings of Ford's actions.

AWFUL PROFITS

Ford testified that although the company produced five hundred thousand cars in 1916, it was his intent to produce one million cars a year. Further, he chose to keep the price stable in 1916, without a reduction, in order to accumulate money for the future expansion of the Ford Motor Company. Stevenson inquired of Ford concerning a recent Edwin G. Pipps editorial in the *Detroit News* wherein Ford expressed his concerns about the company earning "awful profits." Stevenson raised the issue of what the purpose of the Ford Motor Company was, if not to earn profits. To Stevenson, the Dodges, and the general business community, Ford's public complaint about his discomfort with profits were pure heresy, smacking of socialism.

Q. "Dodge Brothers say I ought to continue to ask $440 a car. I don't believe in such awful profits." That is what you stated, wasn't it? "I don't believe it is right." Was that your testament, or wasn't it, or was that Mr. Pipps?

A. You seem to be using the *News* for a Bible, I guess that's all right.

Q. That seems to be your bible?

A. Yes, sure.

Q. Yes, sure it does. Does that express your sentiments now?
A. It did then.

Q. Have you changed your sentiments since then?
A. I don't know. I haven't thought about it since.

Q. You haven't thought about it since. You don't know now whether these are your sentiments or not?
A. No, not altogether.

Q. When would you be able to tell whether you have changed your sentiments, or not?
A. My mind changes quite often.

Q. What is that?
A. My mind changes quite often.

Q. Your mind changes often. Now, I will ask you again, do you still think that those profits were awful profits and not right?
A. Well, I guess I do.

* * *

Q. And for that reason you were not satisfied to continue to make such awful profits?
A. We don't seem to be able to keep the profits down.

Q. You were not able to keep them down; are you trying to keep them down? What is The Ford Motor Company organized for, except for profits, will you tell me Mr. Ford?
A. Organized to do as much good as we can, everywhere, for everybody concerned.

Whether Ford's remarks were sincere or not, they were contrary to and dismissive of the rights of the investors who alone absorbed the real risks of the early days of the Ford enterprise.

INGRATITUDE

Stevenson turned Ford's attention to the disparaging remarks Ford made concerning the Dodges' minimal contribution to the success of the Ford Motor Company, and Ford's lack of gratitude to them.

Q. You said the Dodge Brothers drew out $5,000,000 in dividends, didn't you?
A. Yes, sir.

Q. While they drew out $5,000,000, you drew out $25,000,000, didn't you, and more too, $30,000,000?
A. Yes.

* * *

Q. Who made the first cars that you sold?
A. Dodge Brothers made part of them.

Q. Dodge Brothers made the car?
A. Made part of it.

Q. What part of it did they make?
A. The motor.

Q. What else?
A. The frame.

Q. They made the whole thing, except the tires and the body, didn't they?
A. From our drawings, yes.

* * *

Q. What kind of plant did you have?
A. A barn, I guess.

Q. You had a barn. Mr. Strelow's carpenter shop, wasn't it?
A. I guess it was.

Q. Mr. Stelow's carpenter shop. Dodge Brothers made the completed car, except the rubber tires and the body, and that was taken up to Mr. Strelow's carpenter shop, and the body was put on the car, and then your selling agent sold it?
A. Yes sir.

Q. That was the history of it wasn't it; Dodge Brothers had to

equip their plant to produce those cars, too, didn't they?
A. I guess they must have.

Q. And jeopardized everything they had in the world, didn't they, in the start, to make those cars, didn't they?
A. If you think so, yes.

Q. What is that? I am asking you what you think about it; you know about it.
A. I don't know what they jeopardized.

* * *

Q. You didn't jeopardize anything, did you? Didn't have anything to jeopardize, did you?
A. Well —

Q. What is that?
A. We had our drawings and plans to jeopardize.

* * *

Q. Didn't they have to equip a machine shop to manufacture those cars?
A. I guess they did.

Q. You guess they did; you know they did, don't you, Mr. Ford.
A. Yes.

Q. And they had to buy machinery.
A. Yes.

Q. And wasn't the extent of the purchases they had to make on that account, in their situation, jeopardizing everything they had, if that had not been a success?
Mr. Lucking: I object to that; that is ancient history.

* * *

Q. Have you forgotten what they did?
A. Quite a lot of it, yes sir.

Q. You have forgotten, have you, that they produced the cars that

were sold, to bring the money to make the Ford Motor Company a success, have you?
A. No, sir.

Q. No. There isn't any doubt about that is there?
A. No.

Q. Yes, you talk in this article as though they were stealing something from you, when they wanted a part of what belongs to them. They have got or they own a ten percent interest in your property, don't they?
A. Yes, sir.

Q. They didn't steal it, did they? I said, they didn't steal it, did they?
A. I didn't say that anyone stole anything.

Q. What? You tried to make out that they were ingrates because they wanted a share of the profits that belonged to their property, didn't you?
Mr. Lucking: I object to that. The article hasn't any such language in it at all.

Q. Well we will construe this matter at a later period. Have you ever been offered anything for your property?
Mr. Lucking: He has had phony offers, perhaps. I object to this as being immaterial.
The Court: Answer the question Mr. Ford.

* * *

Q. Can't you recollect anything about what you were offered?
A. No.

Q. Was it a 100 million?
A. It may have been over that.

Q. Was it 200 million?
A. Might have been, I think it was somebody who wanted to know if I would take 200 million dollars for it.

* * *

Q. What did you reply to them when you were asked if you

would take 200 million dollars for your 58 per cent?
A. I said that it wasn't for sale.

Having established one possible market value for Ford's holdings, Stevenson legitimized the financial return that the Dodge Brothers and shareholders were being denied. He skillfully turned Ford's charge of the Dodges' "ingratitude" back on him, showing first that his perception of their ingratitude was ill-founded and self-serving, and second, in light of his own immense fortune gleaned from their risks, an undeserved burden to Ford's shareholders.

Henry Ford maintained for public consumption that he had no particular interest in making money and that the money he made was just incidental to the enjoyment he obtained in "doing good"—that money was just an unavoidable byproduct. But his close associate Mr. Pipp, just three years later, recanted the selfless image that he had painted of Henry Ford.

> "Whatever his reputation may be, the dollar appeals to Ford as strongly as any man on earth. He knows how to make a showing of likeability to the finish and it eventually ends up in Ford's pocket."[60]

FORTY-MILLION-DOLLAR GIVE AWAY

Stevenson then directed Ford's attention to the impact on the shareholders of his current plan to reduce the price of Ford cars from four hundred forty dollars to three hundred sixty dollars in light of the unrequited demand for the car at the larger price. Stephenson was momentarily stunned by Ford's admission that he had not taken the resultant forty-million-dollar thrashing in income into consideration in making his decision. Ford could only offer vague references to "increased efficiency" to justify and, in time, rectify the loss of income. The concept of off-loading forty million dollars in profits in order to encourage a recovery of the profits by increased efficiency in factory employees ran counter to

60. E.G. Pipp, "The Real Henry Ford" *Pipp's Detroit Weekly*, 1922.

basic fundamental business principles. Hundreds of early automobile companies ran aground when profits failed to materialize through lack of sales, and the idea of generating profits through efficiencies, when profits were otherwise available through sales, was unorthodox in the extreme. The idea of rejecting the low-hanging fruit of current product demand to squeeze difficult further efficiencies out of plant and labor was incompressible to a man of business acumen. And likely inhumane to the workers in said plants.

Stevenson challenged the logic of Ford's reasoning. Rolling his eyes, unconvinced and incredulous, he continued his line of questioning.

> Q. Did you take those things into account? You knew that on the face of things, it meant a difference of 40 million dollars in the selling price of the car, didn't you?
>
> A. No, I didn't know that.
>
> Q. You didn't know that. It was a reduction of 80 dollars a car, wasn't it?
>
> A. Yes, sir.
>
> Q. And you sold 500,000 cars the year before?
>
> A. Yes sir.
>
> Q. So with the same production of 500,000 cars, the price being 80 dollars each less, it would equal 40 million dollars, wouldn't it?
>
> A. Not with increased efficiency.
>
> * * *
>
> Q. A little thing like 40 million dollars didn't trouble you?
>
> A. Because it isn't 40 million dollars with increased efficiency.
>
> * * *
>
> Q. Did you realize that in reducing the price of the car $80 that you were cutting off 40 million dollars on the basis of the production and selling price the year before?
>
> A. No.

Q. You didn't realize that?
A. No.

Q. You didn't take that into account at all?
A. No.

Q. Why didn't you?
A. Because we increased our efficiency.

Q. How did you increase your efficiency?
A. In every way in the factory.

Q. How does the reduction in price of the car increase efficiency?
A. Reduces the cost of selling for one thing.

Q. How much effect would that have on the 40 million dollars?
A. Quite a lot.

Q. How much?
A. I don't know but a great deal.

* * *

Q. Now, will you tell us in what particular there would be increased efficiency in the production of the car because of the reduction in the selling price?
A. It makes everybody dig more for profits.

* * *

Q. I am not to be satisfied; I would like to get you to give me some intelligent explanation of what you have done, Mr. Ford, if you can. Your answer doesn't in any way attempt to give anything intelligent on the subject. If you are satisfied with it, I am.
A. Perhaps it doesn't give you any intelligence.

Q. Perhaps not.
A. Because you are not versed in factory practice, or anything.

Stevenson then challenged Ford's alleged generosity toward his workers as it relates to their "increased efficiency." In doing so, he drew a tight-lipped Lucking into the fray. Stevenson began, "When they hustle for eight hours, the way they have to hustle to get that five dollars a day . . . there isn't any hustle in them at the end of eight hours," which prompted Ford to reply, "Do you know anything about the way they have to hustle?"

Stevenson said no, he was not a manufacturer. Ford quipped, "I can see that plainly."

Stevenson then drove his point home: "I am not professing to take care of all of the people in this world, like you, you know."

Alfred Lucking rose to his feet, his jovial face drawn into lines of contempt. "You are sneering at these policies that produced all this money in the past."

Stevenson said, "I am not sneering at any policy. I believe Mr. Ford is very sincere in his desire to improve the conditions of his men. I am ready at any time to accord him all the credit that it is possible for anybody to have in that line; but I still want to say —"

"That he is under a contract to squeeze every cent that he can out of the public, out of his workmen? Is that your claim?" Lucking asked.

Stevenson rose to his full height. He faced the judge directly. "I haven't made any such claim. . . . I am claiming that it is his duty, as the trustee for the stockholders, to earn all the money that he legitimately can earn for the stockholders."

The word "legitimately" hung in the quiet courtroom. Lucking delayed Stevenson's move on to his next topic—Ford's duty as a trustee toward the interests of his shareholders—with a parting shot: "And every cent he can get out of it?"

"I am not saying every cent; every dollar he legitimately can."

This legitimacy lay at the heart of the lawsuit.

Stevenson's clients, as Ford shareholders, saw themselves as the actual owners of the minority interest of the company. They viewed Henry Ford's hijacking of their interests as illegal oppression by the majority shareholder in pursuit of unproven, crackpot economic theories, that bent their anticipated returns to the service of Ford's avid pursuit of grandiose self-interest and autocracy. They perceived him to be fueling his craving for publicity and renown on their nickel. The Dodges were not prone to be treated in such a dismissive manner and they were prepared to fight like hell. They wanted management accountability, not management autocracy.

Back in October of 1916, John Dodge had sent a responsive letter to Henry Ford asking him for information concerning "rumors" that great undertakings and ambitious plans were in the works at Ford Motor involving "the disbursement of a large part of the cash assets of the company. . . . In short, as stockholders, we would ask to be advised promptly as to what plans for the enlargement of the plants, property or operations are underway or under consideration." Dodge requested Ford advise all the shareholders of his plans to radically increase the capital and plant capacity of the company, all plans that were under consideration by the Board.

Ford did not respond to the Dodge letter or advise the shareholders. Instead, he set about obtaining Board approval for his proposed expenditures on November 2, 1916, when he reported the eighty-dollars-per-car price reduction and the new plant expansion as a *fait accompli.*

In the dusty light of the large, elaborate, third-floor courtroom, known by local press as the "throne room," Ford answered questions with extreme evasion concerning his failure to advise the shareholders, his eyes often moving to the pigeons flipping their wings against the outside windows before soaring off into the gray Detroit sky. Stevenson tried to call him back and break his questions down for him in manageable bits.

> Q. We will separate. The furnace plant; you appropriated 11 million dollars for the furnace plant, didn't you?
>
> A. I guess we did, if it says so there.
>
> Q. Without answering Dodge brother's letter, so that you might be stopped from doing that, you went ahead and replied to his letter after you had done what he had requested you not to do, didn't you?
>
> A. I don't know.

Q. You got a request on October 11th to advise him as to what you had in contemplation, didn't you?

A. I guess we did.

Q. You ignored it until after you had done what he was protesting against, didn't you?

A. I don't know.

* * *

Q. You don't know that. You say on the 16th of October, after this letter of October 11th was written to you by Dodge Brothers, you had concluded the arrangement with Riter-Conley, of Pittsburgh, for expending a million dollars. You have said that, haven't you?

A. Yes.

* * *

Q. Yes. Why didn't you give the information to Dodge brothers, stockholders, that they asked for?

A. I guess we were working it out so that we could give them the information.

* * *

Q. Mr. Ford you never advised Dodge brothers of your New York venture [to build a 24-story showroom and offices] either did you?

A. I didn't know that they were directors.

Q. But you knew they were stockholders, didn't you?

A. Yes sir.

Q. And you knew they asked you for information, too, didn't you?

A. About the New York –

Q. About all of the proposed expenditures. That is what they asked you for, wasn't it?

A. It must be, certainly.

Stevenson sought to emphasize Ford's apparent contempt for the very shareholders who carried the early financial risks of the company and enabled him to accumulate his fortune. Stevenson quoted Ford in another newspaper article, drafted by Mr. Pipp, as referring to shareholders as "parasites." Ford denied using the term, but made no effort to correct Pipp's copy. He then contradicted himself, stating that he told a reporter not to leave that word in the article, while denying he ever said it.

Q. You let it stand, published as it was, referring to your shareholders as parasites?
A. Yes sir.

Q. That is what you did, didn't you?
A. I must have, yes.

Q. You didn't attempt to make any correction of it?
A. No. I would be pretty busy at that sort of thing?

Q. You would?
A. Yes.

Next, Stevenson took aim at Ford's assertion that his parasites had cheerfully acceded to his new plans—as quoted in one of Mr. Pipp's friendly interviews. Ford's statement, first published in the *Detroit News* and then also quoted in the Ford Motor Company house organ, the *Ford Times*, claimed that the Ford Motor Company shareholders were eager to reinvest fifty-eight million five hundred thousand dollars in cash in the growth of the company, from the 1916 profits, without receiving any special dividends. When pressed by Stevenson, Ford waffled on the issue as to whether he had planned to put all of the banked profits back into the company for further expansion. Ford also suggested, albeit indirectly, that he had been misquoted. Lastly, he claimed he had not read the articles, in full. How could he possibly affirm what Mr. Pipp claimed he had said?

So, Stevenson quoted from the *Ford Times*. On October, 1916, according to that article, the company had paid out sixty percent dividends and still had "over $58,500,000 to re-invest for the growth of the company. This is Mr. Ford's policy at present that the other stockholders cheerfully accede to this plan." Stevenson asked, "Is this correct?"

Ford replied, "Never saw that before."

> Q. You did not?
>
> A. No.
>
> Q. They would not publish anything in your bible [*Ford Times*] you did not say, would they?
>
> A. They might.
>
> Q. They reproduced this from your other bible? *The News*?
>
> A. That is possibly what they did.

Ford refused to repudiate the statement, only denying that he had ever said it in print. This poignant bit of oversight raised a snicker in the courtroom. And led Stevenson to drive home the salient point, that the Dodge brothers and all of the Ford shareholders received from Ford, not inclusion and elucidation, but the single-minded actions of a driven, autocratic, manipulative, power-hungry, lone wolf.

Stevenson had one last nail to drive into the Ford testimony. A nail which Henry Ford did not see as either sharp or incriminating. A nail provided by the accommodating Mr. Pipp:

> Q. Now I will go back again [Stevenson – reading]: "My ambition," declared Mr. Ford, "is to employ still more men, to spread the benefits of this industrial system to the greatest possible number, to help them build up their lives and their homes. To do this we are putting the greatest share of our profits back into the business."
>
> A. Yes, the greatest share of our profits back into the business. That is all right.

And so, Ford's neglect of his own shareholders entered the court record with no protest on his part; signed, sealed, and delivered by the statesmanlike Stevenson a la the journalistic talents of Mr. Pipp.

Still, the impact of testimony is never a sure thing. Could Ford's exercise in apparent megalomania, an effort to sell his image well in the public mind and to justify his raw exercise of corporate power at the expense of his business associates, be fully appreciated by a judge charged with the responsibility of sorting out the equitable rights of all the shareholders of this fabulously successful, closely held, corporation?

Stevenson closed out testimony of the Defendants by calling Edwin G. Pipp, still editor of the *Detroit News*, to the stand to identify statements by Ford. Barely a month after Woodrow Wilson had declared America's entry in World War I, Pipp spoke with patriotic tones of Ford's commitment to the war effort. Pipp confirmed Henry Ford had said, "Many of our best and brightest young men are going to the front to risk their lives, their all, and in the same spirit we [the rich] should give freely of our incomes that they and our government may lack nothing in the way of equipment and supplies to carry on the campaign." Considering Ford's rabid anti-war campaign blasting all who would enter the European conflict, and his imposition on Woodrow Wilson to personally override Edsel's draft notice into the armed services, the quote was high irony. Ford claimed publicly that he would return all his wartime profits to the government.[61] Again, Ford the humanitarian steps forward when there's money to be made aplenty.

BROTHERS AND OTHERS

Stevenson called John F. Dodge as a witness to the stand. Dodge was a formidable presence—strong, rotund, with a vested belly protruding from his swept-back suit coat. He had a carrot top of red hair crowning his brow. His voice was firm and clear and he betrayed none of the infirmities that would kill him just a few years later. Dodge related his conversation with Henry Ford in the winter of 1916. Ford had stated, in testimony, that the Dodg-

61. There is no evidence that he ever did so.

es wanted him to purchase their shares for thirty-five million dollars, and that if he didn't do so, the Dodges would harass him as much as they could. John Dodge had a different take away from that meeting. Henry Ford had a strong interest in developing a tractor for farmers and began to make plans to create a tractor factory owned solely by he and his son Edsel. He had a problem in that the designs and plans for the tractor were developed using the resources of the Ford Motor Company. The tractor plant issue was high on Henry Ford's list of concerns with his shareholders. After Dodge indicated to Ford that he had no objection to Ford pursuing production of the Fordson tractor as a private, personal venture, Dodge related,

> We discussed Ford Motor conditions in general and finally drifted to the resignation of Mr. Couzens[62] – the reason of Mr. Couzens leaving, and I expressed great regret that he had left and that it would be greatly to the detriment of the company that he had left, and Mr. Ford then stated very emphatically that it was a very good thing for the company that he had left, and that now they would be able to do things that before Mr. Couzens had prevented; that his restraining influence was gone and they were now going to expand and do things that they would like to do, and I asked him what he proposed doing, and he said that they were going to double the size of the Highland Park plant and double the output of cars and sell them at half price, and I told him that if he proposed to carry things to such an extreme as that he could buy out the other stockholders, then he could run the business as he saw fit; he told me that he did not care to buy any more stock, but he had control and that was all he needed, and that was about all of the conversation regarding that. Spent the rest of the time telling about the shortcomings of Mr. Couzens with the aid of Mr. Wills.

Dodge related that until a year before, he had never had a word of

---

62. James Couzens resigned as an officer and employee of the Ford Motor Company, but remained on the Board of Directors until Ford purchased his stock.

criticism for Henry Ford and described the Ford Board of Directors as "harmonious"—up until then. He related that the purpose of a business corporation is to make money and the method of making money does not include primary regard for anything else than the established laws of economics. "My sole idea," he said, "in this matter is to see whether or not the Ford Motor Company should divide some of its earnings with its stockholders before spending them."

On cross examination, Lucking attacked, trying to show that Dodge was not as "humanitarian" as Ford.

> Q. You were opposed to raising the wages to $5 a day?
>
> A. Yes, sir.

Judge Hosmer interrupted Lucking, sternly advising him that were no issues suggested by the question that were before the court. Lucking then pulled out a copy of the November 21, 1903, minutes of the Ford Board of Directors meeting and asked Dodge to read them. The minutes reflected a motion by A.Y. Malcomson, seconded by Ford, to distribute ten million dollars in dividends to shareholders but objected to by Dodge. Dodge said to the Judge, inciting general laughter, "I suppose I did that because I didn't like Mr. Malcomson, who made the motion."

> Q. [Lucking] Isn't it true that you did it because you thought the shareholders would benefit more if the money were used by the company and not distributed?
>
> A. I don't remember.

This meeting had, in fact, occurred fourteen years earlier.

Regarding the 1916 discussion between Ford and John Dodge, raised by Stevenson and revisited by Lucking, Dodge denied making any threat against Henry Ford. "I merely stated that if Mr. Ford wanted to use the Ford Motor Company to carry out his schemes, he should buy out all of the shareholders." He admitted to Lucking, in a cross examination, that he was in the motor business himself, but refused to tell Lucking how much money he was making other than "we are running at a profit." Lucking elicited from him that with the war-time shortage of raw materials, it was prudent to try to control the sources of supply (i.e. iron ore via smelting), a reasonable point, but one which flew in the face of a specific Michigan statutory prohibition limiting manufacturing corporations to manufacturing. When Lucking finished his cross examination of John Dodge, Dodge gathered his girth, nodded to the Judge and resumed his seat next to Stevenson.

Horace Dodge followed his brother to the stand, red hair flashing. He quietly confirmed all the points made by John. Following Horace Dodge, Stevenson again called Ford's friendly editor, Edwin G. Pipp from the *Detroit News,* and Marcus T. Woodruff, editor of *The Dearborn Independent,* to corroborate some of the unflattering statements made by Ford about shareholders. Although pulled hard by Stevenson, Pipp would only testify that Ford showed no interest to him in harming shareholders. Woodruff confirmed that he had heard Ford describe shareholders as "parasites," but he agreed with Lucking that Ford was not specifically referring to Ford Motor Company shareholders at the time.

"PRUDENCE" ON THE ROUGE

Lucking strove mightily to convince the judge that rather than being disrespectful of the interests of his shareholders, that he was acting with far sighted prudence in his actions that would serve them well in the long run.

The defense called a number of expert engineers to show the feasibility of Ford's new iron ore process and the need for Ford to maintain control of its raw materials. When Stevenson suggested the proposed smelting operation was illegal for a manufacturing company under Michigan statutes, one of the attorneys replied, "Well they can do it by having a trustee or some other way a lawyer can tell you about [laughter]."

One of the engineers was unable to field a reply when Judge Hosmer asked him what would happen if the federal government refused to approve changes to the course if the Rouge River that were required for the Ford plant to gain access to the Great Lakes? Ford's plans to develop a behemoth vertically integrated industrial complex relied heavily on his ability to access the plant by water on freighters. He negotiated with the federal government to build so-called Liberty Submarine Chaser boats at the plants, which required water access to the oceans through the Great Lakes. Ford needed the government to not only approve dredging and other changes to the course of the river but to also pay for it. He was ultimately successful on both counts.

When Ford's Chief Engineer, C. Harold Wills—who John Dodge attributed as being the technical brains of the Ford Motor Company—emphasized the need to expand Ford facilities to meet coming demand, Stevenson caught him up.

> Q. I want to know if $25,000,0000 were deliberately cut from the profits of the Ford company in 1916, to give it away or what?
>
> A. It was done to maintain our position in the trade.
>
> Q. Then you deliberately cut profits by reducing the price after experience had shown it was not necessary?
>
> A. The profits were deliberately cut.

He was essentially conceding that there was no discernable business reason to cut profits of the Company and contradicted the Defendants' testimony of the need to protect shareholders by increasing the company's cash position.

Lucking called Ralph Stone, President of The Detroit Trust Company, as an expert to testify that the amount of earnings retained by Ford were not disproportionate to the other companies that he had on a list he prepared. Stevenson countered him by pointing out that the other companies on his list were credit not cash-based companies, hence requiring greater reserves, and that all of them were merely holding companies, rendering the comparison with Ford inappropriate. Stone skulked off the stand muttering that he was not all that familiar with the companies on his list.

Lucking invited Ford shareholder and attorney Horace H. Rackham to the stand for the sole purpose of verifying Ford's answer to the Dodge complaint. But Stevenson insisted upon a broader examination and obtained admissions from Rackham that he was not a "practical man" and knew little about what was going on in the company.

Frank L. Klingensmith, Ford's Vice-President, Treasurer and Board member, appeared as a witness several times during the trial, primarily to answer questions about Ford's productivity and profits history. Lucking recalled him yet again to demonstrate that the Ford Board of Directors was not composed of mere "dummies" responding to Henry Ford's whims. Klingensmith testified about several land deals where the Ford Board refused Henry Ford's requests. Stevenson surgically extracted from Klingensmith further admission that Henry Ford had actually purchased the property himself and then had the Ford Motor Company pay the taxes and later purchase the property from him. Klingensmith also admitted that although there was a Company requirement that all Ford directors be shareholders, he did not in fact own any shares, but rather was "loaned" a single share by Henry Ford to facially qualify for the position.

Following the close of testimony and two weeks of contentious testimony, Judge Hosmer set aside two days for oral arguments on June 6 and June 7, 1917. The "throne room" was packed on both days. Two former judges, William C. Carpenter for the Dodges and Alexis C. Angell for Ford, shared the first day of argument. Angell argued to Judge Hosmer that he would be effectively destroying and "winding up the Ford Motor Company" if he sustained all of the claims in the Dodges' bill of complaint. Carpenter stressed that the Ford shareholders had recently received an unreasonably low rate of return for their investment (1.5% vs. the normal five to ten percent). Hosmer peppered the lawyers with questions. He asked Carpenter whether Ford was not entitled to establish a business monopoly, if he could do so legally, without collusion. To Angell he posed, "Didn't the 'great cost of business' argument made by Ford to justify retention of earnings fade away in the face of the argument that the money was needed to fund a new operation at the River Rouge?"

Alfred Lucking and Elliott Stevenson squared off the following day. With fusillades of high rhetoric, Stevenson suggested that Henry Ford was "guilty of acts which seem to indicate that he considers himself above the law." Lucking, for his part, insisted, "The Dodge brothers are here because they are competitors of Mr. Ford." Stevenson pleaded that the smelter project was illegal for a manufacturing facility under Michigan statute, and that the very large size of Ford Motor Company's retained earnings placed the company in violation of the statutory capitalization limit. He said Ford's purpose was to "crowd out all possible competition," and that Ford's annual salary and regular distribution payments, amounting to nine hundred thousand dollars, rendered him insensitive to the concerns of shareholders. Lucking made his final point that Judge Hosmer lacked jurisdiction to interfere with the business operations of the corporation absent a factual finding of bad faith on the part of Henry Ford.

The kindly, large-boned and gray-bearded jurist thanked the lawyers for their presentations, picked up his notes, and left the bench with the packed courtroom standing in his wake. Just shy of five months later, on October 31, 1917, Circuit Judge George Stedman Hosmer filed his opinion in the case.

Chapter 9

Shareholder's Surge

HOSMER'S HARPOON

The Honorable George Stedman Hosmer was a lawyer's judge—kind in demeanor, schooled in the law, judicious in temperament, evenhanded in decision. Judging from his writings, he was literate and logical—guided by the facts before him. One of the speakers at his memorial service remarked, "On the bench he was kindly, patient, obliging, and always intent on seeing that justice was done in every case. The best of his broad learning, his time, his energy, and his talents were given to his judicial work. Nothing—absolutely nothing appealed to him save the merits of the case. Favoritism, associations, relationship, social and political influence and all else, save the merits of the case, counted for nothing."

> Judge Hosmer was an anomaly in politics. He knew nothing of the so-called "practical politics." The names of precinct and ward leaders, indelibly engraved in the minds of most office holders, meant nothing to him. He was not even an amateur at lining up workers to drum up votes for him. As election time approached he was always a little nervous, knowing his own inability to "play the game." He was a democrat and consequently had to run ahead of his ticket, sometimes thousands ahead to be re-elected.[63]

63. Burton et al., *The City of Detroit, 1701-1922, Vol. 5* (S.J. Clark Publishing Company, 1922).

It was the practice of the Wayne County Circuit Court bench to appoint a three-judge panel to hear important cases, one of whom usually was Judge Hosmer. Not infrequently, because of the respect in which the bar and the Michigan Supreme Court held him, he was appointed as the sole judge to hear complicated and important cases. Hence, his solitary opinion in the *Dodge v. Ford* case. Judge Hosmer based his finding on the technical issues in the case. His decision was much anticipated by the press, the litigants and their lawyers, who hurriedly reassembled in a Detroit courtroom to receive his decision. The atmosphere in the room was charged as he began to intone the written copy of his opinion.

Hosmer avoided commenting on the polemics of the shareholder's dispute over Ford's peculiar views of corporate purpose, and Ford's apparent distain for the interests and contributions of his fellow shareholders. Hosmer did obliquely note Ford's self-interest, and his attitude toward shareholders, in using the assets of the Ford Motor Company to promote the interests of Ford and his son Edsel. He paid particular attention to what had seemed a minor side issue in the case: The Fords had used the assets of the Ford Motor Company to develop the Fordson tractor and transferred those development rights to themselves, when they set up their own tractor plant at the River Rouge site. Hosmer quoted an article in *The Dearborn Independent*.

> In the new tractor plant, there will be no stockholders, no directors, no absentee owners, no parasites," declared Henry Ford the other day in a discussion of modern industrialism. That is, there will be no incorporation, every man employed, during the period of his employment, with the aim will be to make permanent, will share in the profits of the industry, but there will be no dividends to stock either at face or market value.

Hosmer quoted the divergent testimony of Horace and John Dodge and Henry Ford and C. Harold Wills regarding their discussion in January of 1916 concerning the Fordson tractor production issue and dividends. He noted that Henry Ford was not forthcoming with respect to the scope of his planned expansion of the River Rouge smelting facility—a much larger expression of funds and time and corporate concern.

> There is only one conclusion to be reached from this testimony, viz.: that the object of the meeting was to discuss the relation of the tractor to the Ford Motor Company and that the proposed sale of stock by the Dodge brothers came only after Mr. Ford had announced what to them was a complete change of policy with reference to dividends and the proposed extension of the Ford plant. No mention of the River Rouge improvement was suggested at the meeting (n)or does it appear that complainants had any knowledge thereof until a short time before this suit was begun, except for the publication of a newspaper article which, as John F. Dodge testifies, he thought had reference to an individual enterprise of Mr. Ford's and did not relate to the Ford Motor Company.

The court noted that the only further information provided to the shareholders by Ford was a letter sent on November 3, 1916, the day after the filing of the complaint, transmitting copies of the Board of Director's resolutions dated October 31, 1916, and November 2, 1916, appropriating eleven million three hundred twenty-five thousand dollars for a smelting plant at River Rouge, five million one hundred fifty thousand dollars for expansion of the Highland Park manufacturing plant, five hundred sixty thousand dollars ratifying a Ford contract to purchase a building site in New York City, and disclosure of a seven hundred forty thousand dollars appropriation under consideration for the construction of a sixteen-story building in New York City to provide several stories for Ford's use and fourteen stories to be leased to a hotel company.

Judge Hosmer, in his opinion, first addressed the issue of whether Henry Ford's conduct violated Section 2 (monopolization) of the Sherman Antitrust Act. He noted that with the price cutting and large expansion of spending and increase in plant capacity by a company, "suspicions will arise that its motives are not wholly philanthropic; domination quite as much as philanthropy comes to mind." However, he distinguished this case from that of *United States v. Eastman Kodak Company,*[64] where a series of businesses were acquired with the apparent intent to monopolize, by underscoring that the Ford Motor Company growth was the result of legitimate internal growth.

> Experience has shown that price cutting and too great competition may bring evils in its train, but to confer on a court the arbitrary power which must of necessity follow the construction conceded for by the complainants, is to invite far worse consequences. The evidence before the court does not present a case within the *Sherman Act.*

The Judge then turned to the issue of the state corporation statute's limitation of corporate capital stock to fifty million dollars. Alfred Lucking argued that the fifty-million-dollar limitation was not meant to apply to capital derived from internal growth and that, if the legislature had meant to limit the internal growth of a corporation, it could and should have said so explicitly. He further asserted that many other Michigan corporations then actually exceeded the statutory capital limitations. Judge Hosmer carefully reviewed the history of Michigan's statutory limitations on corporate growth. The road was a rocky one. New Hampshire still smarted from a key corporate case, tried in 1819, that had been struck down by the United States Supreme Court.

Hosmer observed that many state legislators were displeased with the decision in the *Dartmouth College* case[65] which held that once granted, a private corporate charter was a contractual obligation and not revocable by a state. Chief Justice John Marshall had reinstated the school's charter, revoked by the New Hampshire legislature, by applying the sanctity of contracts clause of

64. 226 F. 62 (W.D. N.Y. 1915).

65. Famous for the quote ("It's a small college, yet there are those that love it"—Daniel Webster), *Trustees of Dartmouth College v. Woodward,* 17 U.S. 518 (1819).

the U.S. Constitution. This landmark case ultimately assured the rise of the American business corporation.

Hosmer offered that Michigan's corporate limitation was in the spirit of Theodore Roosevelt's efforts to control corporate influence and curb misbehavior. In response to Lacking's claim, the Judge remarked that if the statute was not intended to limit internal growth, it would place an undue burden on a competitor who would be unable to effectively compete with the resources of the Ford Motor Company until the competitor could raise comparable capital resources through internal growth. Hosmer didn't address the possibility of a competitor accomplishing this very end through debt rather than accumulated capital. Finally, he reasoned that the fact of the existence of companies in Michigan with capital assets in excess of the statutory limitations provided no reason for the court to fail to carry out the policy of the state "when its jurisdiction is invoked by one entitled to complain."

> Accumulation may go on and the property acquired become the property of the company so long as its action is unchallenged, but the permitted capitalization, when a stockholder intervenes, must furnish some guide for the action of the court.

Hosmer, being always a reasonable man, stated that the "acquiescence of a shareholder in the past will probably estop him from demanding full relief in the case at bar." He thus limited the Dodges' request for distribution to the fifty percent of earnings initially demanded by the Dodges, with credit for dividends declared for the 1917 fiscal year, while the case was pending. (The Dodges' had increased the size of their demand for dividends distribution to eighty percent during the heat of the litigation; Judge Hosmer chose to honor their original request.)

The Judge found that the construction of a smelting plant was *ultra vires*, beyond the corporate authority of the Ford Motor Company. The *Michigan Corporation Act* specifically excluded the commercial smelting of ore by manufacturing companies. Lucking had argued that Ford Motor should be allowed to smelt ore for its own uses and sell any excess on the open market, since the building of the River Rouge Plant came within the discretion provided by Section 14 of the *Corporation Act*. It reads:

> In addition to the powers hereinbefore enumerated, every corporation organized under this act shall possess and exercise all such rights and powers as are *necessarily incident* to the exercise of the powers expressly granted herein. (emphasis supplied)

The court, again noting that the Company's authorized capital was far below its actual property assets, and that pig iron was readily available to the company "in sufficient quantities," found that an eleven-million-dollar blast furnace would not be considered "necessarily incidental." Judge Hosmer made no specific finding of breach of duty or shareholder oppression by Henry Ford as the controlling shareholder, except as might be implicit in his other findings. He ordered an immediate payment of the fifty percent dividend of approximately twenty-eight million dollars and affirmed the injunction prohibiting the construction of the smelter.

Judge Hosmer's reading of his opinion took under an hour; the repercussions of it would last for decades.

Alfred Lucking announced to a throng of press agents that Ford would immediately appeal Judge Hosmer's decision to the Michigan Supreme Court, and the balding, driven, bushy-browed attorney proceeded to do just that.

The Dodges stepped out into the cool, low Detroit sunshine, popped their derby hats onto their heads and ambled over to Churchill's Tavern five blocks away on Woodward Avenue, where they lit a few cigars and downed more than several pints of cold beer.

Henry Ford, for his part, kicked a door on his way out of the courthouse and plowed grumpily into the back of his waiting vehicle (not a model T), and headed straightaway back to Dearborn.

AWAITING THE APPEAL

In the two years while the Dodge case was pending before the

Michigan Supreme Court in Lansing, Michigan, two major developments occupied much of Henry Ford's attention—the 1918 Michigan U.S. Senate race, and the start and finish of American participation in World War I.

The socialist, populist bent of Henry Ford's views of capitalism, espoused during the Dodge proceedings, continued to enhance his reputation as a new breed of progressive entrepreneur. Although many of his peers, it must be noted, thought him to be quite mad. Ford's surging public popularity caught the attention of the White House, where Woodrow Wilson frequently extended invitations to him to visit and advise the President. Wilson, anxious to break the Senate deadlock over his League of Nations plans, wanted Ford to run for the Senate from the State of Michigan. Ford supported the League idea—anything to secure international peace and keep his cars rolling off the assembly lines. Wilson wrote Ford: "You are the only man who can be elected and bring about the peace you so desire." Ford replied, "If they want to elect me let them do so, but I won't make a penny's worth of investment," and he didn't.

Ford's ego could not resist the stroking or the opportunity to shine in public favor. He entered into both the Republican and Democratic primaries. He barely lost the Republican nomination to Truman Handy Newberry, but won the Democratic nomination to oppose Newberry in the general election. Truman H. Newberry was the brother-in-law of Henry Bourne Joy, the president of the Packard Motor Company. Joy, as a leader in ALAM, had been an active instigator of the *Selden* lawsuit against the Ford Motor Company. Ford relished the chance to bump shoulders and rhetoric with any former foe.

The Senate campaign, however, took a back seat to the start of World War I. Long an opponent of U.S. intervention, and a flame-throwing pacifist, Ford dropped his radical anti-preparedness and antiwar declarations and committed the resources of his company to the prosecution of the War—but not with enormous enthusiasm. His initial efforts were focused on the development of the Fordson tractors to help raise crops in Britain.

Ford's major contribution to the war effort was the sale of Model Ts, which served as necessary ambulance and supply vehicles during the first major motorized warfare. The vehicles light weight, flexibility, and durability rendered them critical military assets. Fifteen thousand of the sixty thousand vehicles owned by the American Expeditionary Force, at its peak, were Fords. French and British Ford dealers, without consent or direction from Henry Ford, began assembling and soliciting Model Ts for the war effort. The Ford dealer in Paris rounded up eleven thousand Model Ts for the French army. The British procured between twenty thousand and thirty thousand vehicles.

In the United States, the military conscripted Model Ts from the civilian population when necessary. Although the Ford Motor Company ultimately produced about one hundred twenty-five thousand Model Ts during the war—a number which Ford proudly proclaimed to all listeners—this was actually a tepid number compared with the production rates of other American auto manufacturers.

When the government decided to dredge the River Rouge to permit navigation by larger ships, Ford contracted to build one hundred ships for them: two-hundred-foot-long, steel, anti-submarine boats, called Eagle Boats. It took three full months to complete the first boat and Ford only produced seventeen boats prior to the November 1918 Armistice. Ford stubbornly rejected Navy guidance and expertise in the construction of the craft, with leaky results. Ford ultimately produced sixty ships for the Navy, but by the beginning of World War II, only eight were still afloat.

Truman Newberry, unlike Henry Ford, apparently had no qualms about "investing" in his Senate campaign. He and other "investors" pumped hundreds of thousands of dollars into Newberry's Senate bid. Ford continued to avoid actively campaigning for the office in the general election. Newberry, a former Secretary of the Navy under Theodore Roosevelt, a lieutenant commander in the United States Navy Fleet Reserve, and commandant of the

Third Naval District of New York, ran a bruising, bare-knuckle campaign of personal attacks accusing Ford of pacifism, anti-Semitism and self-ism in keeping his son, Edsel, out of the military.

Not surprisingly, Ford lost by seven thousand five hundred sixty-seven[66] votes of four hundred thirty-two thousand cast on November 5, 1918, to give the Republican Party a narrow two-seat majority in the Senate. Newberry allegedly spent one hundred seventy-seven thousand dollars on the primary and between five hundred thousand dollars to one million dollars[67]on the general election to defeat Ford. These amounts were many multiples higher than campaign limits allowed under Michigan election laws. Once again, Ford ran his expanding empire without investing a dime—this time for a failed political race.

What, aside from money, kept Ford from winning the Senate seat? Likely, Ford's equivocation on the war and shielding his son Edsel from military service. This last required an act of uncharacteristic humility for Henry. In December of 1917, Henry Ford resigned as president of the Ford Motor Company to be replaced—in name at least—by his son Edsel. Edsel then sought a deferment from the military draft because, as Ford Motors' Chief Executive, he became indispensable to the war effort. Ford executives, many foreign leaders, and even private citizens appealed to Edsel Ford's draft board for deferment. Still, the Selective Service Appeal board at first rejected his request. Edsel Ford penned a hand-written appeal to President Wilson to grant him a deferment. The order granting Edsel Ford's appeal was typed on Woodrow Wilson's private typewriter.

Henry Ford had repeatedly sought the approval of the progressive ex-president Theodore Roosevelt, who bluntly reminded Ford of their differences with regard to the European War. Roo-

---

66. Later reduced to four thousand three hundred thirty-seven in a recount.

67. (two million eight hundred thousand dollars on the primary and seven million nine hundred thousand dollars to fifteen million seven hundred thousand dollars on the general election in today's dollars.)

sevelt had never fully forgiven his beloved father for paying for a substitute to serve for him in the American Civil War. Roosevelt had applied for a commission from Woodrow Wilson, only to be denied. Roosevelt's sons all served honorably and his youngest, Quentin, died in an air crash in France. Several days before the Senate election, the *Detroit Sunday Night Magazine* had published a letter from Roosevelt to Newberry that probably turned the tide in Newberry's favor.

> [Your sons] stand ready to pay with their lives for the honor and the interest of the American people, and while they thus serve America with fine indifference to all personal cost, the son of wealth, Mr. Ford sits at home in ignoble safety, and his father defends and advises such conduct. It would be a grave misfortune to the country to have Mr. Ford in the Senate when our question of continuing the war or discussing terms of peace may arise, and it would be equally grave misfortune to have him in any way deal with the problem of reconstruction in this country.

The Newberry campaign had pounded this home with the slogan, "He kept his boy out of the trenches by Christmas."

Ford loved the press, but only as it flattered his own aims (much like another capitalist-turned-politician of the twenty-first century who deeply adores the limelight). In response to Newberry's jabs, Henry Ford, for his part, rethought his relationship with the press and his ability to manage it. He did not like his son being dragged through the muck. He detested the Senate's embrace of spendthrift Newberry. Through his personal secretary, Ernest G. Leibold, Ford purchased his own media outlet, a newspaper, *The Dearborn Independent.* No more relying on the whims of public thought. Ford would create *Independent* public thought himself.

DECISION

On February 7, 1919, the Michigan Supreme Court, through Chief Justice Russell C. Ostrander, rendered its decision on Ford's appeal, affirming in part and reversing in part Judge Hosmer's decision. Russell C. Ostrander was a respected member of the Court known for his power of analysis and his ability to reduce his thoughts to paper in clear, simple, understandable diction. His colleagues referred to him as "republican of the strictest sort" which seems to mean something different than it might today. He died a mere seven months after the release of the Ford decision. His memorial at the Michigan Supreme Court said, in part:

> The law to him was . . . a living organism, elastic, vigorous and infinitely adapted to the needs and changes of a progressive society. He knew the history of our law and the enormous difficulty with which its principles have been developed and established. He realized the futility of theoretical determinations of right and justice and the infinite perils of disturbing rules tested and approved by long experience, the need of maintaining the uniformity of decisions and the continuity of development.

In affirming Hosmer's ruling on the distribution of dividends, Justice Ostrander was far more pointed about the autocratic and precipitous behavior of Henry Ford. Justice Ostrander, in his opinion, quoted at length from the parties' pleadings and the correspondence between Henry Ford and the Dodge brothers regarding the dividend and the policy decisions of Mr. Ford affecting the shareholders. He noted the shareholder's concerns in their complaint that in the uncertain world following the close of the World War and rising labor and material costs, the expansion of the Company's production capacity was "reckless in the extreme."

He then addressed each of the issues in order, starting with the Michigan capital stock limitation of fifty million dollars. He advanced that "[i]t may be supposed that the legislature looked with disfavor upon an initial aggregation of capital exceeding a certain amount. It cannot be supposed that it looked with disfavor upon a profitable corporate existence." He overruled Judge Hosmer's construction of the *Michigan Corporation Act* as limiting the accumulation of capital through earnings above the statutory limitation. He noted an anomaly in the argued limitation: that a corporation could, through borrowing, exceed the accumulation of actual physical assets in the corporation in excess of the fifty million dollars, but, through the application of debt to the balance sheet, offset on the corporate books the amount of total productive assets recognized as being "owned" by the corporation. This would render a downstream limitation of capital meaningless and ineffective in accomplishing the supposed public policy supporting an absolute limitation in all circumstances.

Similarly, the court rejected the Dodges' argument that the proposed development of the smelting plant was *ultra vires,* holding that because the Dodges, in their complaint, objected to the smelting plant on the basis of policy affecting shareholders and not specifically because it was beyond the power the corporation, the issue was not ripe for a decision. In other words, they rode the wrong legal horse in their complaint.

Ostrander did agree with Judge Hosmer on the determination that there was no evidence of antitrust violations. But, he found, the smelting plant could not be called "inimical to the best interests of the company and its shareholders." And the plaintiffs' further claim against Ford Motor Company for arbitrarily withholding special dividends did require judicial interference.

And that's when Ostrander's ruling grew very interesting.

He noted that the corporate directors' power over the distribution of dividends is "absolute as long as they act in the exercise of honest judgment." Given the prior practice of the directors regarding the regular distribution of dividends, the court felt that the refusal to declare dividends appeared to be an arbitrary action requiring some form of justification. Ford's single man, de-facto control of the company, his plan to drive down profits, and his megalomaniacal expressions of policy, led the court to conclude that he was not acting in the best interests of the company. Ford acted, instead, for his personal gratification and publicity in withholding the dividends.

In short, the plan does not call for and is not intended to produce immediately a more profitable business, but a less profitable one, not only less profitable than formerly, but less profitable than it admitted might be made. The apparent immediate effect will be to diminish the value of the shares and the returns to shareholders.

Justice Ostrander then rebuked Alfred Lucking's fundamental argument that "[a]lthough a manufacturing corporation cannot engage in humanitarian works as its principal business, the fact that it is organized for profit does not prevent the existence of implied powers to carry on with humanitarian motives such charitable works and purposes on the part of the board of directors." Lucking had cited a number of cases where courts of equity approved the directors of profit corporations engaging in incidental humanitarian benefits at corporate expense.[68] The court asserted that the "case presented here is not like any of them. The difference between an incidental humanitarian expenditure of corporate funds for the benefit of employees, like the building of a hospital for their use and the employment of agencies to benefit their conditions, and a general purpose and plan to benefit mankind at the expense of others, is obvious."

Interestingly, the United States Supreme Court in the *City of Oakland* case cited a litany of circumstances in which a court of equity would intervene to protect shareholders. Among them were two arguably applicable to this case— 1) where the board of directors, or a majority of them, are acting for their own interests, in a manner destructive of the corporation itself and 2) or, where the majority of shareholders themselves are oppressively and illegally pursuing a course in the name of the corporation, which is in violation of the rights of other shareholders.

Dodge v. Ford Motor Company, at its core, was a simple case of shareholder oppression: the minority shareholders of the corporation being quashed by the majority shareholder, where the

---

68. *Hawes v. City of Oakland*, 104 U.S. 450(1881) ; *Metropolitan Life Insurance Co. v. Hotchkiss*, 120 N.Y.S. 649 (S. CT. NY) (1909); and, *Steinway v. Steinway & Sons*, 40 N.Y.S. 718 (S.CT. NY)(1896) .

majority shareholder was chasing his idiosyncratic and autocratic daydreams with the captured interests of the minority shareholders. Had Ford and his lawyers focused their arguments and evidence on explaining how Ford's plans would eventually benefit Ford's employees and the company, rather than vague and disconnected rhetoric about avoiding layoffs, the court would probably not have intervened because of the strong power of the "business judgment rule." Henry Ford's unbridled megalomania about serving humanity and his intentional and single-minded tail-spin to corporate profits—while popular among the public—were provocations the court could not ignore.

Justice Ostrander went on to chasten Henry Ford. His words formulate a principal, later identified as "shareholder profit maximization," a principal that became the popular hallmark of the decision, considered in many legal texts, briefs and treatises. To make his point, Ostrander stated the basis for the actual decision in the case. He wrote,

> A business corporation is organized and carried on primarily for the profit of the shareholders. The powers of the directors are to be employed to that end. The discretion of the directors is to be exercised in the choice of means to attain that end, and does not extend to a change in that end itself, to the reduction of profits, or to the non-distribution of profits among stockholders in order to devote them to other purposes.

This statement represents the polar opposite of Henry Ford's view of shareholder rights. In effect, it asserts that shareholder profit maximization is the guiding principal of corporate decision making. While frequently cited, this guideline has never been explicitly followed. It wasn't even the actual basis for the Michigan Supreme Court's ruling. It was merely *obiter dictum* ("said in passing"), that is, a judicial comment made in the course of delivering a judicial opinion, but one that is unnecessary to the decision in the case and therefore not precedential.

The actual holding in the case, the *ratio discendi* (the actual and narrow rule of law, upon which a decision rests), is the rule of law that becomes established precedent under the doctrine of *stare decisis* ("to stand by things decided"). This is the accumulation of narrow holdings viewed as precedent that gives rise to the broad scope of English and American common law. The actual *ratio discendi* in the case was this:

> Courts of equity will not interfere with the management of directors unless it is clearly made to appear that they are all guilty of fraud, or misappropriation of the corporate funds, or a refusal to declare a dividend . . . when a refusal to do so would amount to such an abuse of discretion as would constitute a fraud or breach of that good faith, which they are bound to exercise toward the shareholders.

The Dodges' won their point on the forced distribution of dividends to shareholders. They also accomplished their larger goal of using Henry Ford's need for autocratic control of the Company, without shareholder interference, to move him to buy them out with borrowed money, a move so contrary to his desires and instincts that it only accentuated the degree to which absolute rule in the company animated his personality. Henry Ford achieved a pathway to full corporate dominance, with a green light for plant expansion and the right to begin smelter and other operations at the River Rouge property.

The Michigan Court, reverting to the "business judgment rule," was unwilling to go so far as to interdict the company's plan to build the smelting plant. The Judge dissolved the injunction. The River Rouge project resumed its noisy, gargantuan expansion in Dearborn. It would soon become the world's largest vertically-integrated industrial complex starting, with iron ore shipped to the plant on Ford freighters from the Mesabi Range in Minnesota, to the thousands of Ford vehicles driven off of the assembly line each day.

Dodge v. Ford Motor Company continues to be cited as authority today, not for its dicta but its narrow principal of minority shareholder oppression. It has not been expressly overruled and continues to appear compelling in the case of closely held corporations. Sixty years later, the Michigan Court of Appeals, citing the Supreme Court held in *Miller v. Magline*,[69] in 1977, states that "[i]t is especially true, where one man or family controls and dominates a corporation, that he or they must act in the upmost good faith in the actual control and management of the corporation as to minority shareholders."

Although the decision by the Michigan Supreme Court had mixed results and could logically be viewed as a partial win for Henry Ford, who obtained a go-ahead for his Ford River Rouge smelting operation, Justice Ostrander left Ford with a warning about future conduct of similar ilk. "It is enough to say, perhaps, that the court of equity is at all times open to complaining shareholders having a just grievance."

VICTORY AND DEFEAT

Let that judgmental gavel slam down any way it chose—a narcissist recognizes no law but his own. Henry Ford was not long in developing a strategy for obtaining complete and absolute control of the company without shareholder and judicial interference. While on an extended vacation in California, the elder Ford announced to the L.A. press his intent to form a whole new company with a super Model T vehicle; he aimed to compete directly with the Ford Motor Company to lower shareholder value. Given his similar prior ploy to drive out Alexander Malcomson from the company, the Dodges and the other minority shareholders were not intimidated by his threat. They held fast for fair value as they negotiated buyouts with Edsel Ford, but were happy and eager to cash out of the company. Ford, at the same time, unleashed a group of agents to sound out the shareholders about selling their shares to him. Presumably, concerns about Ford's management style and the lack of effective restraints on his actions and behav-

---

69. 256 N.W. 2d 761 (Mich. App. 1977).

ior were greater incentives on the part of the shareholders to part ways with Ford. The shares flew like pigeons into his cote.

Henry Ford acted fast. He obtained a seventy-five-million-dollar loan from a syndicate of Eastern banks, despite his ongoing disdain for moneylenders. He completed the buyouts by mid-July of 1919. Ford paid the Dodge Brothers twenty-five million dollars; Horace Rackham and John Anderson, twelve million five hundred thousand dollars each; and the John Gray estate, twenty-six million five hundred thousand dollars. But one wily shareholder remained. James Couzens, wise to Ford's pressure tactics and firm in his intent to have his contribution to Ford's success recognized, held out for a whopping twenty-nine million three hundred eight thousand eight hundred fifty-eight dollars. The single share he held for his sister brought two hundred sixty-two thousand thirty six dollars on her one-hundred-dollar investment.

Ford danced a jig when the transactions were complete. He had absolute and complete control of the Ford Motor Company, and with the ownership of *The Dearborn Independent*, he had the means to express himself in any way he chose. Ford could communicate his view of the world to a still-admiring country and attempt to further burnish his reputation and aura as the common man's folk hero. Dictatorial control achieved at last. Upmost good faith be damned.

In 1920, the Dodge Brothers produced one hundred forty-one thousand units to Ford's four hundred twenty thousand units, but that was to be the last year of the lives of John F. Dodge and Horace E. Dodge. The brothers attended the National Auto Show at the Grand Central Plaza in New York, where both brothers came down with what appeared to be influenza. Horace seemed to be the most acutely afflicted and John stood by him throughout the early days of the attack. When Horace appeared to recover, John's condition worsened and, with only Horace present, he passed away on January 14, 1920, in his suite at the Ritz Carlton Hotel, in Manhattan. His lungs were already weakened and scarred by a bout of tuberculosis during his youth. Horace retreated to Florida in hopes that the temperate weather would aid his recovery. There was a heavy presence of Dodge Factory Workers at John's funeral in Detroit, many who served as honorary pall-bearers. Automobile celebrities in attendance included Henry Leland and James Couzens. Notable absentees included Henry and Edsel Ford, Walter P. Chrysler and Alfred Sloan.

Horace Dodge, grieving the loss of his brother whom he cherished, continued living but without a life, until December 10, 1920, when he died in Florida of cirrhosis of the liver and complications from the influenza. His funeral produced even more honorary pallbearers than John's. Both were interred in an Egyptian Revival mausoleum constructed for the Dodge family by the brothers in 1915, in Woodlawn Cemetery.

Henry Ford did not appreciate this patriotic tribute to his rivals. He knew the Dodges were active in freemasonry. This led suspicious minds to conflicting theories about the meaning of the famous Dodge emblem: the letters DB centered inside two triangles. Was the logo a Star of David? Henry Ford's newspaper, *The Dearborn Independent,* suggested Hebrew leanings. The *Detroit Saturday Night Magazine* had this to say: "The theory that they were Jews is quite as sane as any other we have seen in the anti-Semitic antics of Ford's paper."[70] The interlocking deltas actually represented the unity of the brothers, forming a symbol well known in ancient Egypt.

Meanwhile, Ford's appetite for ascendance grew. Although he lost the 1918 campaign for the U.S. Senate in Michigan, Henry Ford had much broader ambitions, looking to the 1924 Presidential race, the ultimate pinnacle to feed his ego and educate the public to his way of thinking. He viewed his route to Washington, D.C., as motoring through the South and rural areas of the Midwest, where his views and prejudices could easily be fanned. He planned to develop his own novel and personally-inspired media empire to shape his image for the contest. Informal polls had him

---

70. "'Hebrewizing' the Dodges," (July 9, 1921).

running ahead of the incumbent President Warren G. Harding. There would be deviations along the way, and Elliott G. Stevenson—attorney extraordinaire—was not yet finished with Mr. Ford.

Part III

Henry Ford vs. The Chicago Tribune ET AL.

Chapter 10

"The World's Greatest Newspaper"

A BREWING WAR AND a war-hungry newspaper drew Henry Ford into public battle, in 1916. The war: Poncho Villa's armed incursions in Texas and New Mexico. The newspaper: the *Chicago Tribune*. A powerful rag with strong opinions (that styled itself as the "World's Greatest Newspaper"), the *Tribune* had embarked on a long editorial campaign promoting U.S. intervention in Mexico. William Randolph Hurst also backed going to war, largely to save his Chihuahuan ranch held by Villa and the Mexican "federales".[71] The U.S. Government had backed a number of Mexican leaders during the Mexican Revolution, beginning in 1910, generally consistent with American investment interests in railroads, mines, oil fields, and ranches producing consolidated cash crops. Therein lay the draw to war—protecting U.S. commercial interests.

Progressive muckraking journalists like John Reed firmly objected to American policy toward Mexico, which generally favored landowners and concessionaires over the interests of poor, dispossessed peons who were fighting for economic freedom from practical servitude. Reed spoke to this regional U.S. bias directly:

---

71. Hearst had to organize a private, one-hundred-man army led by Harry Longabaugh (aka "Sundance Kid") to recover the ranch which was later sold to the Mexican Government for two million five hundred thousand dollars after Hearst died.

> "And yet the Texan is not a particularly bad man. He's just like all the rest of Americans—he doesn't understand the Mexican temperament and doesn't want to; but the Texans come into direct contact with Mexicans, and so they are a little more uncivilized than the rest of us farther north. If you will trace the pedigree of Intervention Shouters, you will find that they are either Texans, or somebody with large interests in Mexico, or somebody who hopes to acquire large interests there under the Dear Old Flag. Or perhaps he might be an American Business Man in Mexico, and that is the worst of all.[72]"

Journalist John Gunther likened the *Tribune* to Texas,

> "What the *Chicago Tribune* reminds me of most is the State of Texas. Like Texas it is aggressive, sensitive in the extreme, loaded with guts and braggadocio, expansionist and medieval. Also like Texas it has its own foreign policy – though one very different."[73]

President Woodrow Wilson, in the absence of an adequate federal army, called up the national guard of the various states including Illinois and Michigan for federal service in Mexico. While he was resistant to declaring war on Mexico, he was sensitive to public pressure for the need to protect the borders. He appointed General John J. "Black Jack" Pershing to command an American force for a Mexican expedition to pursue Villa.

The *Chicago Tribune* announced that any *Tribune* employees who volunteered for a federal call-up of the national guard would have their employment positions held open for them upon their return from service and that they and their families would continue to be supported financially by the *Tribune* while the wage earners were away. The *Tribune* editors encouraged other patriotic companies to do the same and they set up a community fund to support families of recruits.

Enter astute *Detroit Free Press* telegrapher and part-time *Tri-*

---

72. John Reed, "What about Mexico?" *Masses,* June, 1914

73. Gunther, John, *Inside U.S.A.*, The New Press, Ed. Colbert, David, 1997.

bune stringer, P. Whitcomb Williams, who, on a muggy, gray Midwestern summer day in late June, 1916, dialed the Vice President and General Manager of the Ford Motor Company on a hunch. Williams, a garrulous and flamboyant man, asked Frank Klingensmith to comment on the Mexican situation. Mr. Williams, aware of Henry Ford's very public and prolific anti-war diatribes, smelled a story brewing. He asked what Ford planned to do for their employees in the state militia call-up by Wilson.

Klingensmith demurred. Williams persisted. Klingensmith distractedly stated that all Ford employees who left to join the Guard would be treated like all other new applicants for Ford jobs when they returned from service. There would be no Ford financial support for the Guardsmen or their families.[74]

JACKPOT

Williams clapped his hands and fired a telegraph off to the *Tribune* offices in Chicago where editors inserted his story into the June 22, 1916 edition of the paper.

"FLIVVER PATRIOTISM"

> "Ford employees who volunteered to bear arms for the United States will lose their jobs. While most employers have guaranteed not only to give patriotic workmen their old places when they return from fighting their country's battles, but have promised to pay their salaries while they are in service, Henry Ford's workmen will not have a job when they return, much less will they receive pay while fighting for their country. Ford's superintendents refuse to say if there are any Guardsmen employed in the plant, but it is known that some seventy-five men of the militia are Ford employees. No provision will be made by Ford for their wives and families."

On that same day, June 22nd, the *Tribune* was aflame with news

74. Klingensmith later denied making such a statement to Williams, although he had no specific memory of the event.

of the first major confrontation between Mexican and American troops near the border in Mexico, reporting the loss of twenty (actually twelve) American troopers during a Mexican "ambush" at Carrizal, Mexico. The action at Carrizal was, in fact, provoked by American commander Lt. William T. Boyd. Boyd was warned not to try to lead his forces through the town of Carrizal which was controlled by four hundred Mexican government troops. When the Mexican Commander, General Felix Gomez, came out to meet Boyd under a flag of truce, Boyd told an interpreter to "tell the son of a bitch that I am coming through."

All-out war with Mexico seemed likely at the time. Joseph Medill Patterson, co-publisher and co-editor of the *Tribune,* had already joined the Illinois Guard as an enlisted man in an artillery unit and was then marshalling with the Guard in Springfield, Illinois for a train trip to Texas. Patterson's cousin, co-editor and co-publisher of the *Tribune,* Robert Rutherford McCormick, planned a quick departure from Chicago to Springfield to join the 10th Cavalry of the Illinois Guard, of which he was an officer and a horseman. Robert M. McCormick and Henry Ford were on a collision course over politics, reputation and egos.

McCormick was a young, crusty, conservative, pro-military-preparedness curmudgeon, strongly opposed to U.S. intervention in Europe, while advocating the invasion and occupation of Mexico. Although a product of English education and a fan of English tailoring, he was strongly averse to English imperial foreign policy and politics. McCormick attended preparatory school at Ludgrove School in England. Ludgrove was and remains the British equivalent of Groton School in Massachusetts, serving societal elites. McCormick was known to sleep at Ludgrove under an American flag draped across his bed. After his father returned to the U.S., McCormick finished his early education at Groton. Following Groton, McCormick attended Yale (Scroll & Key 1903). He then obtained a law degree from Northwestern University in Evanston, Illinois in 1907. He was a founding partner of the law firm Shepard & McCormick, later to become the legal colossus, Kirkland & Ellis. Although taking the reins of the *Tribune* with his cousin Joseph M. Patterson in 1910, McCormick maintained his position as a partner in his law firm into the 1920s.

At six feet four inches and two hundred fifteen pounds with a ramrod-straight posture, McCormick was an imposing figure. He rode his horses with skill, balance and precision. He spoke with a slight British accent. Although he was basically a shy, introverted man, he was a stubborn purveyor of partisan opinion. He was described as projecting a sort of aloof "confident majesty," and one observer suggested he had "one of the finest minds of the 14th Century [*sic*]."

An unfriendly contemporary described Robert M. McCormick as a "[r]emote, coldly aloof, ruthless aristocrat living in lonely magnificence, an eccentric misanthropic genius whose haughty bearing, cold eye and stately reserve made it impossible to like or trust him."

McCormick had a strong puritan streak, disposed to annoyance by off-color stories. He amused himself with a concealed door on the inside of his office which startled visitors who could not find a way out. It was not unusual for him to send reporters out on peculiar assignments, like visiting the University of Wisconsin at Madison to investigate a story as to whether Wisconsin men were wearing lace underwear. McCormick had an affinity for Alsatian Shepard hounds and English bulldogs and used to enjoy the discomfort of subordinates whose shoes would be ripped apart by his bulldog "Tribby." McCormick prided himself on his physical fitness. When he died at the age of seventy-five, he was buried in the same uniform that he wore in the active military in 1918.

McCormick and Ford had so much in common and yet worlds separated them. McCormick decidedly urban in outlook and experience—Ford determinably rural.

Like Ford, McCormick projected an odd mixture of competence and prescience, sandwiched between layers of eccentricity and quirkiness. He, like Henry Ford, vertically integrated his company by acquiring tree farms, paper mills, and transport ships to convey raw paper for the *Tribune*'s presses to Chicago. He too had a facility for things mechanical. He invented improvements to the printing process and to electric motors. He took credit for having introduced machine guns to the U.S. Army in the Mexican campaign.

McCormick and Ford both opposed U.S. entry into the European war but disagreed on strategy. Ford argued that an American military build-up would eventually trip the country into war, while McCormick insisted that military preparedness was the only way that war could be avoided. McCormick and Patterson, with their senior editorial writers, worked out a clear and consistent *Tribune* editorial policy advocating the American invasion of Mexico, American non-intervention in Europe, and the escalation of American military preparedness in support of both.

PEACE SECRETARY

Following the sailing of Ford's utopian and grandiose peace ship, Oscar II, ("the good ship nutty") to Norway in December, 1915, and its highly visible failure to move the needle on peace negotiations in Europe, Henry Ford hired a young, jowly newspaper reporter to boost his message. Theodore Delavigne, Ford's personal "peace secretary," wrote and published, under Ford's byline, inflammatory antiwar diatribes in news releases, pamphlets and other media accusing preparedness advocates of supporting murder.

Delavigne composed the following for Ford:

> "The word 'murderer' should be embroidered on the breast of every soldier and naval sailor."
>
> "Bismark! Bismark! I guess that is a matter of history. I don't know much about that."
>
> "I don't know anything about history and I wouldn't give a nickel for all the history in the world. The only history worthwhile is the history we are making day to day."
>
> "History is more or less bunk. It is tradition. We don't want tra-

> dition. We want to live in the present, and the only history worth a tinker's dam [*sic*] is the history we make today."

Ford accused bankers and munitions manufacturers of lining their own pockets on the blood of innocents by whipping up war fever. He espoused a form of simple idealistic internationalism, where neither flags nor borders were respected or feared.

> "I am going to keep the American flag flying on my plant until the war is over and then I am going to pull it down for good; I am going to hoist in its place the flag of all nations which is being designed in my office right now. I don't believe in boundaries. I think nations are silly and flags are silly too. Flags are rallying points, that's all. The munitions makers and the militarists and the crooked politicians use flags to get people excited when they want to fool them. . . . Personally, I have been a voter for thirty-one years and in all that time I have voted only six times and then because my wife made me. . . . I used to go to church once a year on Easter Sunday. I don't do that now. The churches probably do go and are all right for those who want them. The best work the churches do is in the country. There they furnish a meeting place for the boys and the girls to get together and mate up. . . . A pacifist I shall always be. . . . I changed my mind only once in my life."

PREPAREDNESS PRESS

The popular media distribution of Ford's views and pronouncements didn't sit well with Robert Rutherford McCormick and the "World's Greatest Newspaper," which had recently and actively supported a one-hundred-thirty-thousand-person march through the streets of Chicago in support of American preparedness. The *Tribune* saw itself as a counterweight to irrational pacifism which it considered a menace to American unity and idealism. It was steadfastly isolationist and unswervingly militant in the protection of American interests. It prided itself on its long history of fighting unpatriotic pacifism going back to the Civil War, when it leveled attacks on the Northern "Copperheads" who opposed the prosecution of the war. While espousing clear versus muddled thinking on the part of its opponents, the *Tribune*, with its own brand of "rococo" journalism, was not known for its consistent objectivity.

On the morning of June 22, 1916, Clifford S. Raymond, a literate and witty editorial writer for the *Tribune,* sat in his office on one of the higher floors of the Tribune Building, with his morning coffee and a copy of the morning paper in front of him. Rain pelted the windows fogging the view of Dearborn Street below. The "Flivver Patriotism" article caught his attention along with the Carrizal "ambush" outrage in the headlines, and the many photos of Illinois Guard soldiers in their campaign hats and "Sam Browne" belts, clambering aboard trains headed for the Springfield mobilization.

Raymond grabbed the paper and hurried down the hall to the elegant office of the head of the *Tribune*'s editorial department, Tiffany Blake. Blake, a lawyer who once worked in the law office of Abraham Lincoln's son, Robert Todd Lincoln, was the courtly and debonair overseer of the editorial comments of the *Tribune*. The two men conferred briefly over the Ford article and Blake directed Raymond to take a cut at an anti-Ford editorial, scolding Ford for his lack of patriotism. Raymond returned to his office and hammered out his draft, then returned it to Blake.

Tiffany Blake, ever cautious, realized that taking on Ford could have repercussions. The man had a tinderbox temper, a deep reservoir of spite and unlimited resources. Blake made a few changes and then tracked down Robert McCormick, who was just then devoting most of his attention to getting out of the office to join the Guard. Blake showed McCormick the draft editorial which indicated that Ford was acting like an anarchist. McCormick's reply as he headed for the door was, "Well, call him one then." They did. On June 23, the *Chicago Tribune* published the editorial entitled "Henry Ford is an anarchist." After referencing the report of his alleged failure to support his employees signing up with the Guard, the comment continued:

> If Ford allows this rule of his shops to stand he will reveal him-

> self not only as an ignorant idealist, but as an anarchistic enemy of the nation which protects him in his wealth. A man so ignorant as Henry Ford may not understand the fundamentals of government under which he lives. That government is permitted to take Henry Ford himself and command his services as a soldier, if necessary. . . . He takes the men who stand between him and service and punishes them for the service which protects him. The man is so incapable of thought that he cannot see the ignominy of his own performance.
>
> The proper place for so deluded a human being is a region where no government exists, except such as he furnishes, where no protection is afforded, except such as he affords, where nothing stands between him and the rule of life, except such defenses as he puts there.
>
> Such a place, we think might be found in the State of Chihuahua, Mexico. Anywhere in Mexico would be a good location for the Ford factories.[75]

Henry Ford immediately issued a denial of the *Tribune* allegations, asserting that the thirty-seven members of the militia among his thirty-seven thousand employees would be re-employed "without prejudice" on their return after their service, and that their families would be looked after. The *Tribune* printed the Ford denial but remained skeptical. The *Tribune* trial marked the beginning of the erosion of Frank Klingensmith's relationship with Henry Ford. He would never recover and was later dismissed on the pretext that he was somehow in league with banks.

BITTER FLIVVER KING

In September, 1916, Ford's attorney Alfred Lucking spurred Ford to file suit against the *Tribune* for libel in the United States District Court in Chicago. Thinking better of standing trial on the

75. Imagine if only the *Tribune* could have seen the future, and if Henry Ford had had a *Twitter* account. Instead, he had to buy a newspaper press.

Tribune's home turf, Ford and his lawyers later decided to bring the case closer to home in the Michigan Wayne County Circuit Court in Detroit. Michigan law at the time required that an aggrieved party to a libel seek a retraction before bringing suit. On May 22, 1917, Ford sent a letter to the *Tribune* requesting the publication of a retraction of the "Ford is an anarchist" editorial and the "Flivver Patriotism" article.

> Your attempt to justify your motives for publishing the article in the *Chicago Tribune* of June 23, 1916, in which I was called an anarchist, has failed to impress me, and your withholding the publication of a retraction thereof, which should not have been necessary for me to request, has convinced me of your insincerity relative to the matter.

In the interim, between June, 1916, and July, 1917, President Wilson had resisted all pressures to declare war on Mexico. But on April 6, 1917, he succumbed to the popular demand for war against Germany and Austria. There was, at the time, a large German immigrant population living in Chicago, and the *Tribune* had been staunchly evenhanded in its coverage of the European combatants, regularly reporting stories from both sides, but reversed itself in the face of Germany's reinstatement of unrestricted submarine warfare against neutral shipping in February, 1917. After Wilson's declaration of war, the *Tribune* was all in on the prosecution of the war.

And then, world history was made. Henry Ford promptly and dramatically changed his mind with the sinking of the liner Lusitania. He lost no time pivoting from avowed pacifist to war munitions producer, although some questioned the sincerity of his conversion. Meeting with Woodrow Wilson, he offered the government the unconditional use of his Detroit manufacturing facilities. He volunteered to construct as many submarine chaser boats and tractors for Britain and France as the government might request. His "conversion" was abrupt, complete and self-serving. In early September of 1917, Ford called Oscar Marx, the Mayor of Detroit, and expressed great interest in personally marching in a soldier-support parade scheduled for September 18. He publicly announced that Ford's Detroit facilities would shut down at 11:00 a.m. on that day to allow his forty thousand employees to attend the pageant with their families.

Not everyone was willing to forgive Ford his earlier opposition to preparedness for war. Frederic R. Coudert, the clever lawyer who represented Panhard and Levassor in the *Selden* case, wrote to him, with some bitterness.

> Has it occurred to you that your propaganda in delaying, obstructing, impending military preparedness may yet in the future result in the deaths of hundreds, perhaps thousands of Americans? The work in France of well-intentioned, but misinformed sentimentalists, sharing your views, has caused that country the loss of probably half a million men. The efforts of pacifists had resulted in the lack of artillery, of machine guns, of ammunition and uniforms, all of which had to be supplied after the Germans crossed the frontier, and this necessitated the loss of the very best blood of France.

The Illinois Guard had released McCormick from service in the Mexican "intervention" in November of 1916, and he'd returned to Chicago briefly before being called by the U.S. Army and reassigned to France after President Wilson's declaration of war against Germany and Austria.

McCormick personally responded to Ford's demand for a retraction on July 11, 1917, citing his being out of town for the delay in answering.

On July 11, 1917, the date of McCormick's letter to Ford, McCormick was still "out of town." He had just arrived on that date in Paris, checking into the Ritz hotel before reporting to General Pershing's headquarters, where he was assigned as an intelligence officer because of his ability to speak French. The *Tribune*, in anticipation of the need for war coverage, opened the Army Tribune office near the Place de la Concorde. McCormick's response to

Ford's request for a retraction was uncompromising.

> We are not enlightened as to your meaning when you refer to our "attempt to justify" our motives. . . . As you have seen fit to force the matter into the courts it will of course be for the court to pass upon our rights and yours; but we do not see how anyone can fairly question our disinterested sincerity in the matter.

McCormick commented on the extensive publicity and advertising of Ford's views which he was able to make because of his "enormous wealth."

> We believed that the views which you publicly expressed were inimical to the best interests of the country, and if put into practice would endanger the security, if not the very existence of governments, and the maintenance of that which we understand is public law.

McCormick continued that the *Tribune* had not charged Ford with being a bomb thrower, but objected to his views which produced a "practical injury" to the country.

> You were sowing a seed which the last year, and especially the present crisis, has shown were to develop the unpreparedness which we all know, and must regret, as a fact today.

McCormick reminded Ford of his admonitions and advertisements which excoriated pro-preparedness newspapers such as the *Tribune*.

> We felt free to criticize your views as you felt to criticize ours, but in doing so used language much more temperate than your own. We think that sober reflection, not embittered by anger, will convince you of this fact.

Noting the fact that Ford had only recently become convinced of the necessity of fighting militarism with militarism, McCormick stated that perhaps there may no longer be differences between them on the subject.

> If so, we shall indeed be glad to comment editorially upon the

> circumstance, and to congratulate the nation that its military policy now has the support of one whose former opposition may cost it so heavily in lives unnecessarily sacrificed.

On July 14, 1917, Mr. Lucking filed Ford's new suit in Detroit. The suit also named the *Tribune's* Detroit distributor, Solomon News Company, in order to obtain jurisdiction over the libel dispute. The earlier suit in Chicago was dismissed.

TRIBUNE AT WAR

Meanwhile, General John J. Pershing and the American Expeditionary Force were in the process of organizing American troop deployments in France. Pershing arrived in Liverpool, England on his way to the continent. There to meet him on his arrival was the *Tribune*'s "eager, lean and toothy" young reporter, Floyd Gibbons. Gibbons was a handsome and dashing veteran of the *Tribune*'s coverage of the Mexican incursion. Gibbons not only knew Pershing, but he also met and interviewed Poncho Villa himself during the Mexican campaign.[76] Gibbons helped set up the *Army Tribune* in Paris and maintained a close connection with General Pershing and his staff. The *Tribune* arranged to donate the net proceeds from the *Army Tribune* to the American Expeditionary Force Command to help them prosecute the war effort.

Gibbons always seemed to be at the right place at the right time to capture a bead on a story. On his way to Europe aboard the Cunard Liner Laconia, a German submarine torpedoed and sank the ship. Gibbons made his way ashore in a lifeboat and telegraphed a first-person account of the sinking to *Tribune* subscribers. While out in the field as a war correspondent in France, a German machine gunner shot Gibbons twice in the arm and shoulder, with a third bullet hitting him on a ricochet through his left cheek and left eye socket and emerging through his helmet.

76. Gibbons once advised Villa not to commence raids during the baseball World Series, because it would drown out the news coverage he would likely get in the U.S.

He lost the eye, but gained a white eyepatch trade mark. In July, 1918, a month after he lost his eye, Gibbons was back covering the allied advance at Amiens.[77] The swashbuckling Gibbons would serve as a living symbol of the *Tribune*'s patriotism and courage, proudly presenting himself in the audience of the courtroom at the trial, in the press rooms, and in the watering holes always close by the court.

Pershing offered then Major Robert R. McCormick a position on his general staff, but McCormick preferred something more dramatic. He entered the French artillery school at Valechon and was later given the command of two batteries in the Fifth Field Artillery of "The Big Red One," First U.S. Army Division. His was the first American Division to encounter the enemy in France. McCormick did actually participate in combat in France being engaged in the American recapture of Cantigny from the Germans. It was during his turn in France that McCormick took to wearing a "tooth brush" moustache, a monocle, and a doleful expression, while toting a walking stick.

FREE SPEECH WARRIORS

McCormick had liberal opportunities to attend to *Tribune* business in Paris, while he was not otherwise occupied. He attended strategy sessions with Weymouth Kirkland in the United States and with Howard Ellis, and other *Tribune* lawyers in the United States and France, who were rounding up witnesses for the Ford trial. Kirkland, forty-two years old, was a dapper and seasoned trial lawyer known for his clever strategic thinking and jury appeal. He was the senior partner and litigator in McCormick's law firm, and McCormick enlisted him as his senior counsel for the trial. Kirkland had a nimble way of calling on juror's own experiences to appreciate the positions of his clients, without oversell-

---

77. It was Gibbons who reported a made-up comment by Pershing, "Lafayette, we are here."

ing them.[78] Kirkland, a native of Gratiot Township, Michigan, was a descendent of John Alden and William Bradford from the *Mayflower*. His great-grandfather fought in the Battle of Waterloo under the Duke of Wellington. Kirkland "read" law under a celebrated Chicago lawyer, Charles Hardy, and then obtained a law degree from Chicago-Kent College of Law in 1901. Kirkland was a prominent litigator who specialized in assisting the *Tribune* to wind its way through difficult First Amendment, libel and antitrust cases. McCormick, at Kirkland's suggestion, retained the services of Ford's dreaded adversary in the Dodge case, Elliott G. Stevenson, as the *Tribune's* local counsel. This choice operated as it was intended—a stick in the eye for Henry Ford.

Assisting Kirkland was a bright, frail, and intellectually curious young man of twenty-six years, who had a passion for First Amendment law, Howard Ellis, the second-name partner of the current firm, Kirkland & Ellis. Howard Ellis received a Bachelor's of Law degree from the University of Chicago in 1914 and Doctorate of Laws degree in 1915. Ellis was engaged in the nitty gritty of preparing and deposing witnesses, including Joseph Patterson and Robert McCormick. He did a lot of this in France. He sailed to France to speak to witnesses on behalf of the *Tribune* (with the ultimate object of joining the French Army to fight the Germans; he was unable to pass the physical for the U.S. Army while in the U.S. and French physical standards were lower). He wrote a number of long letters back to Kirkland describing his interactions with McCormick and other witnesses.

Ellis wrote Kirkland that McCormick was hell-bent on testifying in the trial, and that "the Colonel is strong for fighting Ford hard and bitterly." McCormick wanted to testify to show that the preparedness policy of the *Tribune* and the demand for

78. Kirkland was famous for his courtroom demonstrations to the jury rather than pure argument. He once pulled up a bucket, a potato, and a potato peeler and began peeling to mock a witness in a life insurance case where the death of the insured was in issue; the sailor claimed to have seen the deceased floating by out a porthole, but continued peeling.

war against Germany had been right both ethically and practically. They were also considering bringing in General Pershing to testify, particularly because they were concerned that the entry of the U.S. into World War I would make the events and concerns of the Mexican expedition seem small, petty, immaterial and uninteresting to a jury. They planned to hit Ford hard on his reversal on the war by underscoring the publicity-generating and remunerative nature of his conversion. They wanted to stress the tax exemption available for war profits; and the fact that Ford would be left with a fully-equipped "monster plant" after the war to pursue other financial gains.

Kirkland pursued legal battle strategies with full vigor. He assigned Ellis to firmly prepare many of the *Tribune* witnesses, including McCormick, for testimony and cross examination by Ford's lawyers. Ellis believed that Ford's lawyers would likely seek to favorably compare Ford's musings with those of religious teachers and philosophers. Ellis leaned heavily into the *Tribune* editorial language that called Ford "an anarchist." At one point, Ellis pushed McCormick: "Suppose they ask you whether Christ was an anarchist?" His reply: "If they ask me that, I'm going to yell 'Blasphemy' at them!"

Ellis' letters describe the atmosphere in Paris: the intrusion of the large German gun, "Big Berthe," the constant aerial attacks with sirens blaring, church bells chiming, and sleep foregone. Young Ellis did end up joining the French Army as a private after attending the Ecole Artilliere at Fontainebleau. He did not count on the end of the hostilities in November, 1918, which left him struggling for a way to get out of the French Army to participate in the Ford trial in Michigan before his enlistment term. He had to rely on Gibbons' influence with General Pershing to push the French to provide his release from their Foreign Legion.

While the *Tribune* case was pending and Henry Ford was seeking election to the U.S. Senate, without mounting a serious traditional campaign. He relied on his reputation and his free media connections with newspapers.

In the run-up to the libel trial, the Newberry Senate Campaign' hard-hitting political slams against Ford became popular grist for the *Tribune*'s publicity mill. McCormick tried and failed to get Secretary of War John W. Weeks to publicize the millions of dollars in war-time profits paid to Ford—that were never returned as Ford had pledged. The government would also not release a report on the lack of seaworthiness of the Eagle Boats produced by Ford to chase German submarines during the war.

McCormick, following everything from France, felt strongly that the *Tribune*'s article about Edsel Ford's draft exemption had been tepid. McCormick wanted to stress father Ford's lack of patriotism at trial, a topic he would continue to pursue even after the trial with an investigation exposing Woodrow Wilson's role in Edsel Ford's deferment. Clear fight lines had been drawn, and McCormick wanted a fight. He'd been a major sponsor of Truman Newberry's Senate campaign, happy to see Ford defeated and disappointed in Newberry's lack of competitive spirit after the election. According to McCormick, "I tried to put some fight into Newberry, but Newberry wouldn't fight."

JUDICIAL GUNSLINGER

In the Spring of 1919, the Ford forces were gathering in Detroit for the approaching contest. Alfred Lucking, recognizing the need for more fire power at trial, called upon a friend, Judge Alfred Murphy, to leave the Michigan Circuit Court bench to join the Lucking law firm and the Ford team. Murphy, who shocked his bench colleagues by announcing his resignation from the judiciary after twenty years, said, "I have long thought of getting into private practice. It offers many inducements. Two days ago, Mr. Lucking placed the matter in so attractive a light that I would not refuse." The opportunity for a lucrative fee and notoriety in a lawsuit of international interest compelled this respected judge, who only brought home ten thousand dollars a year.

Murphy held great influence in Detroit. Known for his incisive intellect and his oratorical skills, Judge Murphy often "graced the dais" at patriotic dinners and events around Detroit. He was a thin, severe, dapper man with an intense stare behind a set of round wireless glasses. He was a genial man of immense and imposing dignity. His fellow lawyers and judges considered him "ever more than a lawyer and a judge. He is a master of eloquence, and his voice is always heard in support of every good cause affecting the welfare of the city, state and nation."

Murphy graduated from the University of Detroit with a bachelor's degree and master's degree in the arts. He obtained his law degree from the Detroit College of Law in 1893. In time, he was elected Recorder of Recorder's Court in Detroit, the court of exclusive criminal jurisdiction in the City and he later became the presiding judge of the Third Circuit Court in Detroit, which included jurisdiction over all civil matters in the City of Detroit and Wayne County and all criminal cases in Wayne County, outside of the City of Detroit. Murphy was known for his innovative sponsoring of juvenile courts and workmen's compensation laws in Michigan. Having not refused Alfred Lucking, Murphy set about preparing for the start of the Ford/*Tribune* face off.

The *Tribune*'s local lawyer, Elliot G. Stevenson—acutely aware of Murphy's reputation and standing in Detroit legal circles, and the fifty-one thousand employees Ford had in Wayne County—successfully pushed hard for a change of venue of the Ford suit. He dared not leave the decision in the hands of a Ford-hometown legal hero or a Ford-hometown jury. Circuit Judge Henry A. Mandell of Detroit presided over a three-day hearing to rule on the *Tribune*'s Motion for Change of Venue because of Ford's influence in Detroit. He ultimately sided with the *Tribune* to move the venue elsewhere.

The parties finally agreed on an alternative site for the trial in a sleepy, warm-springs resort town and farming community twenty-five miles north of Detroit, Mount Clemens, Michigan.

Chapter 11

War of Words on the Banks of the Clinton River

BATH CITY

In 1919 Mt. Clemens was a town of about nine thousand five hundred souls and the County seat of Macomb County, named after War of 1812 General Alexander Macomb. Snaking slowly through the center of the downtown was the Clinton River, which provided water access to Lake St. Clair and to the City of Detroit. The town was known at the time for being the "Rose Capital" of the country with thirty acres of rose gardens under glass and also the "Bath City." Its warm sulfur baths were believed to contain powerful healing properties. Several of the large resort hotels with hot springs and wide and long open verandas were reserved by each of the warring sides, for the three-month epic courtroom struggle commencing in May, 1919.

Each side bought their own large entourage of lawyers and media publicists anxious to regale and influence the national and local public with stories and opinions regarding the thrust and parry in the hot, steamy, courtroom then as now, perfumed by the distinct odor of rotten eggs wafting in from the H_2S, hydrogen sulfide, expelled from the salubrious baths. The Ford side reserved rooms at the Colonial Inn, a four-story building with a two-story columned entrance, a wraparound porch and awninged windows overlooking a croquet court and the Medea Hotel, a blockish building composed of red Lake Superior sandstone, with large arches strung along a one-hundred-eight-foot, ground-floor arcade, within a stone's throw of the courthouse. The *Tribune* side decamped to the more sumptuous Park Hotel with a columned wrap around porch and acres of formal gardens on the other side of the Clinton River.

The town was a small island of homes and businesses wrapped in a near endless sea of farmland, occupied in many respects by recent German immigrants, with a distinct taste for spirits and antipathy toward prohibition and a tolerance for its disregard. The 1818 founder of Mt. Clemens, Christian Clemens, established an early distillery there. There is a story passed around in the Macomb County Bar Association about a defense lawyer in a prohibition case who offered himself as an expert in the identification of whisky. He grabbed the bottle and swallowed the offending contents in the courtroom and then moved for dismissal of the case on the basis of a lack of evidence, which was in due course granted. Michigan went dry in 1917 with the Damon Act of 1916, several years before the passage of the 18th Amendment to the U.S. Constitution.

There were plenty of watering holes for the thirsty press corps who descended on the town for the spectacle. In late 1918, Henry Ford arranged for his personal secretary, the massively Teutonic Ernest G. Liebold, with a thoroughly Prussian personality and demeanor, to acquire for him a small local newspaper, *The Dearborn Independent,* to provide Ford with a news platform in which to express and distribute his unfiltered views on matters of public policy and a wide range of other topics on which he cared to hold forth. Ford brought in his old friend, Edwin G. Pipp, the former editor in chief of the *Detroit News,* and others to run the paper and expand its circulation, relying on "interpretations" of Ford's off the cuff and frequently incoherent remarks.

Ford acquired printing presses which he installed in his tractor factory located in the River Rouge complex. The *Independent,* which accepted no advertisements, spread Ford's views and perspectives regarding the *Tribune* suit. far and wide, using Ford dealerships as distributors for his paper as well as his cars. *The Dearborn Independent* was once charitably described as the finest "newspaper ever published in tractor factory." The *Independent* was very much a tool used by Ford in forging the public relations bubble surrounding the *Tribune* trial, churning out story after story of Ford's contribution to the European War effort, Ford's altruism, Ford's humble personality, and Ford's kindness and generosity toward his employees. The *Independent* was later to become an instrument of irredeemable shame for Henry Ford.

Ford and his close staff had an eye on the upcoming Presidential election of 1924 and were stoking the fires of "America First" isolationism, in a constant campaign to remain in the public view. Informal polls had Ford running well ahead of other politicians including the incumbent Warren Harding. Billy Sunday, the notorious professional baseball player turned evangelical preacher, noted with admiration at Ford's media savvy that "Ford has P.T. Barnum skinned a mile." Ford had an elevated appreciation of his power and influence in public opinion, once reciting that "I am the only businessman in the country that can afford to talk on any subject that I please." His rustic, homespun pronouncements and posturing's were widely followed and absorbed in rural America.

Henry Ford established his own personal news bureau in Mt. Clemens to provide copy concerning the trial to small town newspapers all over the country. It was an effort to combat the influence of the *Tribune* with large urban daily newspapers, which tended to identify with the *Tribune*. Both sides smothered the town with private detectives trying to dig up dirt on potential jurors and witnesses that might be called. Ford agents spread rumors in the community that the Ford Motor Company planned to open a new plant in Macomb County to employ thousands of workers. No stone was left unturned by either side in an effort to obtain an edge in the litigation. Some of those stones were decidedly unsavory, including unsuccessful efforts to entice the judge and some of the witnesses with female companionship. The two sides were equally matched and financed with an estimated war chest of about five hundred thousand dollars each. Henry Ford claimed one million dollars in restitution.

The site of the contest was the three-story Macomb County Courthouse standing alone in courthouse square, in the center of the downtown and close to the river. The building was an odd Romanesque style building with a later added single tower on the northwest corner, capped by a pyramidal roof and punctuated by clock faces in each direction. The north facing front of the building contained duplicate doorways covered with classical rounded arches supported by four large Doric columns each and topped with a roof rising to a peak. Inverse curved balustrades guided the stone stairs outward and upward to the second-floor landing of the two separate entrances, which opened to the courtroom beyond. Between the two entrances and outward extended core of the building a stack of two sets of very narrow and tall windows adorned the structure rising to to a center peak of the building. Standing alone on the peak at the front of the courthouse was the mercurial statue of justice. On either corner of the courthouse square stood an ancient cannon with a stack of cannon balls dedicated to the memory of the deceased in the War of 1812, and rededicated as a further memorial to those in the union who died in the more recent Civil War.

Mt. Clemens as a venue presented problems and opportunities for both sides. The proximity to Detroit and the large pool of jurors augured in favor of Ford. His growingly public anti-Semitic beliefs and cracker barrel personality resonated with rural populations. On the other hand, there was a strong patriotic streak among farmers that might be plumbed from the *Tribune* side. The German farmers presented somewhat of a mixed bag, some silently supporting the home country while others anxious to demonstrate their new loyalty to America. Much of the trial would be focused on those elements rather than the facts at hand largely due to a misstep by the Ford lawyers, who in addition to the anarchist charge made the "ignorant idealist" part of the sting of libel, thus opening a wide range of attacks on Henry Ford's personal knowledge of historical facts. One of the realities of defamation litigation is that the plaintiff who claims his or her reputation besmirched opens himself or herself to an onslaught of wide ranging attacks on the reality and integrity of that reputation in the first place. In a sense the complainant becomes the defendant called upon to defend the purity of one's integrity, conduct and reputation, before the practical burden of proof shifts to the actual defendant.

VANITY, SHAME AND SATIFACTION

Vanity, whether springing from a well of real achievement or a smile of blind fortune, can be an affliction from which it is difficult to recover because it is so satisfying to entertain. Jane Austin in *Pride and Prejudice* distinguished vanity from pride. "Vanity and pride are different things, though the words are often used synonymously. A person may be proud without being vain. Pride relates to our opinion of ourselves, vanity to what we would have others think of us." Henry Ford's vanity surfaced from both achievement and fortune and plagued him from his triumphs to his fiascoes. The Ford Motor Company by 1913 had more branch managers, local representatives and salesmen than the other five leading manufacturers. The Company had twenty-eight assembly plants in the largest cities of twenty-two states. In the fiscal year 1916, the Company sold four hundred seventy-two thousand three hundred fifty cars for a resultant fifty-seven million dollar net profit. Ford had clearly established dominance in the fastest growing and most important commercial enterprise in the first half of the twentieth century.

The financial success of the Company, together with the near idolatrous coverage of Ford in the national and local press, spurred a constant thirst for attention and encouraged him to step out and comment on matters of war and peace and other social issues that were of a complexity well beyond his practical knowledge and limited formal education. His involvement in and funding of the ill-fated "Peace ship," the Oscar II, which sailed from Hoboken, New Jersey to Norway on December 4, 1915, underscored his highly visible but ill-considered idealism, widely mocked in the Urban American press as the "Ship of Fools."

A person confident in his pride might subscribe to the "sticks and stones" view that mere "words will never hurt me." To a man consumed by his vanity, words can very much hurt indeed. Shakespeare noted:

> Good name in man and woman dear my lord,
> Is the immediate jewel of their souls:
> who steals my purse steals trash; tis something, nothing
> t'was mine. tis his, and has been slaves to thousands;
> but he who filches from me my good name
> robs me of that which not enriches him,
> and makes me poor indeed.
>
> *Othello*, Act III, scene III, ll 155-61.

The common law of defamation is addressed to remedy the hurt to a person's vanity—to the sense of shame brought on by an attack upon a person's standing or reputation in the public community. It is also imbued with an economic sense of the property value one has developed in one's good name. The community in the common law is generally accepted as the community at large, as opposed to say a disreputable subset (i.e. the Klu Klux Klan). The false attribution of conduct or character to a person which suggests dishonor, disgrace or inadequacy, has historically been a sore point, often spurring some kind of a response in the form of violence (duels), ecclesiastic punishment (excommunication), or judicial penalty (damages). Narcissists, who feed off the need for constant public affirmation of their value and importance, are particularly prone to slights to their public personas and are known to develop reputations as "libel bullies."

The history of defamation law extends back to before the *Lex Salica* in Germany, where King Clovis codified a civil and criminal code, which assigned financial penalties for attributing the words "hare" or "wolf" to another or to demean the virtue of a woman. Early English seigniorial courts and ecclesiastical courts assumed jurisdiction over verbal misbehavior, but with the advent of the printing press and Caxton's establishment of a press at Westminster in 1476, the King's Courts began to develop an interest in regulating the subject. The institutional powers of the Crown and the Archbishop of Canterbury both had an interest in regulating what was published and in punishing what was not approved or not in keeping with a public sense of propriety. After James, the First, banned duels in 1613, the Royal Courts annexed the role as guardians and overseers of the public speech.

The English courts developed a number of unique features in the law of defamation. They developed criminal sanctions for seditious libel for disrupting the peace aimed at controlling publications critical of the state or Crown. Certain false civil imputations were identified as so universally harmful that they were considered defamatory per se, that is that the damage they caused was presumed without the need of evidence. These fell into a number of categories such as the commission of a crime, the contraction of contagious diseases such as leprosy, the plague or syphilis, or anything that would hurt another in his trade or business. A jury was able to enter a damage award on a subjective basis without any guidelines or direction or evidence of damage, which was presumed. False statements that were not defamatory on their face, but required a showing of special circumstances showing the harm, required a showing of damages as well. Truth of the imputation was a defense to a defamation claim.

One of the thorny issues in a defamation action is the actual meaning of the allegedly defamatory words and whether the objectionable words subject to more than one meaning. Lawyers spend a lot of time and effort parsing and dissembling words that are the subject of litigation. Observing a defamation trial one is often reminded of the admonition of Lewis Carroll in *Through the Looking Glass*.

> "When I use a **word**," Humpty Dumpty said, in rather a scornful tone, "it **means** just what I **choose** it to **mean**—neither more nor less." "The question is," said Alice, "whether you can make **words mean** so many different things." "The question is," said Humpty Dumpty, "which is to be master—that's all."

Usually that question is for a jury to decide, although the guidance provided in the English case, *Lord Townshend v. Dr. Hughes* in 1693, is still pretty accurate that the words are to be considered in their "general and natural meaning and agreeable to the common understanding of all men."

American Courts largely adopted and continued the development of the English common law with respect to defamation. Along the way American courts and legislatures adopted a number of qualified and absolute privileges against defamation claims including for example citizen complaints to public authorities and actions by certain public officials. A qualified privilege is one that can be overcome by a showing of malice or bad intent on the part of the defamer. Proof of malice can also subject a party to the imposition of punitive damages, beyond presumed or actual damages.

Both English and American Courts became concerned that defamation actions would have a stifling effect on the safeguarding role of newspapers and other media and developed a further common law defense of "fair comment." That defense guarantees the freedom of newspapers like the *Chicago Tribune* to express statements and opinions on matters of public interest so long as they are not made with ill will, spite or the intent to harm the subject. Howard Ellis, one of the attorneys representing the *Tribune*, became over time one the reigning experts on the media application of fair comment. The defense of fair comment was rendered obsolete in the United States in 1964, when the U.S. Supreme Court constitutionalized the law of libel under the First Amendment to the Constitution in *The New York Times v. Sullivan*,[79] when it overturned an Alabama Sheriff's (public official)

---

79. 376 U.S. 254 (1964).

defamation claim against *The New York Times*, in the absence of showing "actual malice" which it defined as knowledge of the falsity of the statement or reckless disregard thereof. The Court later extended the *Times* privilege to public figures and private persons involved in matters of public or private interest. England, without a constitution, continues on with the "fair comment" defense, but has recently adopted statutes to prevent "libel tourism," by American and other foreign celebrities seeking a more hospitable venue for bringing libel actions.

THE STING OF "ANARCHY"

The substance or the gist of the libel is the sting. In the *Tribune* case the sting was that "Henry Ford is an anarchist." The problem for both sides is convincing a jury what the *Tribune* meant by the word "anarchist" and what objectively the general and natural meaning would be to a rational person reading the term and whether that meaning was defamatory. The *Merriam Webster Dictionary* provides two definitions of anarchist and there actually many more.

> 1: a person who rebels against any authority, established order, or ruling power. 2 : a person who believes in, advocates, or promotes **anarchism** or **anarchy**; especially: one who uses violent means to overthrow the established order.

The first definition is so broad and vague as not to be particularly offensive or defamatory, while the second definition raising the specter of bomb throwing would clearly raise concerns affecting reputation. The *Tribune's* position that it meant the first definition, that could be widely applied to any person whose views were contrary to the established order and whose intent was to overthrow that authority by democratic and peaceful means. Henry Ford argued that it was the second definition, the one imbued with "violent means" that the *Tribune* meant and that people reasonably believed. It could be argued that under the first definition the Dalai Lama or even Jesus Christ could fall within the definition of being an anarchist. Ford and his lawyers believed that the message to the public was that Henry Ford was a bomb thrower, particularly in the context of recent history.

The charge of being an "anarchist" conveyed a much harsher and inflammatory connotation in 1919 than it does today, more like the heat that would be generated for being described as a "terrorist." In 1901, in Buffalo, New York, Leon Czolgosz, a self-described anarchist shot and killed a popular president of the United States, William McKinley, who was succeeded in the presidency by Theodore Roosevelt.

On June 23,1916, there was a reception at the University Club of Chicago for the young new archbishop of Chicago, George Mundeulein, at which a large number of guests became violently ill. Local officials traced the cause to the presence of arsenic in the soup. One of cooks, Jean Crones, whose real name was Nestor Dondoglio, an anarchist, left traces of arsenic in his room. Dondoglio disappeared and was never apprehended. The hundred or so guests affected all survived, but the event left a bitter taste in the public consciousness. Other prominent anarchists at the time like Emma Goldman and Luigi Galleoni were virulent advocates in support of the use of instruments of violence for social goals.

It was, however, the "preparedness day" bombing in San Francisco, California on July 22, 1916 that fanned the public fear and consciousness of anarchists like no other event. It was an early precursor to the modern public reaction to the Boston Marathon Bombing on April 13, 2013 when Dzhokhar and Tamarion Tsarnaev generated mass panic and destruction by igniting pressure cooker bombs along the end of the marathon route killing and maiming many innocents. The parade served as patriotic outpouring in anticipation of the United States entry into World War I. The parade promoters were wary of the potential disruption of the parade by the International Workers of the World ("Wobblies") who opposed intervention in the war, charging that the patriotism was being promoted by financial and munitions interests likely to profit from America's participation in World War I.

The parade, the largest ever held in the City of San Francisco, with a three – and one-half hour procession, supported by two thousand thirty-four organizations, fifty-one thousand three hundred twenty-nine marchers, buoyed by fifty-two bands, hundreds of stars and stripes flapping in the wind, with thousands of whistles and fog horns flooding the air and bleating in the bay, passed through Steuart Street and north to Market St. The perpetrator ignited a steel pipe bomb with metal slugs serving as effective shrapnel buried in a nondescript suitcase. The blast ripped through the bodies of unsuspecting parade participants, tearing off the legs of a young girl, killing ten others and injuring over forty, whose bodies lay prostrate and bleeding on the street and sidewalk outside of the Ferry Building Saloon. Detached body parts and clothing littered the street, sidewalk and bunting in clumps of flesh and pools of blood.

Labor activists Thomas Mooney and Warren K. Billings were convicted of the crime and sentenced to hang, but were later pardoned because of flawed procedure and the prosecution's use of false testimony. Subsequent investigations pointed to the possible participation of Mario Budda, Celesten Ecklund, Alexander Berkman and other prominent anarchists, but in the end there was no confirmed perpetrator identified.

The event that perhaps resonated in the minds of mid-westerners involving anarchy was the Haymarket affair in Chicago on May 4, 1886. Chicago was at the time a hot bed of union organization, spurred by the rapid expansion of industrial production during the gilded age. Labor unrest was high particularly among German and Bohemian immigrants, who were working sixty-hour weeks for a wage of one dollar fifty cents a day. Various labor organizations anointed May 1, 1886 as the target date for the establishment of the eight-hour-a-day work week, with no cut in pay. Business leaders, largely supported by the mainstream press such as the *Chicago Tribune* and *The New York Times,* responded to labor demonstrations with an array of weapons including firings blacklisting, lockouts, strikebreakers, spies, thugs and private security forces. Tactics not very unlike those later embraced by Henry Ford in his labor organizing disputes with the United Auto Workers union.

On May 3, 1886, during a protest outside of the McCormick Harvesting Machine Company, police or Pinkerton detectives hired by McCormick fired into the pro-union crowd killing two McCormick workers. Outraged, labor representatives including the openly anarchist *Arbeiter-Zeitung* "Worker's Times" newspaper distributed leaflets calling for a demonstration in Haymarket Square near the McCormick plant the following day. The speeches at the demonstration were orderly and seemed to peter out toward the end as the weather began to deteriorate. The mayor of Chicago who attended the event left toward the end with instructions to the police not to interfere with the venting. The police disregarded the order after the mayor left and ordered the cessation of the speeches. While the remaining speakers defended from the wagon on which they were perched, the police advanced and someone threw a homemade bomb in front of them leading to hectic chaos with the police shooting randomly and frequently at themselves.

In the end seven police officers and four demonstrators were killed in the melee. Many spectators were wounded, but most sought private treatment in order to avoid being arrested.

The police ended up arresting eight individuals and charging them with the deaths of the police officers. Six of the eight were German immigrants or American born decedents of German immigrants and one American activist, Albert Parsons, and a British activist, Samuel Fielden.

There was no evidence that any of the defendants were involved in the bombing, but they were charged with responsibility because of their failure to actively discourage the unidentified bomber.

A show trial, *Illinois v. August Spies,* et al began on June 21, 1886, in Chicago. Judge Joseph Gary actively favored the prosecution on all issues and dismissed hundreds of potential jurors who might have labor sympathies. He added to the spectacle by inviting comely young women from the audience to sit with him at the elevated bench to observe the proceedings from his unique vantage point. All eight were convicted and seven of the eight were sentenced to die by hanging. One received a fifteen-year sentence. Four of the remaining seven were hanged. One committed suicide in his cell by lighting a blasting cap in his mouth which blew off half of his face. The others had their sentences commuted. All of the convicted were later exonerated by Illinois Governor Peter Altgeld, himself a German immigrant, on the basis of an unfair trial and lack of meaningful evidence.

Following the Haymarket affair, the *Chicago Tribune* was actively involved in whipping up anti-immigrant sentiment among the general public in the Midwest and some commentators blamed the *Tribune* for the executions that were carried out. The Haymarket defendants were variously described as "murderers," "incendiaries," "cut throats," "pillagers," "rioters," "dynamarchists," "bloody monsters," "red ruffians," "assassins," and "fiends." The bombing and the aftermath sparked many attempts to limit further immigration and to deport those who had already arrived. Ironically among those so reviled was a recent German immigrant Friedrich Drumpf, the grandfather of recently elected American President Donald Trump, who arrived from Karlstad, Germany in March, 1886, two months before the Haymarket bombing.

Anarchism was not a subject to be taken lightly and the charge in context of the times arguably implicated an absence of patriotism and imputed the advocacy of violence in the over throw of the government. This was the clear and unambiguous sting of the *Tribune* article that could be presented to the jury. However, not content to address the stigma of "anarchist" alone, Ford's lawyers expanded their claim to include objection to the phrase "ignorant idealist" as well, a decision which vastly expanded the range of defense inquiry and potential challenges of the *Tribune's* lawyers, in front of the trial judge, James G. Tucker, who had a loose conception of the range of evidence relevant to the defense of the charge of "ignorance."

It was hard for the Ford team to dispute the charge of "idealist" and that word alone would not likely to be perceived as actionable, but the charge of "ignorance" cut Henry Ford to the quick. His extraordinary success as an industrialist served a view of himself as full of knowledge and expertise on a vast array of subjects to which he was anxious to share with the general public and did so at every opportunity presented to him. He viewed reputation as something to be earned and savored. He once said, "you can't build a reputation on what you are going to do." He viewed his reputation as the valuable product of what he had earned with his personal knowledge, skill and labor. It was something he had earned, like the accumulation of capital. He was also angry that the *Chicago Tribune* had the temerity to try to sully the very careful image of himself that he had orchestrated in the press since 1903. Ford in 1918 – 1919 became particularly sensitive to attacks on his character and reputation because of the late tactics of Truman H. Newberry during the 1918 Michigan Senatorial campaign.

THE 'HUN' STRATEGY

On Sunday, November 3, 1918, two days before the Michigan Senatorial election, the Newberry camp posted an advertisement in the *Detroit Free Press* accusing Ford of having German sympathies that affected his company's war materials output in World War I. The ad was entitled "HENRY FORD AND HIS HUNS." It attacked Ford for having kept a German born engineer in a sensitive production where he could destabilize the war effort. The ad read in part,

> Carl Emde, a German alien and a German sympathizer, is boss of the drafting work on the Liberty motor at the Ford plant. Henry Ford knows he is a German alien and a German sympathizer, but he refuses to take him off this work. This is not hearsay. It is absolute fact, vouched for by Charles Evans Hughes, whom President Wilson appointed to find out why the production of

> American aeroplanes has been so much delayed, when the American soldiers in France need them so much. President Wilson's confidence in Mr. Hughes is emphasized by the fact that Mr. Hughes is a former justice of the Supreme Court of the United States. His reputation and respect for the truth and for fairness in judgment have never been questioned, even by his bitterest adversaries. Concerning Emde's job, Mr. Hughes says in his report to the President: "IT IS POSSIBLE FOR ONE IN THAT DEPARTMENT TO BRING ABOUT DELAYS THE CAUSES FOR WHICH, IN VIEW OF THE MULTIPLICITY OF DRAWINGS, IT WOULD BE HARD TO TRACE."

Following a number of paragraphs of the same general ilk, the advertisement continued:

> Sacrifice? What about the sacrifice of American soldiers if this German pet of Henry Ford's sees fit to delay the production of Liberty motors and the making of aeroplanes, as he is in a position to do? How many American lives have already been sacrificed in aeroplanes tampered with by German agents? If Henry Ford puts so much faith in the German Emde after all he knows about him, is there any reason why he should not put the same faith in the German Hohenzollern? Since Henry Ford is so fond of this German pet of his, is there no place in his large establishment where he can give Emde work and keep him out of the way of temptation to serve his fatherland, as many other Germans have already served in this country? As Mr. Hughes says: "THERE HAS BEEN A LAXITY AT THE FORD PLANT WITH RESPECT TO THOSE OF GERMAN SYMPATHIES WHICH IS NOT AT ALL COMPATIBLE WITH THE INTERESTS OF THE GOVERNMENT."

The Newberry ad hit the Ford senate campaign in the solar plexus. The campaign struggled to get out a response. It issued the following statement to the press on the following Monday, which was largely buried in the buzz from the pro-German indictment.

> Our policy is to make men, not to break them. In times of panic

> great injury and injustice are often done to innocent persons, and we try to keep our heads.
>
> We would not allow injustice to be done to an old, trusted and valued employee, even though he was born in Germany. . .. We in the plant know that he gave valuable assistance and many suggestions with regard to the development of the Liberty motor cylinders, which are being furnished to all the manufacturers, with a saving of three hundred and forty-five thousand dollars a month to the government over former orders.
>
> From the beginning of the war we have taken the greatest precaution. . .. We have had no interference with our work that could be in any way traced to enemy aliens. . .. The United States Marshal can speak for himself as to our organization and work with regard to that. Mr. Ford was a witness before Mr. Hughes, but he was not asked a single question with reference to enemy aliens, Mr. Emde or anyone else.

Under the Ford reply was printed a statement from the United States Marshal:

> We have had less trouble with enemy aliens in the Ford plant than in any other large plant. If there is any blame with regard to the Ford plant, it should be on the marshal's office and not on the Ford people. The Ford company did not employ a single German alien without a permit of the marshal's office.

Henry Ford's campaign manager, ironically of German descent, Edwin Gustav Pipp, told Ford that the "Hun" ad cost him at least ten thousand votes, particularly in rural areas of the state, well above Newberry's margin of victory. Elections as we know have consequences and Ford's defeat had many ramifications for the Democratic Party and the country, not the least of which was the loss of control of the United States Senate and the defeat of Woodrow Wilson's plan for the League of Nations.

The impact of the "Hun" ad was not lost on Henry Ford and his lawyers, who quickly seized on patriotic and anti-German immigrant feeling to try to salt the potential jury pool by painting the *Chicago Tribune* as being Pro German in its leanings. They arranged for their agents to compile a list of editorials and writings published by the *Tribune* to suggest that the *Tribune's* saber rattling about war with Mexico was in support of German and their own private interests and not the product of patriotic fervor. Ford published the compilation in two pamphlets under the title of *The War Record of The Chicago Tribune*. The front page of the first volume recites that it is "submitted to the People of Illinois, Indiana, Iowa, Wisconsin and Michigan." It leads with the statement that "your attention is particularly challenged, however, to the editorial of April 4, 1916 entitled 'Realpolitik for America,' (page 4 herein) in which the *Tribune* recognizes that Germany would welcome war between the United States and Mexico – and then to the editorial of April 21, 1916, entitled 'Bitter Fruit' (page 5 herein) in which the *Tribune* deliberately advocates war with Mexico. Respectfully. THE COMPILERS."

The *Record* contains many *Tribune* quotes taken out of context and quotes many statements that are not editorial opinions. Ford also flooded Michigan newspapers with ads extolling Ford's wartime production efforts.

Ford's lawyers asked for repeated continuances from starting the case between November, 1918, and May, 1919, which *Tribune* lawyer Stevenson thought was to poison the well of potential jurors with propaganda. The delay also resulted in the loss to the *Tribune* of its most powerful potential witness, Theodore Roosevelt, who relentlessly roasted Ford and his son Edsel around the country and in particular, Detroit, for their opposition to military preparedness and the European war. Roosevelt died unexpectedly at his home in Oyster Bay, New York on January 6, 1919. The *Tribune* for its part was not shy about parading Ford's own words to raise questions about his patriotism.

In February, 1919, the *Tribune's* local counsel, Elliot G. Stevenson, wrote to Weymouth Kirkland, the *Tribune's* main counsel, suggesting that he arrange for service upon Henry Ford of a libel action in Illinois based upon the "*record*" of Ford's public statements about the *Tribune*. Ford was scheduled to pass through Chicago by rail on his return from a vacation trip in California. Kirkland chose not to surrender to the temptation and to keep his eyes on Mt. Clemens. The trial finally started in May, 1919, with twelve jurors picked from an array of forty-eight. The Court provided each side with twelve peremptory challenges, with the twelve jurors being selected from the remaining twenty-four after their *voir dire* examination and challenges for cause. The jury impaneled by the Court contained eleven farmers and one road inspector, hard duty for many for ninety-three days of trial during the growing season.

Presiding over the trial was Circuit Judge Honorable James G. Tucker, a handsome but sleepy-eyed jurist, with a large head of rumpled hair, a modest judicial intellect, and a noticeable lack of focus and control in the courtroom. A sign leading into his courtroom offered, "If you spit on the floor of your own house, do it here. We want you to feel at home." Tables for counsel were set up to accommodate up to ten lawyers on a side and their clients. Behind the lawyers were tables assigned to the fifty or more news outlets covering the trial. The jury box, with twelve seats, stretched out facing the judge and the witness stand. The balance of the courtroom contained crammed-in seating and overflow standing room to accommodate the curious crowd leaning in to hear the witnesses. Many of the witnesses were women who were not otherwise occupied in the fields or in their homes. The courtroom windows were opened wide to catch any whiff of fresh air and the sulfurous aromas of the local baths. Outside of the courthouse the Gratiot Avenue trolley plied back and forth between Mt. Clemens and downtown Detroit.

Chapter 12

Sturm Und Drang

THE LEGAL STORM CLOUDS were gathering. After three days of questioning to seat the jury, the stage was set.[80] One of Henry Ford's principal attorneys, former Wayne County Circuit Judge Alfred Murphy, rose on the morning of May 19, 1919, to address the all-male jury of eleven farmers and a road inspector. The small, whited-walled courtroom overflowed with lawyers, clients, newsmen and the curious. The morning would be Murphy's to use to state Henry Ford's case to the jury. The intense jurist-orator pulled out his handkerchief to clean his lenses, replaced them on his nose, thrust his thumb in his waistcoat and stared briefly at each juror before beginning. He glanced briefly at Col. Robert M. McCormick and his cousin Joseph Medill Patterson, the *Tribune* publishers, vigorous young men sitting intently at the *Tribune* defense table. He nodded knowingly to his client Henry Ford and his son Edsel and slowly began.

Murphy painted a picture of Henry Ford as a kind and humble man, who despite his immense wealth, dedicated himself to humanitarian causes and shared his wealth and success with his employees. Ford, he said, was an avowed pacifist, who hated war and tried to stop it. He vociferously denied the *Tribune*'s premised facts for the "anarchist" editorial. He insisted that the Ford Motor

---

80. *The Trial Transcript of Henry Ford v. The Chicago Tribune et al*, is located at the Benson Ford Research Center, Dearborn, Michigan at Accession 53, Boxes 5 and 6.

Company did plan to return the jobs to Ford National Guard employees returning from the Mexican encounter. He said Ford did plan to assist their families while their breadwinners were away protecting the southern border of the United States from Mexican bandit raids. The story in the paper, he intoned, was a contrivance, motivated by personal malice directed toward Henry Ford.

Murphy insisted that despite the *Chicago Tribune's* depiction of him, Henry Ford was also a patriot. When President Wilson announced that a state of war existed between the United States and Germany and Austria, Murphy said Henry Ford was the first industrialist to step forward and offer the assets and services of his company to assist the war effort.

Murphy projected a narrow, pejorative view of the term "anarchist," asserting that the meaning of the term incorporated "one who advocates the violent overthrow of the government." An anarchist he insisted was a "bomb thrower," and that was precisely the stigma the *Tribune* intended to convey to its readers. He argued that the *Chicago Tribune*, of all newspapers, having experienced in its own city the arsenic poisoning of some of its illustrious citizens and the execution of four labor activists as anarchists, following the Haymarket bombing in 1886, would be intensely sensitive to the dark implications of the term *anarchist.*

Murphy offered his view of the motivations of the *Chicago Tribune* in disparaging Henry Ford as an anarchist. He suggested that the *Tribune* served a large German immigrant population and that the leadership of the paper was serving German interests when advocating for war with Mexico. He said the Germans would have liked nothing better than to have the military resources of the United States tied up in a war with Mexico. He said Robert McCormick's mother had a friendly relationship with the former German ambassador to the United States, Count Von Bernsdorff. Further, Murphy said that the Ford team would show to the jury that the *Tribune* McCormicks had financial interests in the reaper McCormicks' International Harvester Company and in the Standard Oil Company through marriage to a

Rockefeller, and both companies' interests would be served by an American invasion of Mexico.

Lastly, he portrayed the personal pain and anguish suffered by Henry Ford, at being accused of being an anarchist, a suffering which no amount of money could truly relieve; and the necessity for the jury to send a message to the press that the defaming of individuals for personal goals would not be tolerated in America.

No man lives or walks this soil who has the sanction of that emblem, who has given his country in the hour of need, all of his resources, all of his mind, and pure heart and soul — no man did more than this plaintiff without thought of reward.

After the noon break, it was Weymouth Kirkland's turn to expound on behalf of the *Tribune*. With more than a hint of anger in his voice, he rose to defend McCormick and Patterson. He reminded the jury that not only did both McCormick and Patterson volunteer for the Mexican campaign, they also put themselves in harm's way in Europe. Patterson endured two hundred ten days of fighting and suffered injuries requiring hospitalization. McCormick experienced one hundred eighty days of combat in an artillery bombardment in the first action involving American troops in France. Kirkland contrasted their service with that of Edsel Ford, whose father, Henry Ford, managed to pluck his son out of the selective service call-up to keep him safe at home, with a call to his friend Woodrow Wilson.

Kirkland stressed the damage done to the military preparedness movement in the United States by Henry Ford's radical pacifist utterances and questioned the sincerity of Ford's "conversion" to patriotism. He chronicled the chaos on the Mexican/U.S. border necessitating American intervention in Mexico. The purity of the *Tribune's* motivation in advocating for intervention in Mexico, he claimed, was in response to atrocities perpetrated by Mexican bandits on American citizens in Texas and New Mexico. He underscored the negative impact of Ford's posturing on the ability of the army to properly mobilize and arm the National Guard.

Kirkland noted that the late President Theodore Roosevelt also strongly advocated intervention in Mexico. He embroidered a vivid description of the conditions of anarchy pervading the border and described in detail the humiliation of American soldiers captured by the Mexicans at Carrizal, where American "Buffalo Soldiers" were stripped naked and marched through the streets of the town. He recounted the cold-blooded murder of women and children in Columbus, New Mexico, by marauding Mexican invaders.

Kirkland ridiculed Murphy's suggestion that Robert McCormick's mother would have her son "go down and be shot at" by Mexicans "for a few greedy dollars" in her pocket. He stressed that the *Tribune's* main motivation and concern had been the American lives at stake because the Army and the National Guard were inadequately equipped with antiquated weapons while their opponents had up-to-date machine guns—all due to a lack of preparedness. The *Tribune*, he insisted, was not pro-German but pro-preparedness, and the conditions of anarchy that reigned at the border had cried out for intervention and the immediate upgrade of military defenses. Ford's anti-preparedness harangues impeded public support for military spending and properly equipping the Army.

The definition of *anarchist* sketched by Kirkland was much broader than Murphy's. He posed it as a philosophical leaning that could, but didn't necessarily, include an embrace of violence. He described it as the philosophical opposition to the use of force by government in obtaining public ends. He noted that the *Tribune* editorial made no suggestion of Ford being a "bomb thrower" or an endorser of violence. The *Tribune* had a public duty, he said, to comment on the views and actions of a "public figure" like Mr. Ford that placed the lives his countrymen at risk, and that the *Tribune* accepted its duty with the utmost honesty and good faith, using language and imputations substantially less inflammatory than those adopted by Henry Ford when he himself described American soldiers and sailors as "murderers."

He told the jury that even a verdict in favor of the Plaintiff of "six cents" would be an affront to the *Tribune.*

MOBILIZATION

The opening statements presaged a long and bitter contest, a veritable legal storm, that required a firm, controlling hand on the scope of the evidence allowed. Without it, the trial could spin with a wide, wild centrifugal force into a broad range of issues that had only marginal relevance to the principal issue at hand: Was Henry Ford an anarchist?

Judge Tucker had a very loose and slippery grip on the rudder of the dispute. Following opening statements, he set aside a full week for exhaustive and exhausting arguments by the contentious lawyers concerning the law of libel and the defenses and evidence applicable to the case. The attorneys argued over the definition of *anarchy*; whether it was a duty of the judge or jury to determine the meaning of the term; and whether the term was inherently defamatory. They argued over the relevance of statutory definitions of *anarchy* and the common everyday meaning of the term. Alfred Lucking argued that the definition of *anarchy* inherently included the incitement to violence. Elliott Stevenson likened the description of Ford to Clement Vallandingham and the "Copperheads,"[81] Northern politicians who opposed the Civil War and who generated vigorous political opposition to the prosecution of the war, but did not incite active violence.

One newspaper, at least, predicted that unless the trial judge sailed tight to the wind on his evidence rulings, the Ford/*Tribune* lawsuit was sure to drag on.

> So important to the case will these rulings prove, that close observers of the trial are eagerly awaiting the day when they must be drawn – the day when it must be determined whether the evidence will be held down to the issues raised in the Tribune editorial headed "Ford is an Anarchist," or whether the testimony will include

---

81. The Copperheads represented an extreme wing of "Northern Democrats." They represented a traditionalist faction that revered the tenants of Jacksonian Democracy.

the vast issues of preparedness, national defense, and pacifism.[82]

The *Tribune* lawyers embraced the law of a prominent British case, *O'Brien v. The Marquis of Salsbury*[83] in which the appellate court affirmed the principal in the defense of "fair comment" that a statement of fact can be a statement of privileged opinion where it appears to be a deduction derived by the writer from other disclosed facts. In short, the *Tribune* argued that in calling Henry Ford an anarchist, while on the surface a statement of fact, was actually a statement of privileged fair comment opinion, because it was based on the other facts recounted in the editorial, in other articles and generally known to the reader. One can call a soldier a "murderer," which seems defamatory but is not defamatory if, in the context of the statement, it is clear that one is expressing an opinion that all persons engaged in war are murderers.

Each side challenged the other over what evidence should or should not be allowed in the trial, while Judge Tucker engaged in blissful reverie, ruing his absence from the slippery banks of his favorite trout stream. He lamented, "I have been talked almost to death," but appeared to be no closer to making definitive decisions for the effort. He took the many issues under advisement without ruling. During the course of the trial he frequently dealt with most of the bitter arguments over admissibility of evidence with a "Let it stand temporarily" response, which largely avoided addressing the real issues head on.

While the lawyers were haranguing the Judge over the nuances and complexities of libel laws and defenses, the witnesses and forces for both sides assembled like medieval armies preparing for siege and assault. Henry Ford's principal lieutenant, Ernest G. Liebold, arranged to move the entire Ford Motor Company headquarters operation from Dearborn into the Medea Hotel and a number of empty office buildings in Mount Clemens, so that Henry Ford could run the Company from there during the course of the trial.

---

82. The *Yale Expositor*, May 22, 1919, p. 6.

83. 54 J.P. 215, 216 (1889).

After several New York and Boston newspapers signaled a lack of interest in covering the trial, Liebold set up the *Mount Clemens News Bureau* to provide daily copy by wire to small and medium-sized newspapers around the nation. Looming over the clatter of typewriters in the Ford newsroom was a large national map stitched with thousands of red (pro Ford) and blue pins (anti-Ford) indicating friendly and unfriendly local newspaper outlets. The Ford news bureau accumulated two hundred sixty daily and two thousand five hundred seven weekly "friendly" newspapers to service.

Liebold also developed his own local intelligence network to spy on the jurors, the witnesses, the Judges, the lawyers and the clients. Many of the spies would hang around the lobby of the Colonial Hotel, the Park Hotel, and the Medea Hotel. They would record the comings and goings of anybody having to do with the trial and anything overheard in the lobbies. The *Tribune's* witnesses created a stir in sleepy Mount Clemens. Many of them were from the Texas and New Mexico border area and adorned with big hats, large belt buckles and high-heeled boots, normally accustomed to holding spurs. Liebolt dispatched a former U.S. Marshall from Texas, then working in Ford's Sociological Department, to make connection with the Texans and glean from them their anticipated testimony. Any out-of-towner who checked into a Mount Clemens hotel was immediately surveyed and identified.

Liebold became concerned that a certain comely but shadowy lady from Cleveland, without an adequate explanation for her presence in town, seemed intent on worming her way into a level of intimacy in the Ford side. She once stopped Henry Ford in the lobby of the Medea Hotel, but was brushed aside by Liebold. The lady apparently hooked the attention of Alfred Murphy, enticing him on long, late night walks, returning after 10:00 or 11:00 p.m. Liebold arranged to have the lady hustled out of town. Liebold's spies also carefully detailed the after-hour exploits of the *Tribune* lawyers at the infamous Edgewater Beach Club on nearby Lake St. Clair, where fashionably dressed Grosse Pointers were known to embrace gambling, drinking and general frivolity with enthusiasm.

One important piece of intelligence exhumed by Liebold's agents was that *Tribune* attorney Stevenson planned to cross examine Henry Ford on his knowledge of well-known events of American history. Alfred Lucking set to preparing Ford for this public courtroom grilling. But Lucking was continually frustrated in delivering his crash course history lessons; Ford would divert attention outside the room to low-flying airplanes and unusual birds, while refusing to focus on the issues at hand.

MAY 26, 1919

On Monday morning, the trial at last set sail with Henry Ford's lawyers at the helm, presenting Ford's case as the plaintiff. Sitting in the audience and distracting the crowd was the European war hero with the white eye patch and left arm in a sling, in full military regalia, Floyd Gibbons. Gibbons attended the trial, at the invitation of the *Tribune*, during a brief interlude from his book tour celebrating his first-hand account of the American Expeditionary Forces in France, *And They Thought We Wouldn't Fight.*

The early days of the Ford case were largely smooth sailing, with his lawyers calling employees from the personnel and sociological departments to refute the *Tribune*'s claims that Ford workers would not be allowed to retain their jobs following service with the National Guard. They also defended the efforts Ford took to look after soldier families in need. Lastly, the attorneys sought to enshrine Ford's overall generosity to his employees with his radical five-dollars-per-day profit-sharing plan. This was a foil the defense would attack by showing Ford's largesse was a very small faction of Ford's "profits" and came at the expense of mind numbing, repetitive, and exhaustive labor by Ford employees.

JUNE 4, 1919

On this afternoon, the Ford team shifted its focus to a direct attack on the *Tribune.* One of Ford's lawyers read a deposition given by Edward Goldbeck. Goldbeck, a sometime *Tribune* feature writer, was born in Berlin and served seven years in the German army. He was a decided anti-Bolshevik and anti-socialist, who occasionally presented the German view of issues in *Tribune* give-and-take forums. Although presented to show pro-German bias by the *Tribune*, Goldbeck testified that his views were not controlled by the *Tribune,* and that Captain Patterson once asked him to help recruit support from German-Americans against Germany.

JUNE 5, 1919

Next, the Ford Team read depositions to the jury of various Standard Oil Company and International Harvester Company Executives as well as that of a McCormick uncle, married to a Rockefeller, to highlight Col. McCormick's family interests in companies who had a financial interest in promoting war with Mexico. Their purpose was to establish *Tribune* "malice" in attacking Ford for his opposition to "preparedness" for the Mexican campaign.

JUNE 6, 1919

In the morning, the Ford lawyers read the Deposition of Elinor Medill Patterson, Captain Patterson's mother, who recounted her friendly and social relationship with Count von Bernsdorff, the engaging German Ambassador to the United States. Ford's team presented this evidence, capping off his opening case, to demonstrate Mrs. McCormick's, and by association and relation, her son's predisposition to favor Germany.

The defense rallied to end the afternoon and the entire week with a mesmerizing account of the Brownsville, Texas train wreck and Mexican bandit attack, through the riveting testimony of Mrs. Nellie S. Austin, whose husband and son were brutally executed by the bandits on the border.

JUNE 9, 1919

The *Tribune* defense opened its case with a full, weeklong onslaught of horrific stories from the Mexican border. The stories showcased the vital reasons for the *Tribune*'s concerns about anarchy and the need for military preparedness, illuminating its "good faith" in its attacks on Henry Ford. The *Tribune* called store owners, post masters, wounded soldiers, marshals, cattlemen, customs officials, immigration officers, railroad workers and foremen, firemen, and a string of widows whose husbands were killed in the Mexican raids. They called a surgeon to describe mutilations of the victims of Mexican attacks. The courtroom rocked with the heavy clump of Texas boots and the heavy bodies of those denizens of the southern frontier.[84] The Ford team largely waived at the passing pageant offering little or no cross examination, and complaining loudly at the lack of relevance and materiality of the parade of evidence.

Closing out the week on a high note, the *Tribune* called Floyd Gibbons, still in full uniform and Sam Browne belt, white eye patch and arm sling, to testify to his experiences on the southern border with Pershing, Poncho Villa, and the 1914 battle of Marco, Arizona. Gibbons delivered on the stand. He reported that many Mexicans had superior weapons, including German Mouser rifles. By the weekend, the citizens of Mount Clemens felt wistful, missing the presence of the clean-living, strong-limbed, clear-eyed and alert men of the border who "gained many friends in town."

JUNE 16-18, 1919

Floyd Gibbons again assumed the stand on Monday, awash with his usual swagger. He testified about the humiliation of the U.S. Negro soldiers caught and stripped by Carranza soldiers. Gib-

---

84. The *Tribune* compensated its southwestern witnesses with a ten-dollar-per-day fee and a free trip to Niagara Falls.

bons also gave his direct observations of Col. McCormick and Captain Patterson doing their duty in National Guard service on the border. He described the impact of the lack of preparedness on the performance of the Army on the border and in France. Alfred Lucking was constantly on his feet sputtering his objections to the testimony because Gibbons did not personally witness the limits on preparedness he described.

On the next day, Gibbons testified that he never thought about Germany wanting the U.S. to engage in a war with Mexico until the Zimmerman cable.[85] He stated that he saw no evidence of German propaganda in Mexico.[86] He reiterated his view that a lack of equipment hampered Army performance and that Villa and his rebels had better equipment.[87] Lucking constantly objected as to the relevance of the testimony.

During one of the arguments before the Judge, Stevenson exploded, "Ford spent millions undermining the American effort in Mexico." Lucking responded, "It was only $30,000."

Judge Tucker, after reflection, concluded that the issue of how much or how little preparedness is necessary from Gibbons' perspective was irrelevant and barred further testimony from him on the sorry condition of America's army. As he arose to step down from the stand, Alfred Lucking asked Gibbons, "Did you have any pro-German tendencies?" Staring at Lucking through his one eye and waiving his sling, he answered, "Hardly!"

William J. Abbott, a journalist with the Hearst newspaper syn-

---

85. The infamous January, 1917 secret dispatch by Germany to Mexico, intercepted by British intelligence, offering Mexico a return of parts of the U.S. in the event of a German/Mexican alliance bringing about a successful war with the U. S. The disclosure of the Zimmerman cable locked President Wilson into a course of events leading to his declaration of war on Germany and Austria, three months later.

86. There was in fact a growing German presence and influence in Mexico on President Carranza's regime at the time. See Tuchman, Barbara, *The Zimmerman Telegram: American enters the war 1917-1918* pp 90-91.

87. Villa drove a Ford.

dicate described an interview he had with Ford. Traveling with Ford in Stockholm on the Oscar II, Abbott said they viewed ample evidence of the futility of ending the war by peaceful means. And yet, Ford—understanding this truth—continued to cripple U.S. preparedness.

Irving Bacon, a Ford Motor Company sketch artist and head of the Ford Motor Company art department, attended the trial. Stevenson called Bacon from the audience to ask him to describe the "Flag of Humanity," a universal, non-national flag Ford had his art department design, in opposition to national flags. Its blue background symbolized universal mankind and fraternity. During Bacon's examination by Stevenson, Murphy rose to interrupt him. Stevenson rebuked Murphy. "When I raise my hand like this [raising hand] I am still talking." Stevenson then turned back to Bacon, and suggesting cowardice, asked, "Was there any yellow in that flag?"

Stevenson quoted from an R.E. Ackerman interview of Ford in the *North American Independent Magazine* as saying that the sinking of the Lusitania and the liner Sussex were insufficient cause for the U.S. to break with Germany. He also quoted well-known Henry Ford views opposed to preparedness.

The *Tribune* called Henry A. Wise Wood, a New York aeronautical engineer and inventor of a high-speed printing press, who was a member of the conference committee on American preparedness, and a former member of the Naval Advisory Board. Wood described a meeting he had with Henry Ford where Wood hoped to show Ford the error of his ways. He said Ford mistrusted the opponents of Germany and agreed with Germany on the sinking of American ships conveying supplies to the allies. Wood ended his testimony with a statement, "I considered him a dirty American."

JUNE 19, 1919

Thursday was a very short day, largely because of the oppressive heat in the courtroom. The constant whirr of electric fans did little to cool the building. Mr. Wood was still on the witness stand. A *Tribune* attorney introduced a letter to Mr. Wood from Theodore Delavigne, thanking him for a newspaper article quoting Mr. Ford. The defense called Henry Ford to the stand to identify Mr. Delavigne, a man who was alleged to be the actual author of numerous inflammatory articles appearing under Ford's name "He was my publicity man," Ford said. He then returned to his chair behind his lawyers.

This was a rare appearance of Mr. Ford in the courtroom. Both he and the *Tribune* owners were occupied in running their respective businesses. Ford, with his headquarters essentially moved to Mount Clemens, could be seen in his hotel and his daily walking excursions in the countryside near the town. He was accompanied by associates and newsmen, who reported that he could identify every bird, tree and flower that they observed. He enjoyed demonstrating his agility for a fifty-six-year-old by leaping ditches, vaulting fences, and challenging others to foot races.

Alfred Lucking tried to elicit Wise's appreciation for Ford's pro-labor reputation in establishing the five-dollars-per-day wage in his factories. Wise told the jury that it was his understanding that Ford considered it a good economic, not humanitarian proposition, because the employees had to work at high speed. Said Lucking,

> Q. Don't you know that Mr. Ford had thousands of applications for jobs because of his reputation for fair dealing?
>
> A. I have read so.
>
> Q. Don't you know it is so?
>
> A. No. Machinists prefer to drive their machinery, not be driven by it. I have heard the men in my shop talk that way.

JUNE 20, 1919

Friday began with the appearance of an expert witness on the subject of anarchism—Jesse S. Reeves, professor of International Law and Political Science at the University of Michigan. Reeves was an open-faced man with a slightly receding hairline. He was then chairman of the University of Michigan Department of Political Science. The *Tribune* called Reeves to establish that Henry Ford's public utterances were consistent with other well-known anarchists. He identified an interview with Ford by Edward Marshall[88] and responded to the Ford pronouncements contained in the Interview.

> Q. (Stevenson) I want to ask you, if you find in the article referred to, in which Mr. Ford expressed his views, anything that is identical in substance with the teachings and writings of well-known and recognized anarchists of the World?

Alfred Lucking, flushed in the face, rushed to object. "Every anarchist in the world has a great many ideas in common with millions who are not anarchists." Murphy also objected. "It strikes me that clearly calls for mere opinion and the mere judgment of this witness, and that is incompetent." Stevenson responded, "How do we propose to prove, in one respect, that he was an anarchist? First that he advocated views that were the common views of anarchists that were well recognized the world over." The Judge seemed puzzled, staring briefly out the window. "If you have any authorities, I think I would like to see them, and that is all. The argument won't help us any. I have got the idea right. It is rather a new problem for me."

Judge Tucker, after waffling, eventually decided to take Reeve's testimony. Reeves declared, "So far as I am aware all anarchists hold as one of their tenants, one of their principals of belief, the idea of one brotherhood, instead of national patriotism." Further, "all anarchists, with whose writings I am familiar, express the idea that government is something that has been imposed upon and slipped over the people." He identified antipathy toward military service as an anarchistic meme. Their attitude is "why should any

---

88. Marshall was a journalist who ran a private news column syndicate out of the *Chicago Tribune.* Having been in Theodore Roosevelt's "rough rider" unit in Cuba, Marshall famously corrected the mythical record that there was a "charge" up San Juan Hill. They walked up. The horses were still in Florida.

man who does not want to be a butcher, be compelled to learn the soldier's trade?" Reeves thus cross-referenced Ford calling soldiers and sailors "murderers."

Referring to the Marshall article airing Ford's views, Stevenson queried Reeves:

> Q. Did you find the expression in the first two or three paragraphs there, anything indicating the views of well-recognized anarchists?
> A. Yes, there is an idea expressed there that will be found common to all anarchists.
>
> Q. What is that idea?
> A. Opposition to military service, and especially obligatory military service, under the guise of patriotism.

Reeves noted the Ford desire to destroy and abolish all armies and navies, and his disdain for the false sentiment of patriotism, which he believed leads men to sacrifice themselves for something, which is not really in their own self-interest. Reeves then cited other famed anarchists: Russian Prince Kropotkin; Mikael Bakunin, a Russian proponent of violent anarchism; Leo Tostoy, the leader of the peaceful anarchists; a Frenchmen, Pierre Joseph Prudhon, and an American, Benjamin R. Tucker, as leading lights of anarchist dogma and practice. Reeves said that he had read an article entitled "Humanity and Sanity," written for Ford by Theodore Delavinge, and found it consistent with the views of his identified anarchists.

Ford, no great student of literature or philosophy, with the possible exception of Emerson, spent the greater part of the day in the Ford Motor Company Mt. Clemens office tracing sales reports for the Model T.

JUNE 23, 1919

The Ford lawyers deferred the cross examination of Professor Reeves until June 24th, to give them more time to prepare.

The *Tribune* put a number of "filler" witnesses on the stand on Monday. Herbert Brand, a *Tribune* reporter, assigned to interview employers about payment of wages to guardsmen during the Mexican call-up, testified that only twenty of a thousand employers agreed to assist their guardsman employees while they were protecting the border. The *Tribune* presented his testimony to demonstrate that it had not singled out Ford for inquiry and that the paper was justified in its concern about the lack of interest among manufacturers in supporting the troops.

P. Whitcomb Williams, the stringer who started the controversy, testified as to his communications with Frank Klingensmith, where Klingensmith rejected the idea of special treatment of guardsmen. Williams reported his conversation to the *Tribune* which then ran what Williams asserted was a balanced and fair representation of Ford Motors' policies.

Julia Orloff, a volunteer with the Patriotic Fund, worked to help families of guardsman called to duty. She described her early difficulty in getting help from the Ford Motor Company for some guardsmen's families. Several Michigan guardsmen then testified that they never heard any announcement regarding Ford maintaining jobs for returning guardsmen.

JUNE 24, 1919

The Ford team recalled Professor Reeves on Tuesday, for cross examination by Alfred Lucking. Reeves reiterated the "index fossil" of anarchism in his view is:

> That patriotism — that there is no such thing as a patriot – the attitude especially with reference to the national flag – that soldiers are murderers – I think those are not common thoughts of most writers who are not anarchists.

Lucking inquired as to whether Ford's views were consistent with Christian doctrine. Reeves responded, "Not unless that belief is brought in antagonism to the idea of nationalism." Asked by

Lucking to define anarchism, Reeves responded:

> An anarchist, I would say, in the first place, is . . . I think a man who promotes by action, or by propaganda, a state of anarchy, either by interfering with the efforts of government to put down a condition of anarchy, or by directly promoting it himself by propaganda or action.

Lucking proceeded to grill Reeves on the similarity of Ford's anti-preparedness views to prominent writers, poets, and theologians, who were not generally acknowledged to be anarchists. Reeves dispatched Christian doctrine and eminent theologians relating to the brotherhood of man as relating to matters of personal belief, within the religious realm, and not a political doctrine in opposition to nationalism. He said, "[R]eligion is essentially a matter of belief. Otherwise Marcus Aurelius, who taught a perfect code of morals, would be the founder of a religion which he is not." Reeves distinguished the views of Henry Ford from those of Woodrow Wilson noting that "there is no antagonism there between the idea of nationalism and the world brotherhood." Lucking challenged the soundness of Reeves' methodology, suggesting that cherry picking sentences from a man's statements, without context might lead to great misconception. Reeves agreed, but stated that it frequently illustrates the general tenor and context of an article.

Lucking moved on from religion to reference writers, starting with Ralph Waldo Emerson. Emerson issued anti-war musings during peace time, and Reeves held that context was here essential to determine anarchistic leanings.

> Q. An anarchist?
>
> A. No sir, a transcendentalist. . . I should have to say that one would have to take into consideration the context and circumstances surrounding the publication to say that a particular sentence, picked out of man's words, is anarchistic, especially when I know that Emerson was not an anarchist.

Reeves continued to insist that Ford's remarks in the context of the likelihood of imminent war in Europe, rendered him an anarchist.

Lucking tried to emphasize the penchant for violence among anarchists, to differentiate them from Henry Ford.

> Q. They believe in killing and destruction in order to abolish government?
>
> A. Some do.
>
> Q. The men that are popularly known –
>
> A. (Interrupting) I think that Tolstoy is very popularly known as an anarchist, and he certainly does not.
>
> Pressed by Lucking, Reeves drilled down to the core:
>
> That is the fundamental principle of anarchy, Mr. Lucking, that mankind is at heart all right, and if you let him alone, he will accomplish his own salvation in the course of time.

Challenging Reeves with quotes from Benjamin Franklin, Dr. Samuel Johnson, James Russell Lowell, Alfred Lloyd Tennyson and others, Lucking tried to set a trap for Reeves. But one day had not been enough for a crash course in the annals of anarchism; Lucking showed his naiveté by starting out with a book of Emma Goldman's writings, a book he had obtained from the University of Michigan library. Anarchist Goldman famously advocated for direct action and even violence.

> Q. What do you say of this definition from Goldman's anarchism, and other essays, printed by the University of Michigan by the way?
>
> A. The University of Michigan has never published any article of Emma Goldman's and you know it.
>
> Q. I beg your pardon; I saw it on the bottom here.
>
> A. You cannot judge a book by what is on the outside of it.
>
> Q. Just a moment; don't get excited.
>
> A. I have a right to get excited, when you impute – that is the University of Michigan library.

Q. They have it in the library at least?

A. Of course they have.

After reading and questioning Reeves on a number of sections from Goldman's book, Lucking looked down at the book and appeared to read the following "Goldman quote" from it:

> With a few honorable exceptions, the United States Senate is a composition of ignorance, selfishness, personal avarice, political greed, stupidity, blatancy, flamboyance, asininity, to be equaled only by the same composition to be found in the House of Representatives of the United States Congress, because in the opinion of the majority, it is of exclusive importance that bills and measures of personal advantage should be considered.

Lucking asked Reeves whether his recitation was consistent with Reeves' understanding of Ford's views. Reeves answered,

> I think Mr. Ford went a great deal further than these men that they were actuated by personal ambition. Mr. Ford, as I say, rather thinks that the politicians generally are pretty near habitual criminals as I look at it.

Reeves, while noting that the statement was "rather strong," failed to see anything anarchistic in it. Lucking then confessed to presenting a ruse.

Q. It is from the printed war record of the *Chicago Tribune*.

A. I say, I knew it was not in the book you pretended to read.

Q. You did know it?

A. Yes, because it didn't sound like Emma, because she would not have made a few honorable exceptions. . . . Oh, I have seen that done frequently.

Q. That is the reason that you judged that; is that the reason?

A. I have seen that done so frequently, Mr. Lucking, pretending to read out of a book, when you are not.

Lucking, with a sheepish smile, slowly returned to his seat.

Stevenson, on redirect examination, sought to expand the concept of anarchism from the total destruction of government to the mere rendering of government ineffective.

> Q. In what is the common factor [in anarchism]?
>
> A. The opposition to the use of force by government.
>
> Q. Whether that opposition is based upon an entire destruction of the government, or rendering the government incapable of discharging its functions, the result is the same, is it not?
>
> A. Yes, sir.

Stevenson sought to establish that the term "anarchist" was broader than the concept of inherent violence and Lucking pushed the idea that Ford's musings were not inherently anarchistic. The intellectual give and take over these issues were not likely to generate a rise out of the distinctly rural members of the jury.

Following Professor Reeves, the defense called William Colnon, a reporter for the *Detroit Journal.* Colnon pulled no punches. He described the interview he had had with Henry Ford to see whether Ford would pay the difference between National Guard salaries and Ford's salaries for Ford employees called up for the Mexican intervention. Ford told him, point blank, that he thought men joined the army because they were lazy and shiftless and did not want to work. Then, John H. Dunnenwind, an editor for the *Detroit Free Press*, testified that he had spoken to the stringer, Williams, about his conversation with Mr. Klingensmith, and Dunnenwind had confirmed by telephone with Mr. Kingensmith the substance of that conversation: that Ford had no plans to rehire workers who returned to Detroit after completing their service with the Guard.

JUNE 25, 1919

The following morning, Wednesday, there was a buzz charging through the courtroom as the lawyers for both clients huddled at the bench in front of the Judge—that is, all except Elliott Stevenson, who had not appeared. Stevenson's automobile had sideswiped another vehicle, the night before, on Lakeshore Drive in Grosse Pointe, and he suffered a leg injury. Defense counsel put on a number of minor witnesses during the balance of the week. The parties and the court were essentially treading water, while awaiting Stevenson's return.

JUNE 26, 1919

Judge Tucker used this additional time, without Stevenson, to finally reach a decision on the scope of evidence he would allow in the case. He took a liberal tack. Tucker advised that he would rule that any evidence which indicated Ford's views and actions and justified the *Tribune's* criticism was material to the case. Which is to say, he completely let go of the rudder.

> I don't think it makes any difference. I think that anything [that] indicates Mr. Ford's anarchistic tendencies is material. I don't care where it comes from . . . and on the proposition, I feel that anything was done for the purpose of hindering or preventing the government from making such preparation as it saw fit to make, whether much or little, or adequate inadequate is material.

A stunned silence among the Ford lawyers sucked all the remaining oxygen out of the room. Lucking and Murphy faced the prospect of a long hot summer to come. The Judge adjourned the case until the following Monday in anticipation of Stevenson's return.

JUNE 30, 1919

The week dawned with the *Tribune* gearing up its preparedness campaign. Clifford Raymond, a *Tribune* editorial writer, took the stand and guided the jury through the evolution of the "anarchist" editorial and how it related to the *Tribune*'s concerns over the government's lack of preparedness to both deflect the border incursions and to stave off the European war.

JULY 1, 1919

The defense then called the young, boyish, and charming Captain Joseph Medill Patterson to the stand. Patterson, the co-editor and co-publisher of the *Tribune* and the cousin of Col. Robert M. McCormick, related his history with the *Tribune*, his experience as a voluntary enlisted man in the Illinois Guard on the Mexican border, his later service as an officer in the American Expeditionary Force in France, and his wounding and hospitalization in service of his country. Like a balm on the courtroom, Patterson's fresh, vigorous story kept the devilish heat at bay—here was a countryman all could admire. Even in ninety-seven-degree heat with ninety-four-percent humidity and not a breeze to be had, Patterson evoked a pure unadorned patriotism that every man could admire.

JULY 2, 1919

Next in line, Col. Henry J. Reilly testified. The military affairs writer for the *Tribune* was strong – jawed and tight lipped, and seemed almost undressed without his Sam Browne belt and his tin doughboy helmet pushed rakishly forward on his head. During the war, he had commanded the famous and highly decorated 42nd "Rainbow" infantry division in France. His regiment was popularly known as Reilly's Bucks. Reilly, who viewed the Mexican incursion from different perspective than Gibbons, described Japanese and German interests operating in Mexico from 1913 to 1916, where he was a war correspondent, and the general impoverishment of the citizens of Mexico. He described conversations that he had with Captain Patterson, Col. McCormick, and Tiffany Blake of the *Tribune* on preparedness.

> My attitude was simply that the United States stood in the midst of a good many real and potential enemies . . . it would be foolish to delude ourselves about our having any real friends; that every

> nation worked for its own self-interest; that we had ideas about democracy and fair play that did not appeal to a great many other people on this earth and the only thing for us to do if we were going to be able to follow a square policy, and not have to knuckle down to everyone when we put our foot down, would be to be properly armed.

The jury then listened to a reading of the deposition of James W. Gerard, a lawyer and judge, who served as Woodrow Wilson's Ambassador to Germany from 1913 to 1917. The German government asked Gerard to leave Germany in January 1917. Gerard testified that Henry Ford's peace ship, the Oscar II, was known in the American embassy as the "good ship nutty." He stated that German official opinion was that the United States did not want to fight and could not do so if it wished. He stated that Germany, in 1915, regarded pacifist propaganda such as that issued by Ford as being favorable toward her.

He went on to say that the Kaiser warned him that America had better look out after the war; that the German Admiral Alfred von Tirpitz had plans to use the combined British and German fleets, after vanquishing Britain in the war, to attack the United States. "The last thing the Germans wanted was preparedness here," he said.

Tiffany Blake, the *Tribune*'s Editorial Chief, ended the session, explaining why he approved Raymond's incendiary editorial. He said he approved the characterization of Henry Ford as an anarchist "[b]ecause at the time when the United States was in grave danger, he advocated the destruction of our army and navy; because he said he didn't believe in patriotism; because with the world in flames, he opposed preparedness; because he said the flag should be pulled down and because he said the soldiers were murderers."

The Judge then adjourned the case until Monday, July 7, to allow sufficient time for Mr. Stevenson's recovery and the much-anticipated clash between Col. Robert M. McCormick and Henry Ford.

Chapter 13

The Dog Fight

JULY 7, 1919

The first day back in court held few fireworks. Tiffany Blake, the boy-faced, soft-spoken, chief editorial writer for the *Tribune,* resumed the stand and under the patient examination of *Tribune* counsel, Waymouth Kirkland, continued his justification for the "anarchist" editorial. "The motive of the editorial was to offset the anarchistic influence of Mr. Ford." "The *Tribune,*" he said, "desired to support the government in its efforts to protect Americans in Mexico and on the border. If this protection was not offered the administration would not have deserved the name of government. Troops were called for. Mr. Ford did all he could to prevent a response to this call." He went on, "The *Tribune* did what it could to support the call, and as an incident to that support, criticized Mr. Ford."

In rounding out his presentation by Mr. Blake, Kirkland read to the jury a number of *Tribune* editorials from the 1913 to 1916, where it originally stood for caution with President Wilson, through an eventual separation with him, when the paper became convinced that the President's policy of caution failed to create "apprehension in the breasts of the Mexican administration."

JULY 8, 1919

The following morning the defense surrendered Tiffany Blake to

Alfred Lucking for cross examination. Elliott Stevenson, hobbled by his injury and supported by a cane, was back roaming the boards of the courtroom. Lucking devoted a half hour to reading early *Tribune* editorials showing that in the early days, the *Tribune* advocated that the Mexicans be allowed to work out their own destiny.

Lucking tried to establish that the *Tribune*, in initially opposing war with Germany over the submarine question, was at one time *with* Ford. "The *Tribune* had that right," Lucking said. "It was reluctant to enter the war and so was Mr. Ford." Blake acknowledged that the *Tribune* differed from Woodrow Wilson and others over Germany's submarine policy, until the sinking of the Lusitania, an unarmed passenger vessel, without a prior search. The *Tribune* opposed the carrying of munitions on unarmed passenger ships and separately opposed any embargo on the shipment of supplies to any country. Blake insisted that the interests of the *Tribune* were "[t]hose of the United States, 'first, last, and all the time,' that is the test we wish applied to all of our utterances at any stage of the world war."

Lucking put it to Blake that because of Ford's continued reluctance, the *Tribune* stigmatized him as an anarchist. Blake replied, "I don't know what you mean by stigmatize." "I mean," said Lucking, "that you desired before that editorial was written to attach an opprobrious epithet to him." "No," said Blake, "We meant to characterize him as an anarchist."

> Q. Why?
>
> A. Because his position in opposing defense measures in a time of danger was notorious. He was for pulling down the flag. He said patriotism ought to be abolished.

Lucking made little headway in his examination of Blake, as the dapper Chicagoan crossed his arms and dug in his heels in defiant justification of his editorial. The Judge, ever cognizant of the multitude of farm chores awaiting members of the jury, dismissed them early. The lawyers, tense and aware that the real clash of hounds was imminent, were glad to have the additional time to prepare.

JULY 9, 1919

Colonel Robert R. McCormick, thirty-eight, stepped forward and raised his right hand to be sworn as a witness. McCormick, sun-bronzed, sitting tall and ramrod straight in the witness chair, accepted full and personal responsibility for the anarchist editorial. Henry Ford and his son Edsel directly faced him for the first time in the trial behind their phalanx of seven lawyers.[89] The *Tribune* had subpoenaed the Fords for cross examination in its case, and they sat together behind their lawyers awaiting their turn.

McCormick described his early visits to Russia, England and France as a war correspondent in 1915 at the battlefronts. On his way home, he stopped to visit Lord Kirchner and Marshal Foche, the commanders of the British and French armies. He refused an invitation to visit Germany under high escort. He enlisted in the First Illinois Cavalry when he returned, where he achieved the rank of Major. The First Illinois sent him to the Mexican border in 1916. On the day the Lusitania sank, he called the Guard again to join the first cadre of troops to be assigned to participate with the American Expeditionary Force in France. The First Illinois converted into an artillery unit and McCormick accompanied his unit to France in 1917, where he was promoted to Lt. Colonel and finally Colonel. He served on the General Staff in France before being reassigned as commandant of Ft. Sheridan, Illinois. He was mustered out in 1918. While he was serving on the Mexican border, McCormick related that he had read about the massacre of American troops at Carrizal Mexico, by Mexican soldiers armed with machine guns. McCormick collected a fund to obtain machine guns for American troops, but couldn't find any guns to be had.

Lucking objected that McCormick's machine gun story was immaterial and Kirkland replied that it went to show McCormick's state of mind at the time of the editorial. Kirkland added, "Ford was the reason he couldn't get machine guns." Judge Tucker

---

89. The *Tribune* most always had ten lawyers in the courtroom at any given time.

ruled that Kirkland's comment was improper and directed that it be stricken from the record.

Continuing with his testimony, McCormick stated that he had heard of Ford's attitude toward Guardsmen going to the border. He said the paper's motive in publishing the editorial had been to discourage other manufacturers from adopting similar policies and to hopefully infuse Mr. Ford with a sense of patriotism. With his famous toothbrush moustache occasionally twitching, McCormick, answered questions frankly and courteously. He tended to grab the bit and run with it with extended comprehensive answers, often accompanied by his pounding one meaty hand into the other for emphasis. Clearly, the man felt his obligations to country very keenly.

Under cross examination by William Lucking, Alfred Lucking's brother, McCormick addressed the editorial itself. McCormick testified to a highly anxious state of mind when he approved the anarchist editorial, as he was expecting an imminent Mexican invasion. He again insisted that his purpose had been to encourage Ford to modify his stand. Newspapers sway opinions, and he'd hoped to sway Ford's. When questioned about his personal holdings, he said that he personally owned sixteen thousand five hundred shares in seven percent preferred stock in International Harvester founded by a relative, Cyrus McCormick, but Cyrus McCormick had no interest in the *Tribune.* He admitted that he and Captain Patterson continued to draw thirty thousand dollars each in annual salary form the *Tribune* while they were in the army in France, but other employees at the *Tribune* drew no salary supplements. Dig as he might, Lucking found little pay dirt in McCormick's testimony.

JULY 10, 1919

Under Lucking's questioning, McCormick reasserted that the *Tribune* was activated by "American motives" in printing the anarchist editorial. He described the history of the *Tribune*, from its founder Joseph Medill in 1850 to the present. He mentioned his close association with Winston Churchill, the First Lord of the Admiralty, H.H. Asquith, the British Prime Minister, Sir Edward Grey, the British Foreign Minister, and other British and French notables.

Lucking then challenged McCormick's description of the Mexican incursion as an "invasion," reading to him a letter from Woodrow Wilson to the press asking that it not be referred to as an invasion. McCormick responded, "That doesn't alter the fact that it was an invasion." Lucking offered that there wasn't an "invasion" because President Wilson had an agreement with the Mexican president for the U.S. to enter Mexico to capture Poncho Villa. McCormick responded that only President Wilson thought there was an agreement. McCormick said he didn't prefer President Carranza's word to Wilson's, but that Wilson may have been mistaken. "You remember," said McCormick, "that Carranza troops attacked American detachments twice—at Parral and Carrizal." When Lucking suggested that President Wilson had better information that any newspaper, McCormick replied, "He certainly had some misinformation. One of the government agents in Mexico turned out to be a German spy."

Lucking questioned McCormick about the probability of an American war with Mexico aiding Germany. McCormick, refusing to take the bait, replied,

> It would not have diverted shipments of munitions to the allies, for what we were shipping would not have been needed for an expedition into Mexico. It would have restored order and thus facilitated the movement of supplies, which the allies were getting from Mexico and it would also have built an American army, which we did not have at the time, as Germany well knew.

At one point, during their extended parries, McCormick suggested to Lucking that he refrain from resting his hand against his lips so that his voice would carry better. Leaving the stand, McCormick smiled broadly at Lucking and announced, "I have had a very pleasant time," which drew an objection from Murphy as being "insolent."

Stevenson then abruptly and unexpectedly called Ford's "Teutonic" personal secretary, Ernest G. Liebold, to the stand and demanded to know the whereabouts of the so-called "peace flag" designed by Irving Bacon. Liebold crudely denied any knowledge of the flag, which during the course of his examination appeared to strain credibility. He eventually agreed to mount a search for the flag and to produce it, if found.

JULY 11, 1919

Stevenson turned his attention to Edsel B. Ford, then the President of the Ford Motor Company. Young Edsel described his "meteoric" rise to the command of the Ford Motor Company despite his lack of any formal education. He had not likewise risen to military service.

Q. You are not a member of the National Guard?

A. No, sir.

Q. Nor any other military organization?

A. No, sir.

Edsel, obviously nervous, frequently drew his fingers over his nostrils. He looked very much of a younger version of his father and shared with him a habit of frequently drawing his hand over his face and chin. He projected an endearing image of a "diligent schoolboy." Sensing juror empathy toward him, Stevenson adopted a distinct and unusual paternal tone toward Edsel Ford, as he led him through a recitation of the financial history of the Ford Motor Company. Stevenson's announced purpose was to show that the 1914 "profit sharing plan" adopted by the company was "humbug" and a misnomer, because only a small share of Ford's profits were distributed to employees leaving an astonishingly large sum of thirty million dollars in profits for the shareholders.

Edsel Ford testified that the earnings for the Ford Motor Company in 1916 had doubled to sixty million dollars and Stevenson suggested that the monies paid to Ford employees were "amply earned" and since the earnings of the workers didn't change with the increase in Ford earnings, that the Ford employee compensation plan could not reasonably be called a profit sharing plan. The Luckings objected that Ford's largess was substantially larger than any distribution the *Tribune* had ever made to its employees. Stevenson's real purpose in examining Edsel Ford was to demonstrate that Henry Ford had more than enough money and didn't really need any more and that he suffered no real damage as a result of the publication and Ford's generosity toward his employees was less than claimed.

Lucking, on cross examination of Edsel Ford, used the opportunity to praise the Ford Motor Company as the pinnacle of capitalistic altruism. He cited a list of Ford Motor Company contributions to the war effort—Liberty airplane motors, nine thousand artillery caissons, two million light weight helmets, sixteen or seventeen tanks with a thousand more on order at war's end, and hulls for Liberty anti-submarine boats. Edsel Ford quietly and without posturing made the case that Ford had enthusiastically performed its patriotic duty in support of the American war effort.

On redirect, Stevenson sought to get Ford to admit that the government, in effect, forced the Ford Motor Company to perform war work. Ford responded, "No that is not true. The government controlled raw materials, but I think we could have continued [making cars] on a limited basis."

> Q. But you would have had to lay off thousands of men and wreck your organization?
>
> A. Yes, it would have wrecked the organization.

Lucking succeeded in showing through his son, Henry Ford's contribution to the American war effort despite his personal misgivings about war in general. Henry Ford, like all Americans, had struggled with the horrors of war and done his best to resist

American intervention, yet then when the War was entered, Ford contributed greatly to his homeland's military success. Lucking stroked the "common man" sympathies for all they were worth: Ford as champion of the masses and a patriot when the chips were down.

JULY 14, 1919

The Monday dawned that all of Mount Clemens and much of the country were eagerly anticipating—the appearance of Henry Ford on the witness stand for cross examination. Ford appeared wearing a conservative gray suit and a round-collar shirt. He appeared nervous and fidgety, and spoke in a barely audible voice. Stevenson led him through the formation of the Ford Motor Company in 1903, with an initial capital of one hundred fifty thousand dollars.

Blood did not fly. Fists were not thrown. In fact, the first day of Henry Ford's testimony was mostly taken up with Stevenson reading early *Tribune* editorials complimentary to Henry Ford. Ford remarked, at recess, "I have not made up my mind yet whether this is a Sunday school picnic or a dog fight."

The only apparent struggle, on day one of Ford's cross-examination, came about due to a telegram that Henry Ford had sent to the Secretary of the Treasury; both sides wished to introduce it into evidence. Lucking and Stevenson crossed verbal swords, and the Judge, saying, "What difference does it make who offers it?" received it as a joint exhibit.

The picnic then resumed till day's end.

JULY 15, 1919

The dog fight began on this sultry summer morning. Stevenson asked Ford to agree that after the initial favorable editorials in the *Tribune*, Ford and the *Tribune* "split" on the "rock" of "national preparedness." Ford demurred. Ford admitted his personal ignorance of history and that he believed that history was largely "bunk." Nor did he have much use for music or other forms of art. Stevenson directed his attention to a pamphlet, ghost-written for him by Theodore Delavigne, entitled *Humanity and Sanity*, most of which Ford had never read. Stevenson read aloud the pertinent damning sentences. And then quoted comments attributed to Ford by the journalist Edward Marshall. Ford listened with pacific countenance and easily confirmed his view that soldiers, including General Pershing and General Grant, could legitimately be classified as "murderers." The courtroom temperature rose several degrees.

Feeling the heat, Ford leaned back in his chair. He crossed his left leg over his right and grasped his left knee with hands in a defensive "fortress posture." There was an interruption in Ford's examination when the so-called "flag of humanity" or "peace flag" made its appearance in the courtroom. The flag measured fourteen by seven feet with a white globe of the earth on a blue background. There were two gold bands across the globe with a large red band across the equator. When Stevenson struggled to unfurl it, Ford grabbed one end saying, "Let me help."

Stevenson's interest in the flag was as a flag of anarchism in opposition to American preparedness for war. Ford clarified earlier testimony, saying that he had no objection to the concept of "preparedness" only unnecessary or "overpreparedness."

Q. Do you believe it is the duty of government to defend its citizens?

A. Yes, sir.

Q. How?

A. By getting prepared up to date.

Q. But in 1915-1916 you were advocating disarmament?

A. Yes, for the whole world.

Q. President Wilson was one of those who urged the preparedness you call murder.

A. Overpreparedness. I am strong for preparedness now.

Q. You were not in 1915.

A. I thought our preparedness at the time was adequate.

Q. Do you think now that war is murder?

A. Not for the oppressed.

Stevenson, tossing a challenge, advanced toward his quarry. "I shall inquire whether you are a well-informed man, competent to educate people." Advancing, he said, "What histories have you read?" Murphy interrupted with a vigorous objection. Stevenson reminded the Court that one of the libels complained by Ford was the attribution of "ignorant idealist."

Ford volunteered, "I admit that I am ignorant about most things." He asked to qualify an earlier answer about his lack of interest in the arts. He said he was beginning to appreciate art and music, particularly the banjo.

Laughter erupted in the courtroom.

Murphy, reverting to his argument, stated, "Adam didn't have any history and I think he got along very well," leading Waymouth Kirkland to retort, "Yes, and Adam got into trouble."

Returning to the issue, Ford stated, "In all of the history of civilization I cannot find one man who justified war." Stevenson countered, "Do you think that you can provide for the future and cars wisely with reference to the future without knowing the history of what happened in the past?"

Ford snorted into his hand. "When we got into war in the past it didn't amount to much for us."

Stevenson kept Ford skating around the hole of an admission that he was an ignorant idealist, but Ford would not fall in. "I don't admit that. That would mean that I was ignorant of everything." Still, Stevenson sought to highlight Ford's ignorance.

Q. What do you consider the fundamental principles of government?

A. Justice, I think.

Q. That is all.

A. That will do.

Stevenson asked Ford about a Delavigne ghost written article under Ford's name related to preparedness providing instruments of murder. "I know what it means," said Ford, "yes, sir, if you put it a little plainer, I could understand it." Stevenson asked him to read it himself, aloud for the courtroom. Ford declined to read it, claiming to be without his glasses. Lucking objected again to the line of questioning related to Ford's knowledge of government, history or civics.

Judge Tucker responded, "When a man on cross examination on the witness stand is charged with being an ignorant idealist mustn't he submit to an inquiry as to all things that go to make up an ignorant idealist?"

Stevenson continued plumbing the depths of Ford's ignorance. Ford stuck his foot firmly into the muck.

> Q. Do you know whether there have been any revolutions in this country or not?
> A. There was, I understand.
>
> Q. When?
> A. In 1812.
>
> Q. Don't you know there wasn't any revolution in 1812?
> A. I don't know that; I didn't pay much attention to that.
>
> Q. Now can you tell us anything about the revolution in 1812?
> A. About aggression, I guess.
>
> Q. You don't know what the War of 1812 was about?
> A. No.
>
> Q. Were there any other wars that you know about.
> A. Spanish American War.
>
> Q. Do you know what that was about?
> A. To free Cuba, I guess.
>
> Q. You didn't read history?
> A. Not very much.

Q. Then you don't know of general facts of that sort in detail then?

A. Not very much, no sir.

JULY 16, 1919

One day was not enough for investigating Ford's "ignorance." Stevenson continued his probe. Ford declined to read any written document Stevenson presented to him, citing the absence of his glasses. He said he didn't bring them, because he could read pretty well without them but not carefully. Was Ford dyslexic? How could this brilliant businessman have so great a fear for print? Ford again danced around the "ignorant idealist" issue until he grew tired of dancing. "Whether I am an ignorant idealist? If it will do any good, I will admit that I am an ignorant idealist."

Q. If you admit that it will foreclose the question.

A. I will admit it just to foreclose it.

Q. Not just to close it; if you will admit it as a fact we will stop the inquiry.

A. I don't know whether it is a fact or not, that is for the jury.

Q. If you don't admit it there isn't anything for the jury to find out.

Failing to obtain a clear admission, Stevenson pressed on, obtaining a more stunning revelation of ignorance.

Q. Did you ever hear of Benedict Arnold?

A. I have heard the name.

Q. Who was he?

A. I have forgotten just who he is. He is a writer, I think.

Q. A writer?

A. I think so.

Q. What subjects do you recall he wrote on?

A. I don't remember.

Q. Did you ever read anything he wrote?

A. Possibly I have but I don't know – – – I don't know much about him.

LUCKING: [INTERJECTING] "There is an Arnold who is a prominent writer."

STEVENSON: [TO FORD] "What is that. I don't quite catch your answer. These statements behind my back are out of order."

JUDGE TUCKER: [TO LUCKING] "The difficulty is that the jury can hear your statement, I cannot lots of times."

FORD: "I could find a man in five minutes who could tell me all about it."

Q. You could find a man who could fill your place in the United States Senate could you?

A. I never wanted to go to the United States Senate.

Q. I might add that the people did not want him, but I won't your honor.

MURPHY: "That remark is uncalled for your honor."

JUDGE TUCKER: "I think it is myself."

Stevenson's callous cut regarding Ford's Senate loss portended pointed commentary from unfriendly newspapers.

The *Buffalo Express*: "It is not always wise for a great educator of public opinion to allow himself to be placed in the on the witness stand."

The *Milwaukee Journal*: "Mr. Ford's haziness about school book fundamentals cannot be fairly regarded as part of his supposed equipment for the United States Senate."

The *Portland Oregonian*: "The State of Michigan was spared a great humiliation when it failed to elect Ford to the United States Senate."

The *Baltimore News*: "Mr. Ford is evidently a genius in the matter of quantity production of automobiles, but is there a man who in viewing his exposure of his lack of knowledge of history, of government, of the meaning of ordinary words, will say that he is fit to legislate for a great nation?"

Tucker warned both sides about further offhand remarks within the hearing of the jury. Stevenson complained that Ford's counsel made one hundred twenty-five objections on behalf of Ford the previous day and were on track to break the record. Stevenson expressed his dismay at Ford's continued failure to bring his glasses to court and vowed to subpoena them if necessary.

Stevenson asked Ford whether he knew when the United States was created. Ford, plainly nettled, said that he didn't know, but could find out in a few minutes. Asked to tell the jury what his idea of an *idealist* was, Ford responded, "Well an *idealist* I think is a person that can help make people prosperous. I think I can do it a little." The *Tribune* team proceeded to read a number of preparedness speeches by Woodrow Wilson and others into the record. Lucking requested that Ford be allowed to leave the stand during the reading. Stevenson offered Ford a chair near himself, which Ford politely but briskly refused, grabbed his hat, and left the courtroom with Lucking.

Upon the resumption of testimony, Stevenson asked Ford if he knew what the United States was composed of before the Revolution. "Land, I guess," he answered, smiling. Ford acknowledged knowing of the Declaration of Independence, but didn't know any details. The courtroom was abuzz as the reporters scrambled to get to their wire services. Many were shaking their heads in disbelief that a man of such renown and consequence could appear so unconstrained by levels of knowledge within the basic reach of school children.

JULY 17, 1919

Stevenson, this morning, drew Ford's attention to a magazine article about him entitled, "Industry's Miracle Maker," written by the socialist journalist John Reed.[90] The unfailingly admiring article painted Ford as a democratic person more comfortable chatting

90. Reed, the author of *Ten Days That Shook the World*, about the Bolshevik Revolution and the subject of the movie *Reds*, is one of only several Americans buried in the Kremlin.

over a back porch with neighbors rather than hobnobbing with the social elite of Grosse Pointe. Stevenson queried Ford as to how a man living in a million-dollar house surrounded by security guards could find the opportunity for "cracker barrel" discussions with neighbors. Ford just smiled. Ford, at one point, told Reed that he thought the cause of the war was German beer and French wine, because alcohol caused the nations to be suspicious of each other.

Reed's flattering description of Ford's appearance with his "well-balanced complexion," "wavy silver locks," and "Yankee nose" caused Ford to blush, the women in the courtroom to giggle, and the men to laugh, as Ford held up his index finger for the reader to stop the description.

The tittering stopped when Stevenson asked Ford about a Reed quote, saying Ford wanted to pull down the stars and stripes. Ford didn't recall it.

Stevenson suddenly interrupted the reading of the Reed article to call advertising executive Kirk B. Alexander to the stand. Alexander related conversations that he had had with Ford where Ford opined that if Germany had not invaded Belgium first, Britain and France would have done so. Ford also told Alexander, in December 1917, that the Kaiser was ready for peace. Alexander further testified that Ford spent eighty thousand dollars to publish his antiwar diatribes written by Delavigne.

When Ford returned to the stand, he testified that he knew Reed; that he did tell Reed that he didn't give a nickel for all the history of the world. Reed concluded his article by stating, "He [Ford] has a mind of appalling simplicity." Reed referred to his subject as "poor ignorant Mr. Ford," but apparently intended it as a reflection of his admiration for him. Admiring or not, the charge of Ford's being an "ignorant idealist" had been beautifully laid out by John Reed.

JULY 18, 1919

Stevenson completed Henry Ford's first week of testimony by focusing on the substance of the *Tribune* editorial itself. Ever the reluctant reader, Ford threw a giant gasp into the courtroom, admitting he rarely read beyond the headlines of newspaper articles. To him, the *Tribune*'s editorial title "Henry Ford is an Anarchist" proclaimed loud and clear that the *Tribune* accused him of being a "bomb thrower." He admitted that the purpose of a headline is to reflect what is contained in the body of the article, but he rarely ventured below the headline.

Alfred Lucking stood up and intoned the Ford position that the headline, standing alone, is actionable libel. Stevenson complained to the Court about the constant barrage of interruptions and objections to his examination flowing from the Ford lawyers, arguing that one third of the transcript of the proceedings thus far contained Ford objections.

Tucker ignored his complaint and Stevenson continued, "You will hardly deny the charge that you are an ignorant idealist Mr. Ford, you said so twice yesterday."

Ford smiled, "Well Mr. Stevenson, you can get me to say black is white."

Stevenson asked if he hadn't been fair with Ford. Ford said, "Yes," and Lucking jumped again into the fray. He called Stevenson's line of questioning "brutal." "This brutal to a fine man, a modest man who hates to appear in public; who does not wish to be here. I submit that it is brutal."

Stevenson said, "You don't think that Mr. Ford, do you?"

Ford just smiled.

Stevenson then called Ford's attention to his previous testimony, admitting ignorance of most things about the Army and Navy. Stevenson then excused Ford for two hours while Waymouth Kirkland took the stand to read the testimony of General Erasmus Weaver before the House Committee on Military Affairs. Weaver contradicted, in detail, one of Theodore Delavigne's articles that attacked Weaver's views as to the adequacy of America's coastal defenses.

Returning Ford to the witness stand, Stevenson again raised the question of his ignorance. This was a key point to win, as the

Tribune editorial had proclaimed, "A man so ignorant as Henry Ford may not understand the fundamentals of government under which he lives." Ford had apparently read that far. He turned to Tucker and asked, "Does he want me to say that I don't know anything about government?" Tucker remained silent, and Stevenson continued. "I have asked you a number of questions and I don't want to press you as to whether you are a well-informed man, competent to educate the public, or an ignorant man who ought not undertake to educate the people, but in view of what you have said, you would not question that *ignorant* is a proper characterization of you?

Lucking jumped to his feet, flushed with anger, yelling, "That is objected to as brutal and inhuman." Ford, ignoring Lucking, responded. "As I have said Mr. Stevenson, I am ignorant of most things."Tucker held the question as proper, and Stevenson turned to Ford with a grin.

> Q. Have I been brutal, Mr. Ford?
>
> A. No, sir.
>
> Q. Again, is he [Lucking] talking thru his hat?
>
> LUCKING: "This is another illustration of what I have said, that Mr. Ford is willing to confess anything against himself. This is as absolutely brutal an examination as I have ever heard.
>
> JUDGE TUCKER: "Mr. Ford cannot be treated any different from any other witness, nor do I think he would care to be."

Lucking's blood pressure shot through the roof of the very high courtroom ceiling. Stevenson fingered through his notes with an air of satisfaction. Henry Ford stepped down from the stand to take a long stroll among the birds at river's edge. Journalists covering the trial remarked on the different personalities of Henry Ford, in and out of court.

> On the street, Mr. Ford is an easy going, emphatic sort of person. He will talk without hesitation on subjects ranging from the tail feathers of a bird to the motives which inspire governments. He

> is mild and genial with those with whom he comes in contact. In court, under cross examination, the manufacturer has been low voiced and diffident in his answers. His easy conversational style has been displaced by replies almost monosyllabic.[91]

JULY 21, 1919

Lawyers on both sides consumed the morning with arguments before the Judge on the scope of cross examination regarding the issue of "preparedness." Thus, Henry Ford had a relatively mild start to the day. The Judge agreed to permit testimony concerning the parties' views but refused to allow outside testimony regarding the state of preparedness in the United States.

The Court permitted Stevenson to read into the record an interview of Henry Ford published in the *Chicago Tribune* on May 25, 1916. In the interview, Ford expounded on the virtues of disarmament and the uselessness of history. "It means nothing to me. History is more or less bunk. It's tradition. We don't want tradition. We want to live in the present and the only history that is worth a tinker's damn is the history we make today." The reading of the "History is Bunk" quote drew objections and rebuttals in the press.

Henry Ford resumed the stand shortly before noon. Debate heated up immediately. Ford resisted Stevenson's efforts to get him to admit that a state of anarchy existed on the Mexican border—preferring to call it a "riot" instead. John Reed, the red rabble-rouser, had been deposed, and the Judge admitted this deposition. Without varnish, Reed shared journalistic insights from his Ford interview. Reed quoted Ford as saying that he didn't believe in boundaries, that after the war he was going to pull down the American flag forever and set up a "flag of all peoples."

You could almost feel the cloth between Stevenson's and Ford's outstretched hands.

Reed stamped the end of the day with this unforgettable quote: Ford called most soldiers "lazy, crazy and out of a job."

---

91. The *Brooklyn Daily Eagle*, July 21, 1919, at 3.

Ford continued his hunkered down responses to Stevenson's questions in a constant diffident soft monotone that spectators, newsmen, and even lawyers, had to strain to hear. His appearance on the stand much belied the confident arrogance of his public proclamations.

JULY 22, 1919

Stevenson concluded his cross examination of Henry Ford at about 10:30 in the morning, turning him over, with some noticeable relief by Ford, to his attorney, Alfred Lucking. Stevenson ended his examination by stressing Ford's opposition to an unprecedented Anglo-French loan by U.S. private bankers. Stevenson established that Ford, in his opposition to the loans because bankers were involved, was inexplicably and blissfully unaware that these loans were backed by the guarantees of the French and British government and the loan proceeds used fund allied purchases of food and goods from farmers and manufacturers in the United States. He spoke, again, of Ford's insensitivity to the sinking of the Lusitania: "They were fools to go on that boat because they were warned." Stevenson also raised a final question about Ford's ability to read.

> Q. Mr. Ford, I have some hesitation, but I think in justice to yourself, I should ask this question: I think the question has been created by your failure to read some of these things that have been presented to you, that you could not read; do you want to leave it that way?
> A. Yes, you can leave it that way; I am not a fast reader and I have the hay fever, and I would make a botch of it.
>
> Q. Are you willing to have that impression left here?
> A. I am not willing to have that impression, but I am not a fast reader.
>
> Q. Can you read at all?
> A. I can read.

Q. Do you want to try it?

A. No, sir.

Q. You would rather leave that impression?

A. I would rather leave that impression.

Ford's obvious nervousness evaporated when Lucking took charge. The twitchy fidgeting ceased. Ford relaxed into his chair and his voice became noticeably stronger.

"I will make short of it," said Lucking, smiling, "under orders."

Ford testified that he paid little attention to his income or what was done with it. He testified as to his investment of millions of dollars in the Henry Ford Hospital in Detroit. He described his development of a hospital for war-displaced Belgians in England, indicating that he had no idea of its cost. He said that all of Ford Motor's factories were devoted to some form of war work. And yet Ford answered Lucking's questions with as many "I don't knows" as he provided to Stevenson. He said that he was eager to get away for a camping trip in the Adirondack Mountains with Thomas Edison and John Burroughs. He described himself as being extremely interested in birds and said that the only federal legislation that he actively promoted was for the protection of birds.

Q. If Mr. Stevenson came to your farm could you tell him a few things about birds?

A. Yes, just a little.

JULY 23, 1916

Stevenson recalled Ford, one last time, to ask about Edsel Ford's deferment. Ford answered that Edsel was a great relief to him and that his son had wanted to enlist, but that Henry Ford had discouraged it. He said that Edsel had been offered several military commissions, which would have allowed him to continue doing what he was doing, but Edsel didn't want to camouflage the situation. Stevenson asked Ford whether he assumed responsibility for his son not enlisting. Ford replied, "Yes I think I did."

Q. He is more useful to you in the factory?

A. Yes,

Q. The draft board disagreed with you?

A. I think so.

Edsel Ford's draft deferment was a major source of contention against Ford in the Newberry Senate Campaign. Stevenson wanted to end his examination of Ford by showing how, despite his financial contribution to the war effort, he still had no real skin in the game and was not by a long shot a fully committed patriot.

One of the wire news services reported that the long strain of the trial appeared to be taking a toll on the jury, some of the members of whom were elderly. The court scheduled a two-hour rest at noon to allow them to recover their stamina.[92]

Following Henry Ford, Stevenson called John R. Lee, the former head of the Ford Personnel Department, an eight-year Ford insider, who testified that Ford strongly believed in universal disarmament. Lee confirmed a number of Ford's outlandish pronouncements in the Edward Marshall article, one in particular: "Murderer should be placed on the breast of every soldier." Said Lee, "He thought we should sink our navy and disband our army." Despite being under contract to build "Liberty Boats," Lee said, "that without qualification he did not believe in the navy." Lee said that Ford told him that he didn't blame men for leaving Europe to avoid military service and that he employed men from every warring nation in his plants.

JULY 24, 1919

The defense, again following the anti-Ford, roadmap used against

92. UPI, The *Mount Carmel Item*, July 23, 1919.

him in the Senate campaign, presented Edward F. Clement, a member of the American Protective League, to show that Ford was harboring pro-German and potentially dangerous workers in his factory. This nonprofit, right-wing, vigilante volunteer organization, loosely affiliated with the U.S. Justice Department, gathered information on disloyal and pro-German activities during the war, particularly within factories producing clothing and war material.[93] Clement said that he was assigned to snoop in Ford factories, and he and his Ford cohorts identified two hundred fifty Ford employees with potentially pro-German leanings. He identified one man as being interned. Clement said that if a man was suspected of pro-German leanings, Clement assigned the investigation to an "operative" within the suspect's department. When the government eventually issued an order requiring enemy aliens to carry permits, a total of six hundred seven were identified at Ford of thirty thousand workers. In response to a question by Murphy, Clement related that his group made no recommendations regarding prosecution. They just reported the information to the government.[94]

Mr. F. Edward Spooner testified that he knew both Henry and Edsel Ford, and he heard Henry Ford say that he would withdraw his funds from any bank of his that participated in the Anglo-French loan.[95]

Lastly, Stevenson complained to the Judge that the defense was having difficulty closing its case because it could not locate James A. Conners, the witness for Ford who earlier testified that Mr. Klingensmith told him the Ford Motor Company would care for its 1916 called-up employees and their families. Steven-

93. The APL claimed at one point to have two hundred fifty thousand badge-carrying members in six hundred American cities.

94. There is no proven record of significant pro-German sabotage or espionage occurring in Ford plants.

95. The 1915 Anglo-French loan for five hundred million dollars by private American banks was adamantly opposed by German agents and sympathizers in the United States.

son claimed to have new evidence that would cast doubt on Conners' veracity.[96] Stevenson read into evidence the deposition of Conners' mother who claimed that her son was not dodging subpoenas, but she was unable to identify his whereabouts. This was a thin and ultimate futile effort to discredit Conners' testimony and the *Tribune* side closed its defense case with more of a whimper than a clang, awaiting Ford's presentation of rebuttal.

JULY 25, 1919

The trial kept all in attendance "on their feet," but none so actively as Judge Tucker. He spent a lot of his time moderating and responding to the arguments and objections of defense counsel, regarding the rebuttal testimony being offered by the Ford lawyers. They called Bishop Charles D. Williams, an Episcopal Minister from Detroit, to counter the earlier expert testimony by Professor Reeves. When Lucking asked Williams, "What is an anarchist," he answered, "One who believes, advocates and works for the elimination of government and does so by violent means." Lucking quoted a number of Ford utterances advocating for a world view rather than the nation's point of view followed by, "Is there anything in that that is particularly anarchistic?" Williams said no, there was not. In the argument between counsel that followed, Murphy asserted that the ideas of Mr. Ford were those of the Christian religion and generally held by Bible philosophy. Allowed to proceed, Williams said Ford's remarks were not particularly anarchistic but rather sentiments appearing frequently in the bible such as "Love thy neighbor as thy self."

When Lucking asked whether Williams thought Quakers were anarchists, the defense objected and those objections were sustained by the Court. When Stevenson asked Williams what he thought of Ford's statement that to his mind the word "murderer" should be embroidered on the breast of every soldier, the Bishop

96. Conners apparently lied under oath about his marital status.

only said that he could not recall such teachings by anarchists. He said Ford's opposition to conscription was not anarchistic, and that Carlyle, Emerson and others had said that war is murder. He admitted that Ford's statements that he would abolish the army and navy were "very strong," and that he "would not care to undertake to answer" questions about them.

The Bishop indicated that many of Ford's observations were ones that he himself held. Stevenson objected: "We are not trying the Bishop for being an anarchist." The Bishop replied, "I am afraid that my turn is coming because if this is anarchy, I agree with it mostly. The Bishop quoted from the forty-sixth Psalm, "Come behold the works of the Lord, what desolations he hath made in the earth. He maketh wars to cease until the end of the earth; he breaketh the bow and cutteth the spear in sunder. He burneth the chariot in the fire." Quoting from Isaiah, the Bishop said, "And they shall beat their swords into plowshares and their spears into pruning hooks; nation shall not lift up sword against nation; neither shall they learn war anymore."

Anger flashing across his face, Stevenson honed in on the difficult witness in cross examination.

Q. Do you believe in the doctrine of non-resistance?

A. No, I don't.

Q. It is the belief of anarchists?

A. Yes, and the belief of Christians, who are not anarchists, as well.

Q. I asked you if it was not the opinion of anarchists. Will you be good enough to answer the question?

A. Anarchists teach that and Christians teach that. I am going to tell the truth and all the truth.

Q. When I asked you if anarchists taught that, was it necessary for you also say some others taught it?

A. Yes, if I tell all the truth.

Q. Disarmament is the doctrine of anarchists, too, isn't it?

A. And others.

Q. Now Bishop . . .

Not all of the press covering the trial were impressed with the Bishop's performance. "Henry Ford had a trying time on the witness stand, even his friends testifying to disadvantage. A bishop on his oath declared that the sentiments attributed to Ford are found all through the New Testament. And every practical person knows that the New Testament is hopelessly 'idealistic' for this enlightened age. Any nation taking that direction would go to smash in short order."[97]

JULY 29, 1919

Alfred Lucking led off the final week of testimony with more rebuttal, calling the Vice-President and General Manager of the Ford Motor Company, Frank Klingensmith, to the stand. Klingensmith denied that he had ever heard Henry Ford make antagonistic remarks about the government. He denied that he had ever told the *Tribune* stringer, Williams, that Ford would not hold jobs for called-up Guardsmen or help out their dependents during the Mexican incursion. Klingensmith suffered from major credibility problems when he could not remember what he had said to others on the same subject, and what he did actually say to Williams. He could only say that it wasn't what was printed in the *Tribune.*

The Ford side then called Professor William A. Dunning, Chair of the History and Political Philosophy Department of Columbia University, as an expert witness on the subject of anarchy. Lucking led Dunning through each of the Ford utterances earlier condemned by Professor Reeves as being anarchistic, and Dunning found them to be "commonplace"—liable to be said by anybody. Dunning didn't specifically refute Reeves' testimony but

97. The *Topeka Daily Capital,* July 28, 1919, at 4.

rather pointed out that those views were also held by non-anarchists. Lucking asked him,

> Q. How about having the word "murderer" embroidered on the chest of every soldier?
>
> A. The idea of embroidering it is perhaps new.
>
> Q. Rather suggests a woman?
>
> A. Certainly no man ever said that.

The deposition of journalist Edward Marshall, offered into evidence by the Ford lawyers, indicated that those words were first used in Marshall's presence by Jane Addams, the Chicago social worker, author and activist, and that Marshall had put them into Ford's mouth for the article; Marshall said that Ford accepted his adoption of the phrase.

JULY 30, 1919

Stevenson, on cross examination, elicited from Dunning the agreement that anarchists believed their doctrines would improve the lot of mankind. Lucking objected, "Counsel is trying to make out that the *Tribune* was highly complementary in calling Mr. Ford an anarchist." Stevenson rejoined, "We are showing that we did not call him a bomb thrower." Then, turning to Dunning, Stevenson said,

> Q. The desire of anarchists to benefit mankind is shared by most American's, isn't it?
>
> A. I think so.

Dunning testified that there are a great variety of anarchists—some believing their doctrine essentially Christian and others who find Christianity anathema. He said many anarchists are pacifists and many, like Emma Goldman, advocate violent means. He said that all anarchists were opposed to military service. Stevenson then read to him a Ford quote, "It seems to me that there is not much difference between a republic, a monarchy and an empire; they are all ruled by a little group of interests who have special privileges."

Q. Isn't that genuine anarchist teaching?

A. Anarchistic and socialistic.

Q. The anarchists and socialists agree on that?

A. I think so.

In the course of his testimony, Dunning mentioned that there were many anarchists who could not read. Stevenson responded, "Neither can Mr. Ford."

LUCKING: Oh, no, Mr. Stevenson, that is unfair!

MURPHY: Your honor, we object, Mr. Ford was suffering from hay fever. We insist that it be stricken out.

With all the lawyers standing and talking at the same time, Stevenson's voice topped them all, "Mr. Ford said he could not read, didn't he?"

Judge Tucker, drawn yet again to his feet, advised everyone to sit down and requested Stevenson to reserve his comments for closing arguments.

AUGUST 1, 1919

Henry Ford left Mount Clemens, for the last time, with few sighs or regrets. Traveling to New York to meet up with Thomas Edison, H.H. Firestone, and John Burroughs, Ford sought solace in his auto camping trip in the Adirondack Mountains. Meanwhile his lawyers called another expert, Frances W. Coker, a professor of political science at The Ohio State University. Coker provided a fawning endorsement of Professor Dunning's expertise and prestige ("everybody uses his book") and insisted that Henry Ford was a capitalist who believed in property, supported the state, was an advocate of government, and could not "in the wildest flight of imagination be called an anarchist."

The Ford lawyers recalled Dr. Samuel S. Marquis, the head of

Ford's Sociological department,[98] to explain the mystery of the Ford "world peace flag." Marquis accepted full responsibility for the flag's design. He had mentioned the flag to Henry Ford, but Ford neither approved nor disapproved of it. Marquis described it as "sort of a shop flag," representing the 50-plus nations of the Ford workers. He described the gold bands round the globe as representing prosperity and the red band at the center representing the phrase, "He hath made of one blood all the nations of the world."

Curious that the shop flag had been so very hard to locate.

AUGUST 4-5, 1919

A hazy August day kicked off the final courtroom events. Alfred Lucking put on a long series of witnesses with often hazy and contradictory testimony as to the initial Ford policy regarding the treatment of Ford employees called up by the National Guard for Mexico duty. Witnesses also attempted to explain the tardy relief provided to some of the Ford Guardsmen's dependents. Several witnesses testified positively about Ford's ability to read and write. They included William J. Cameron, a writer for *The Dearborn Independent* whose duty it was to translate Henry Ford's thoughts into "Mr. Ford's own page" in the paper.

The final witness in the case was Clinton DeWitte, the superintendent, of the Ford English School for Ford employees. DeWitt described Henry Ford's efforts to make Americans out of his foreign-born workers. He said the school's motto was "Help the other fellow" and the school cheer was "Siss boom bam, hurrah for Uncle Sam."

"We always run patriotism and home together in our lessons," he said. He related that the school purchased small American flags in batches of five thousand to give their students upon graduation.

---

98. Ford's Sociological Department was charged with the intrusive responsibility of determining whether Ford employees were living family centered Christian focused lives so as to qualify them for the "profit sharing" largesse of the company,

DeWitt closed out the evidentiary portion of the trial on a high note of Ford patriotic fervor, describing the school's graduation ceremony in which the graduates, dressed in raggedy European clothing, would step into a huge, smoking "melting pot" stirred from above, and climb out the other side dressed in "smart," tailored American clothing on the other side, fully homogenized and absorbed Americans.

Chapter 14

Verdict on Verdict

THE TRIAL, LIKE THE Clinton River adjacent to the courthouse, was winding wearily to the sea. The Court took the day, August 6, 1919, to hear arguments on the Court's instructions to the jury. Judge Tucker set four days for oral arguments by the attorneys, August 7, 8, 11 and 12. The extraordinary widespread national coverage of and interest in the Ford/*Tribune* trial had generated many impressions, conclusions and verdicts both personal and professional.

The *New York Tribune* assessed the impact of Henry Ford's testimony in newspapers across the country.

> The consensus of opinion seems to be that the Detroit manufacturer who is suing the *Chicago Tribune* for $1,000,000 for calling him an anarchist is, outside of his own business, an impulsive, warm hearted, untutored child with an active mind and wobbly judgment. The editors point out that Mr. Ford does not think consistently, and not being given to thinking about anything but the automobile business does not stop to think where he places himself when he permits a literary hired hand to flood the country with literature on Henry Ford's views of war and peace.

The Sioux City Iowa Journal: "He is disclosed as a man with a vision distorted and limited by his lack of information. The public has been disillusioned and if Mr. Ford has not been, he has failed to learn one of the most valuable lessons of the trial."

The New York Times: "Mr. Ford's apparent ignorance upon

many subjects that an ordinary school child has a certain familiarity with . . . is not so much vanity as it is assumption. The victim of the disease comes to believe that, having accomplished great things in one practical line of life, he is qualified to give an opinion on almost any subject, to teach other men to do almost anything and to reform the world in some particular manner not at all related to his own experience. If he fails, if he makes himself ridiculous, if he wastes his own money and other people's time he sighs that he was right, but that the world in general was not bright enough to take advantage of the opportunity he offered."

The Nation magazine: "Now the mystery is finally dispelled. Henry Ford is a Yankee mechanic, pure and simple; quite uneducated, he cannot rise above the defects of his education, at least as to public matters. So, the unveiling of Mr. Ford has much of the pitiful about it, if not the tragic. We would rather have had the curtain drawn, the popular ideal unshattered."

The Salina Evening Journal: "The examination of Henry Ford as a witness for himself seems not unlike a mental vaudeville performance as such an exhibition of mental disorder and incompetence, the cynic must sneer, the satirist smile and the philosopher sigh. If there never has been a valid argument for classical education before, there is one now in the revelations of confusions, the limitations and the contradictions of this remarkable man's untutored mind."

Ford, by getting on the witness stand, had done more harm to his public image and personal reputation than any offending newspaper editorial could do for him, and he came to blame Alfred Lucking for getting him into the soup. While a number of newspapers across the country continued to report respect and even affection for "ole Henry," it was clear that his public image had taken on more dramatic torpedo hits than the Lusitania.

FINAL ARGUMENTS

Eleven lawyers spoke for the combatants, with early prosecution arguments drilling down to Ford's humble beginnings and perceived character, his spectacular rise, and his unconventionally liberal treatment of his employees. The defense focused on the importance of free speech and a vibrant and vigilant press. Both sides wrapped themselves in the flag of patriotism. Weymouth Kirkland, in his address, stressed the patriotic willingness of Gold Star[99] mothers to sacrifice their own children to serve the country, in contrast to Edsel Ford's deferment.

> There are many gold star mothers in the United States today who believe in patriotism and willingly and gallantly gave their sons to die for their country, because they thought that the flag ought not to come down.

The last three lawyers to address the jury were the silver-tongued Judge Alfred Murphy; the persistent and eloquent Elliott Stevenson; and the intensely vehement Alfred Lucking.

JUDGE ALFRED J. MURPHY, ESQ.

Judge Murphy described Henry Ford as a "gentle, simple-hearted man, without pretense," who considers his reputation a "pearl without price." He described five distinct "lies" in the *Tribune* publication: 1) Ford employees would lose their job places in a Guard call-up; 2) Ford would make no provisions for the dependents of Guard employees; 3) Guardsmen families would have to get along in any fashion possible; 4) If Guardsmen returned, they would have the same footing as all other applicants for employment; and 5) The same rule would apply to all Ford employees everywhere.

Murphy stated that the *Tribune* chose to chastise Ford with the "whip of words" and that the term *anarchist* should be taken in the common, usual and ordinary meaning—one given to inciting violence. He recalled the Haymarket bombing and the University Club poisoning by alleged anarchists in Chicago. He argued that

99. The "gold star" concept started with service flags in World War I, where families displayed flags with blue stars for each service member in the family and changed the stars to gold when a service member died.

the *Tribune* was motivated by its pro-Germanism, and that the McCormick and Patterson families had deep interests in inciting war with Mexico. He reminded the jury of Henry Ford's own statement that he didn't need any more money. ("I don't want any more money. The more money I have the more trouble I have.") Murphy insisted that Ford was standing on principle in bringing action against the *Tribune,* not pursuit of money for its own sake. He wanted the jury to send the *Tribune* a message that it could not trifle with an honorable man's reputation in pursuit of the paper's separate agenda. The only way the message could be affectively delivered was with the award of significant damages.

Murphy was careful to point out that the only salve or recompense to Ford for his anguish of his damaged reputation was an award of money and requested the jury consider an award for each one of the four hundred eight thousand publications of the offending "anarchist" editorial to each of the *Tribune* subscribers. Referring to Ford's performance on the witness stand, Murphy mentioned that Ford was too busy making history to recite it. In fact, he claimed, a man "may be wise yet ignorant." Murphy mentioned Jesus Christ, the "Master," soliciting humble, ignorant fishermen to serve as his apostles. He noted that neither Charlemagne nor Oliver Cromwell could read or write. He offered that this "kindly man was too courageous to tell you how he suffered."

Murphy then recited a parable of a woman who had slandered her neighbor and asked her pastor for forgiveness. The pastor instructed the woman to find a goose and remove all of its feathers and cast the feathers to the wind and when finished set about recovering each of the feathers and when done, return to him and they would discuss forgiveness. Defamation was no small thing. He ended with an appeal to patriotic service, saying, "You will have rendered a patriotic service which is comparable to the highest service to be rendered by anyone for the republic," which prompted a scattering of applause in a corner of the courtroom. This drew a prompt and harsh admonition from the Judge. Stevenson responded, "I suppose in as much as it is confined to a lot of old ladies over there, there is no harm done."

ELLIOTT G. STEVENSON, ESQ.

On the morning of the final day of argument, Elliott Stevenson, dressed in a contemporary dark blue "sack" suit, with a prominent white handkerchief, brushed his white moustache and stared down the jury. He reminded them that there was no mention of bomb throwing or poisoning in the *Tribune* editorial—the *Tribune* objected to Ford's discouraging service to the nation. The *Tribune,* in this libel case, had been "forced to open the mind of Henry Ford" for their viewing. How shocking it was to find Ford so ignorant of the fundamentals of government. Ford's performance in the courtroom and his refusal to bring his glasses to court raised the probability that he could not read at all.

Stevenson argued that Ford, through the media, had "hypnotized the American people;" that the *Tribune* editorial "Ford is an anarchist," had had no effect on Ford's reputation. The editorial "might well have poured water off of a duck's back." He reminded the jury that in August, 1916, after the "anarchist" publication, Ford was elected as a Republican candidate for President of the United States by the Michigan Republican party.[100] Here, Stevenson paused for effect. "My God, gentleman of the jury, think of what it is to be libeled that way."

Turning to Judge Murphy's goose feather parable, Stevenson stated that the story was suspicious because he was unaware of any Christian church imposing impossible conditions for forgiveness.

> Gentlemen of the jury, it has occurred to me what an awful predicament Henry Ford would have been in if he had gone to that pastor and asked for forgiveness for the slanders that he

100. This actually occurred before the publication and Stevenson corrected it but still insisted that Ford's nomination for the Senate in Michigan carried the same point.

> had uttered, and the libels he had published against millions of American citizens.
>
> * * *
>
> And this pastor says, "Mr. Ford," in the language of Judge Murphy, "go and catch enough geese for each man you have slandered." Said Stevenson, "God grant that he may talk to the birds. He would need it in that time."

Stevenson recounted that just fifteen days after the *Tribune* called Henry Ford an anarchist, Ford came out with the first Delavigne ghost written articles "denouncing everybody as a traitor, a murder, who was in favor preparedness." Then, Stevenson referred back to John R. Lee's testimony that it was in fact James Couzens who had urged the Ford Motor Company to adopt the five-dollars-per-day wage plan. Stevenson said, in a wondering way, "[I]t is kind of funny, how Henry Ford gets credit for everything going on in the world."

Next, Stevenson attacked the image of Henry Ford as portrayed by his lawyers:

> Now that you here got him, gentlemen of the jury, he comes in here and plays the baby, and asks you, and his counsel ask you, "Why I am gentle, I am mild, I am kindly. Didn't I establish an educational department? Didn't I the next year turn my factory over?" What has that to do with 1916? [The year the Tribune editorial appeared.]

Stevenson reminded the jury, that during his cross examination of Ford's expert, Bishop Williams, he brought Williams to admit that a condition of "practical anarchy" existed on the Mexican border because of the absence of a government force to govern, and that a man who actively undertakes to promote practical anarchy would be an anarchist, a "practical anarchist," but not in the philosophical sense. Quoting from the Williams testimony transcript, Stevenson posited the key question:

> Q. Now, then, supposing this situation is presented, that upon

> the border of Mexico, in Texas, there had continued for several months, I will put it, a state of anarchy such as I have described to you, and the President of the United States appealed to Congress . . . that he didn't have troops enough, even to protect the border . . . Mr. Ford started propaganda for the purpose of preventing the President and the government having that additional force, wouldn't that be anarchistic? Wouldn't he be an anarchist?

That question was never answered due to Judge Murphy's objection—it was merely an opinion. Stevenson, facing the jury, argued with heat,

> But, gentlemen, when I asked the question that brought it right home to Henry Ford, "Wasn't Henry Ford an anarchist when he did those things?" [Murphy said] "I object." He knew what the answer would be, because it could not be but one answer. Then they say that we have not shown that Henry Ford is an anarchist.

Stevenson turned to the Ford argument that Ford could not have been an anarchist because of his war work. Stevenson reminded the jury that the war work began in 1917, a year after the *Tribune* had called Henry Ford an anarchist. He noted Edsel Ford's testimony that but for accepting the war work, Ford's factories would have sat idle. Addressing Ford's record of philanthropy, Stevenson noted the passing of Andrew Carnegie the day before, who gave three hundred fifty million dollars to charity. By comparison, he said, "Ford is a piker," drawing general laughter in the courtroom.

In concluding his argument, Stevenson drew a comparison of the patriotism of Ford with that of Colonel McCormick and Captain Patterson. While Ford was discouraging men from enlisting, McCormick was out raising funds for machine guns to outfit his unit. Patterson joined the Illinois Guard as an enlisted man, currying officers' horses and digging trenches. They were both among the first one hundred thousand men to land in France with the American Expeditionary Force.

> [W]hen I asked this gentleman who drew this flag, whether there

> was any yellow in Henry Ford's flag, he did not remember, but you remember gentlemen, when you saw the flag there were two great streaks of yellow [actually gold] right through the center of it. But there was not any yellow on the flag that Colonel McCormick and Captain Patterson carried. They are soldiers of the country, proud of the fact, and they went and served their country; and now they [the Ford's] ask you, gentlemen of the jury, ask you to declare them libelous, sympathizers with Germany, disloyal. Why gentlemen, the truth shall be determined by their conduct.

Stevenson chastised Ford for his "insidious appeal" in trying to make the people think he was their friend, and that all other capitalists and rich men were bad. He compared Ford to Clement Valandingham and the Civil War "Copperheads" who actively opposed the war. He quoted Abraham Lincoln: "He who dissuades one man, one man from volunteering, or induces one man to desert, weakens the Union cause as much as he who kills a Union soldier in battle." Stevenson suggested that Edsel Ford's "slackening conduct" would likely be buried by subsequent alterations in the historic record and public relations.

Stevenson ended his closing argument with simple strength:

> Gentlemen of the jury, do justice between these men. Say to these men who were slackers, and who were disloyal, and who were untrue to their country, to accept a verdict of the jury; and find him properly characterized as an anarchist; and say to these young men who went forth to defend their country [pointing to McCormick and Patterson], you did well to serve your country; you shall not be characterized as being libelous.

ALFRED J. LUCKING, ESQ.

Following the noon recess, Alfred Lucking rose stiffly to the podium, his bald head glistening. Wearing a black cutaway coat of the fashion of a generation before, Lucking began by addressing "my friend's address." He described Stevenson's words as a "very powerful appeal to arouse the passions, and the prejudices and the partisanship" of the jury. He mentioned that the only prevention of Bolshevism in the country is the same kind of treatment by all employers toward their employees as exemplified by Henry Ford. He challenged Stevenson's remarks about Ford libeling others: "Mr. Ford has never called anyone a murderer." He said a Ford reference to Packard Motor Company President, Henry Joy, as an "apostle of murder" was merely calling him a "preacher of murder" for advocating war.[101] Lucking said, "I do not charge Mr. Stevenson with deliberately falsifying or misleading you. It is simply the excitement, the partisanship, the extravagance of the moment, that is all." Stressing the importance of the jury trial as a replacement for duels in resolution of conflict, Lucking said, "Why, Henry Ford and his friends would have taken their shotguns and they would have traveled to Chicago and required the libeler to pay the penalty."

Henry Ford, he stressed, placed Detroit on the map of the world, and his case was being watched all over the continent and beyond. He acknowledged a newspaper's right of fair comment, but argued that the question to be determined is whether they have "unbridled license to attack private citizens, or public citizens, for that matter." "The question of the right of private reputation and private character to have it, to keep it, to hold it free from attack, is in this case."

Lucking described the anarchist editorial as having been written "in cold blood" and placing Henry Ford on the same plane as the Haymarket bomber and the University Club poisoner in Chicago. He noted the *Tribune*'s hypocrisy in not paying wages to enlisted employees during their service in the Great War, when McCormick and Patterson continued to receive *Tribune* stipends. He argued that the *Tribune*, throughout 1916, knowing that "Germany was crazy to get us into a war with Mexico," kept advocating war with Mexico.

---

101. Ford and Joy crossed swords over "preparedness" in separate newspaper articles.

Addressing Klingensmith's testimony, Lucking said that if Klingensmith gave the *Tribune* misleading information, it was just that—misleading information, and that it wasn't surprising that Klingensmith's memory was hazy from some years ago. He insisted that Ford at all times planned to take their Guardsmen back and to assist their families during the Mexican campaign, and the fact that the *Tribune* failed to retract when Ford insisted they were mistaken was clear evidence of malice. He remarked that the stringer who reported to the *Tribune* knew that the *Tribune* was hostile to Ford and deliberately set out to gather information that would provide the powder to lambast him.

> Wiping the sweat from his forehead, Lucking turned to the question of Ford's ignorance. There are a million subjects of human knowledge, and no man can master more than one. On all others he is an ignoramus, and if he knows one well, and has a smattering of a few other things, he is a well posted man of this world, and no man has a right in public print to vilify him over the world by saying he's an ignoramus.

He asserted that Henry Ford had created one of the wonders of the world "in putting that great engine together and making it work like a human being; aye, a thousand times more precisely than it is possible for any human bring to work." And yet, like all men, Ford had limits. It troubled Lucking not a whit that "they denounce him as ignorant, before the world. Of course, he is, of certain facts; of most facts. So is everybody else."

Lowering his voice and adopting a more conversational tone, Lucking shared an anecdote regarding compartmentalized knowledge. He told the jury a story about John Marshall, the brilliant first Chief Justice of the United States Supreme Court, out riding in a horse and buggy one day. Marshall ran over a sapling that lodged between the buggy and wheel, impeding further progress. Marshall called to a farmer and asked him to find an ax and chop down the sapling. The farmer suggested that he just back up his horse some, which disengaged the sapling. When

Marshall left a dollar for the farmer with the proprietor of the local tavern, the farmer commented, "That fellow is a very fine man, but he is the biggest fool I ever saw in my life."

Lucking offered that the "Mexican border business is very greatly exaggerated." He noted that the border people who had taken the stand "threw a little slur on Mount Clemens" because of the expressed desire to return to the border as soon as possible, and that many of the witnesses had seen "just one particular raid." He chastised the *Tribune* for wanting the U.S. to seize Mexico, saying that Presidents Taft and Wilson felt it would ruin the American reputation to do it. "Grabbing territory is what caused this great war in Europe." He let that idea sink deeply into the jurists' hearts and minds. Then, Lucking offered Ford's more benevolent attitude toward Mexico, in training one hundred forty Mexican nationals "to carry back to Mexico the practical operation of the gospel of Henry Ford."

"There is not a scintilla of evidence that this man is an anarchist, not a scintilla," he argued. He reminded the jury that they had the word of Floyd Gibbons, the *Tribune*'s one eyed war correspondent, sworn to by himself, that there never was any necessity of calling the Guard out at all. "What remained in the heart of Henry Ford," Lucking said, "was war makes a man a wild beast – a savage." Lucking fully embraced the Christian references and comparisons by Bishop Williams, who had suggested that individualized statements by the "prince of peace," plucked out of context, could suggest an unmeant intent. Lucking continued:

> If some of the definitions that counsel produced here before you of anarchists are correct, they would include George Washington, John Adams, Thomas Jefferson, all of the signers of the Declaration of Independence, all the men who attended the Boston Tea Party, and thousands and thousands of patriots who fought against the established laws that had existed for a century and a half in this country, under the Control of England.

Finally arriving at the issue of damages, Lucking stated, "A small verdict is practically the same as a verdict for the defendant." He warmed his argument by degrees. "And I ask you, if you believe with us that this is a villainous libel, to punish them and punish this persistency, with which it has been shoved here on to you until the last minute by, proper and adequate damages."

Then, his face flushed, Lucking grabbed the lectern with white knuckles, eyeing each juror with intensity.

> Now, gentlemen, time is fleeting. They say, what was it June, 1916, not just what it was in February, 1917. Ah, gentlemen. If a man is an anarchist in June of this year, he is an anarchist, the next year just the same. The leopard does not change his spots, and the anarchist does not reverse his character. But, on the 15th day of September, 1915, one year before these articles, Mr. Ford said, "If any enemy attempts to come on our land, all that I have and all that I am is at the feet of the President."
>
> * * *
>
> [in 1917, just after the U.S. entered the War] He took the first train to Washington, and there in the center of our life and government, he laid at the feet of the President of the United States, all that he had, all his organization, all his plants and his time.

JURY INSTRUCTIONS

The morning of August 14, 1919, dawned under patchy clouds, in Mount Clemens, with intermittent rain storms. The air was close and humid. Of the dozens of litigators who served in the trial, Joseph Patterson was the only party present. Judge Tucker began reading his instructions to the jury, outlining the law of libel and its defenses. He told the jury that the *Tribune* publications in issue were libelous, *per se*, that is, on their face, without explanation. He made several findings regarding the evidence presented as a matter of law. He told the jury to ignore any claims of personal financial interest or pro-German sympathies made by Ford against the *Tribune*. Despite weeks of testimony on the subject, he told the jury to ignore the concept of "preparedness" as an issue, except as it reflected on the good faith of the *Tribune*.

Tucker advised the jury that the most common definition of *anarchist* was a "murderous, dangerous person; possibly a bomb thrower." He also read to them a number of other possible definitions including the "absence of government as a political ideal." The Judge told them that it was their exclusive providence to determine, in the circumstances, what was meant and what was understood by the reader in the publication. He instructed them on the defense of "fair comment" as an expression of the writer's real ideals and honesty as a writer.

On damages, the Judge told the jury that only "general damages" would be allowed because there was no proof of special damages. He said the jury could add to the damages a factor for malice, if they thought malice was present in the publication. He told them to apply "your own hard-headed sense of damages," if any, to Ford's feelings and reputation. If they found that the *Tribune's* publications were made in "good faith," he said, "you may reduce damages in your good judgment."

THE JURY SPEAKS

The jury entered the jury room at 9:55 a.m. and arrived at a verdict just ten hours later. There was a large crowd outside the courtroom together with a band returning from a picnic. In the echo of fiddle tunings and the wash of a mid-August sunset, the jury took its seat. Rows of attorneys, a phalanx of sweating journalists and a smattering of patient spectators held their breaths in the sultry, close courtroom.

Orvey Hulett, the jury foreman, read the verdict in a low, nervous voice. "We find the *Chicago Tribune* guilty and attach a verdict of six cents." The crowd burst out of the courtroom to where the crowd cheered and the brass instruments from the picnic band rang forth. Attorneys for both sides seemed stunned. Quickly recovering, they all declared victory and vindication.

The verdict had been a compromise verdict. This group of twelve men, with differing views, did not want the months spent in the courtroom to go for naught in a hung jury. Col. McCormick sent an investigator, C.D. Hagerty, to interview each of the jurors after the verdict. None of the jurors thought Ford was an anarchist, and most bought into the "Ford is a good man argument." If it were Delavigne on trial, they said, they would have pasted him. Even though Ford accepted responsibility for his writings, they did attribute to him the acid of Delavinge's writings. None of the witnesses thought that the Texas witnesses were essential to the outcome. Most thought Ford's "'teachings,' but not the man" were anarchistic. A strong minority thought him a fool.

The jury had high praise for Judge Murphy, Alfred Lucking, and Waymouth Kirkland but were strangely silent about Elliott Stevenson. Col. McCormick and Captain Patterson impressed the jury as being nice, straight up men. They thought that Ford had not been particularly harmed by the *Tribune* publication and thought that Ford's lawyers made a mistake in initiating the litigation. The compromise verdict was intended as a "gentle warning" to the *Tribune* to be more careful. Several jurors seemed totally at sea, with little or no understanding of what they heard or what they did in response.

Henry Ford, much like those jurors, did not seem to fully appreciate what had happened to him. While the jury was out, Ford and his fellow campers had stopped for lunch in Hartford, Connecticut, where he was interviewed by the press. Awash with the energy that comes of proximity to nature and good company, Ford said that he had not heard anything about the trial for a week. He said, "I am no anarchist and they will see if I am ignorant." When asked about his cross examination by Elliott Stevenson, he answered, "He said he would keep me on the stand for five days, when he thought he would make me read, but you noticed I didn't, didn't you."

THE PRESS REACTION

The press reaction to the verdict was swift and uncharitable.

The Salina Daily Union: "No one believes that Henry Ford is disloyal or ever was, but his conduct during the early days of our trouble with Germany certainly did arouse our suspicion. Our opinion has been that the man was notoriety crazed. He thirsted for publicity and did everything his hired men could think of to get into print. The *Tribune* performed a public service in unmasking him."

The *Great Falls Tribune*: "Perhaps the most useful lesson to be derived from this long trial is the folly of going to court to obtain a financial plaster for rudely wounded feelings. Henry Ford and his six cents of damages further accentuates a truth that many a plaintiff in libel suits has learned before him."

The *Leavenworth Times*: "At this distance, it looks like a victory for the Chicago paper. The trial certainly showed Ford up in a very unenviable light."

The *Daily Gate City and Constitution Democrat* (Keokuk, Iowa): "Henry Ford as a witness made a sorry appearance. How simple minded he is and how flatterers have worked him, his testimony showed; and the question arises in some minds if lawyers, who had his true interests at heart would have advised him to bring action against the Chicago newspaper. They knew, as he did not, what an ordeal he would have to pass upon the witness stand. They realized, as he did not, how ill-equipped he was to meet it, how his testimony would be read throughout the land and how the revelations of his intellectual limitations would mortify him all through life."

The *Albuquerque Journal*: "It is doubtful if Mr. Ford's reputation was damaged appreciably by the *Tribune's* charge. But there is no doubt that it suffered seriously during the trial through his own admissions on the witness stand."

And, lastly, an opinion which resonates in our day, with the difficulties of a President trained in business only, facing the lack of transferability of skills honed in the private sector to the complex needs of effective governance.

The *San Bernardino County Sun*: "Mr. Ford's success in business does not imply the ability to handle the work of government well. A man can make a fortune in business, but may be abysmally ignorant of things which are essential to success in government. No doubt the majority of business men are generally well informed, yet the fact remains that their brains are developed along the channels leading to success in business and may be totally undeveloped or only slightly developed, along the channels which lead to successful public administration or legislation."

THE COMMON MAN HERO

Despite Henry Ford's broad decline in the esteem of newspaper editorial writers, he remained remarkably and tenaciously popular among his base support in the rural Midwest, the West and the South, where regardless of his experiential and educational deficiencies, his fans revered him as a straight talker, a truth teller—isolated by his enormous wealth from the need of maintaining political correctness or to kowtow to the Eastern financial elite. Historian, David L. Lewis, ascribed Ford's "real genius" in maintaining free personal media coverage to a two-pronged formula which seems to have resurfaced in American politics today: first, do things that nobody else does, which makes news, and second, do familiar things in unfamiliar ways.[102] There were those who objected to Ford's potential candidacy for the presidency because they felt that he was already too powerful and would have difficulty separating his political interests from his personal economic interests. "Ford could openly do business and conduct politics. He would have the best of both worlds. When he sold a car, he sold himself, when he sold himself, he would sell a car."[103]

FORD'S REACTION

Yet, the verdict, and the press reaction to the verdict, cut Ford

---

102. Lewis, David L., *The Public Image of Henry Ford: An American Fold Hero and His Company*, Wayne State University Press, Detroit, (1976), p.217.

103. Wik, Reynold M., *Henry Ford and Grass Roots America*, University of Michigan Press, Ann Arbor, (1972), pp. 176-177.

to the quick. The award of six cents slapped him in the solar plexus. The press pummeled him on all sides. This very public beating triggered, within Ford, two widely different reactions. The positive reaction gave rise to Ford's enormously generous contribution to understanding American cultural history and industrial development—the Edison Institute, which was later renamed the Henry Ford Museum and Greenfield Village in Dearborn, Michigan. The second and very negative reaction led Ford into a closed tunnel of isolated paranoia, where his worst instincts could sprout and grow like weeds. His darkest impulses fed off events in the courtroom. He swore to his associates that he would never again submit himself to humiliation in a courtroom. He would wall himself from any invasion of his privacy that he did not invite.

The Ford Motor Company continued to prosper between 1920 and 1926, selling half of the automobiles and trucks made in the United States. During the 1920s, Henry Ford received more personal publicity than any man in the United States, except Calvin Coolidge, who succeeded Harding to the presidency after Harding died in a San Francisco Hotel, in August, 1923. In a Spring, 1923 pre-presidential poll by *Collier's* magazine, Ford led all candidates, including then President Warren G. Harding, who was unable to muster support from a majority of his own party. While Ford declined to publicly rule out a presidential bid, the death of Harding and the rising popularity of the "Sphinx of Northhampton," he elected to endorse Coolidge in December, 1923, after Coolidge hinted to him that he would support Ford's efforts to acquire the Muscle Shoals dam and nitrate plant[104] owned by the government on the Tennessee River in Northern Alabama.

---

104. The government built Muscle Shoals dam and nitrate plant during World War I to produce nitrate for munitions and also fertilizer. Congress, led by Senator George Norris of Nebraska, rejected Ford's bid as being too low.

Part IV

Sapiro vs. The Dearborn Publishing Company ET AL.

CHAPTER 15

Farmer Wars

BIGOTRY

HENRY FORD WAS AN anti-Semitic bigot. He didn't hate individual Jews. He had friends who were Jews like his one-time neighbor Leo M. Franklin, a rabbi who he sometimes stopped to visit on his way to his factory in Highland Park, Michigan. He had business associates who were Jews, like famed Michigan architect Albert Kahn, who designed many of Ford's factories and the Gaukler Point home of his son, Edsel, in Grosse Pointe. He was genuinely surprised when they began to withdraw from him. He did hate the concept of Jewry, as he perceived it. He hated the urban, unassimilated, foreign, money-grabbing, power-wielding concept of the race that he saw as fundamentally responsible for all of the world's ills. He considered many Gentiles in the banking and finance world as "Jews"—people who never farmed or worked with their hands, but prospered from the hard work and creative ingenuity of others.

Ford was not alone. High levels of anger, fear, and distrust welcomed the massive immigration of European and Russian Jews into the urban centers of the United States in the last quarter of the nineteenth century. The social and economic unrest generated by the International Workers of the World (I.W.W. or "Wobblies") and other unions, who were constantly agitating for better working conditions and higher pay, was often laid at the feet of Jewish leadership. Henry Ford, for all of his contributions to the urbanization of America, always saw himself as a farmer and friend and protector of farmers. He had a profound dislike of Wall Street and fervently stressed the virtues of rural life. He built things with practical uses and heartily endorsed "honest labor" as opposed to what he perceived to be the parasitic enterprises of banks and Jews.

Ford's distrust of Jewish abilities seemed to rise from his personal bank of faults. Determinably anti-intellectual, Ford managed his keen inability to articulate his thoughts through the presence of a circle of secretaries and employees to serve as his "interpreters." Ford consigliere, Harry H. Bennett, described Ford's principle talent as excellence in the judgment of the technical aptitude of other men. Ford flourished in the realm of the mechanical. He was insensitive to the impact of words of hatred and condemnation on the feelings and lives of others.

REBIRTH OF HATRED

On August 16, 1915 at 10:00 p.m., on a sweltering Georgia night, an organized group of twenty-eight men broke into a penitentiary at Milledgeville, Georgia, handcuffed the warden and forcibly removed a thin, thirty-one-year-old, Ivy League-educated, New York Jew. They pulled him from his cell dressed only in a night shirt. They led him to a caravan of seven cars that slowly made its way to Marietta, Georgia at a top speed of eighteen miles an hour. The terrified young man maintained his dignity as best he could until his arrival in Marietta. The caravan, on reaching Marietta, pulled up to a large oak tree with a table below. The assembled gentry of Marietta pulled Leo M. Frank from one of the automobiles, threw a rope with a noose over an arm of the tree, stood Frank on the table with his neck placed in the noose and kicked away the table, leaving Frank swinging and gasping for air. They had wrapped his legs in a blanket to protect his privacy.

Those present included a judge, a former governor, several lawyers, a U.S. Senator's son, a state legislator and several local business leaders. They described themselves as the "Knights of Mary Phagan." A local jury had convicted Leo Frank of the murder and sexual assault of thirteen-year-old Mary Phagan, who worked for Frank as a laborer in a Jewish-owned pencil factory. The jury convicted Frank based on thin and highly questionable evidence, some of it provided by a black janitor, who many now identify as the probable perpetrator. The Georgia Governor, George M. Slayton, convinced of the questionable nature of Frank's conviction, in an act of unusual political courage, commuted Frank's sentence from death by hanging to life imprisonment.

Newt Morris, the Judge present, stepped forward to prevent the crowd from mutilating Frank's body, telling them "whatever sin the living Frank committed, he has a mother and a father—have mercy on him." A bystander, Robert E. Lee Howell, repeatedly stepped on Frank's face after they cut him down. They drove Frank's body to Atlanta in a Ford Model T. Fifteen thousand people gathered in Atlanta to view Frank's body. J. G. Woodward, the Mayor of Atlanta, remarked, "When it comes to a woman's honor, there is no limit to which we will not go to avenge and protect it."

The execution of Leo Frank was the first and only lynching of a Jew in America. It sent shock waves through the Jewish community in the South and the Northeast in particular, sparking a migration of Jews from the South. Half of Georgia's population of three thousand Jews moved elsewhere following the lynching. The condemnation of the lynching in Northeastern newspapers drew hostile and angry responses in the South and other parts of rural America. Then came the movie that lit an explosive fuse of barely latent tribalism and resentment among white, Protestant Americans.

A galloping troop of "Christian crusaders," furiously driving their pounding chargers through the southern countryside made an electrifying and heart-thumping spectacle. Their cross escutcheons were emblazoned on their chests and their steeds' caparisons. The white hoods of the knights and their garments flapped in the wind as they pounded in unison to the rescue of

Dr. Cameron, the "kindly master of Cameron Hall," and his wife and daughter who were holed up in a rickety cabin, fighting off a hoard of Black Reconstructionists laying assault and siege to the building and bent on their destruction. The music and imagery of D.W. Griffith's *Birth of a Nation* had a deep and lasting impact on the culture and politics of the United States in 1915.

The movie spurred a rebirth of the Klu Klux Klan that year at Stone Mountain, Georgia, an event that included members of the Knights of Mary Phagan. It kindled a blaze of rural populism to rescue America from the perils of European immigration and the threat of papist and Jewish religious beliefs. Secret societies like the Masons, the Knights Templar, and the Knights of Pythias flourished, as did the Klan, whose reach permeated all of rural America, not just the South. Bolshevism and Socialism, which were then taking root in Russia and parts of Europe, were wrongly identified as products of the Jewish elite due to the prominent involvement of several highly visible Jews like Leon Trotsky (Lev Davidovich Bronstein). These systems enraged the sensibilities of Klansmen nationwide. Michigan, Henry Ford's own state, developed one of the largest contingents of the Klan in the Country, amassing a staggering eighty-five thousand members by 1920.[105] The inflammatory rhetoric of reactionary American populism surged between 1915 and 1925.

In 1919, a number of industrial strikes showed American labor unions flexing their muscles, but these strikes were forcefully suppressed in the context of widespread fear of communist infiltration of American industry after the October, 1917, Bolshevik Revolution. The 1920s in America were characterized by a widening middle class, urban prosperity, a resurgence of "America First" Nativism, anti-immigrant fever, and a wide-spread hostility toward Communist activism, thought to be sponsored in large part by Jewish interests. Almost half of the country lived in rural

105. An interesting Michigan statute took a great deal of the mystery out of the Klan. It was illegal in Michigan to wear a mask unless you were going to a party.

areas and were dependent, one way or another, on agricultural production for their livelihoods. These livelihoods were in serious jeopardy due to the European agricultural resurgence after World War I; American farmers (who had planted gigantic numbers of crops for the world's wartime needs) suffered price drops and a rise in land prices—"thank yous" for their hard work, which drove many farms into bankruptcy. Recessions fuel resentment and desperate social movements.

At the same time, in the cities, Jacksonianism or Jacksonian Democracy enjoyed a widespread resurgence: antipathy toward banking institutions and the resistance to what was thought to be the political dominance of a greedy and privileged minority, non-producing middlemen, brokers, agents and corporate owners. The "New Jacksonians" saw themselves as an oppressed majority of white males who were left behind and excluded from the larger prosperity of the country, victimized by foreign immigrants who took jobs and subverted the security of the country with ill-considered and dangerous foreign, communist and socialistic economic ideas. They were eager to be protected and rescued by the Knights of the Klu Klux Klan.

The Klu Klux Klan gladly inherited the mantel of extreme middle class Protestant political and social movements. In 1924, John Moffatt Mecklin, a Professor of Sociology at Dartmouth College, published a highly readable and insightful analysis of the rebirth of the Klu Klux Klan that remains relevant today.[106] The Klan, he noted, "makes a powerful appeal to the petty impotence of the small-town mind." Mecklin claims that it was "simply impossible to estimate the 'educative effect' of the 'film masterpiece,' the *Birth of a Nation*, upon public sentiment."[107]

Henry Ford and his populist and exclusionary "America First" agenda provided a disturbing parallel of interest between himself

106. *The Klu Klux Klan: A study of the American Mind*, Harcourt Brace & CO, N.Y., 1924.

107. Mecklin, supra, at 121.

and the Klan. A commentary by a Michigan newspaper reporter describing an outdoor KKK initiation near Clawson, Michigan, strikes the mood of the times.

> "Henry Ford for President!" shouted a stentorian voice. "Hurrah!" from the throats of a thousand or more . . . white clad members, like ghosts in the twilight, were on guard entirely round the woods from the roadway (as close as your correspondent could get) the hooded forms, moving among the trees, presented a unique spectacle. . .. Some of the speakers blessed with powerful voices, could be heard . . . more than a mile away. The reflection of the fiery cross could also be seen for miles and attracted many to the vicinity, and they enjoyed a splendid display of fireworks."[108]

Mecklin tracks the widespread popularity of Griffith's movie, which he calls "essentially a small-town amusement:"

> [I]n the Ford, the small townsman's means of locomotion, in revivals, the small town's type of religion; in Fundamentalism, small town theology, and in the enthusiastic reception of Mr. Bryan's[109] denunciation of evolution, which fits the small town's idea of science.[110]

Victoria Saker Woeste, in her epic study, *Henry Ford's War on the Jews and the Legal Battle Against Hate speech,* agrees. "The family farm, the one-room school house, and racial and ethnic homogeneity all dovetailed with a profoundly conservative and Christian fundamentalism."[111]

Enter a man to lead the charge, Henry Ford.

---

108. Quoted in Fox, Craig, *Everyday Klansfolk: White Protestant Life and the KKK in 1920s Michigan*, Michigan State University Press, East Lansing, 2011 at 10.

109. William Jennings Bryan.

110. Mecklin, supra, at 220-221.

111. Stanford University Press, Palo Alto, (2012).

PRESIDENT BY ACCLIMATION?

Henry Ford, still licking his wounds from the *Chicago Tribune* trial, still harbored an interest in attaining the Presidency in 1924. Ford gladly turned the sights of his newly acquired newspaper, *The Dearborn Independent,* to mining his identification and solidarity with the rural Protestant mindset—populism gold. He chose a very easy target. He would fund an attack on the Jews. Ford had earlier planned an attack on the Jews as part of his ill-fated 1918 U.S. Senate campaign, but his advisors talked him out of it. Chastened by the close loss of the Senate seat, Ford would follow his own instincts in future political forays. In this effort, he was enthusiastically supported by his personal secretary, Ernest G. Liebold. Former *Detroit News* and *The Dearborn Independent* editor E. G. Pipp remarked, "And no one more ruthlessly executed Ford's anti-Semitic directives, because no one at the Company, perhaps even the boss, hated Jews more than Liebold did."[112] On another occasion Pipp offered that "the door to the Ford mind was always open to anything Liebold wanted to shove into it."[113]

Ford urged his unofficial campaign manager and newly appointed *The Dearborn Independent* editor, E.G. Pipp, to get on board Ford's "southern strategy" of anti-Semitism. Ford announced, "You fellows are afraid to print those attacks on the Jews. Now I want them printed and I will take the full responsibility." Pipp later wrote that "the campaign was carried on, not only with Ford's approval but by his orders."[114] Pipp stressed,

> When Ford launched the attack on the Jews he was a candidate for the Presidency of the United States, firmly so in his own mind. He figured that the prejudice in the small communities

---

112. E.G.Pipp, "Ford's Recantation Analyzed," *The American Hebrew*, July 15, 1927 ("Pipp II"), at 347.

113. Baldwin, Neil, *Henry Ford and the Mass Production of Hate*, Public Affairs, N.Y., 2001, at 95.

114. Ibid.

> throughout the United States was so strong that he would gain three, four or five votes there for every Jewish vote that he lost.[115]

Ford was not so much running for the Presidency as he hoped to be appointed by popular acclaim. He held himself out as a practical businessman who could get things done. In a 1923 interview, Henry Ford stated,

> I can't image myself today accepting any nomination. Of course, I can't say what I will do tomorrow. There might be a war or some crisis of the sort, in which legalism and constitutionalism and all that wouldn't figure, and the nation wanted some person, who could do things and do them quickly.[116]

During the 1920s, Ford received more publicity than any other American, except Calvin Coolidge.[117] Ford reveled in the limelight, and in the populist propaganda he was able to disseminate in his own newspaper. According to Pipp, newspaper coverage linked with Ford's name as the "greatest" was "meat and drink to him."[118] There were, of course, unflattering books published by people who knew him closely, like Samuel Marquis and E.G. Pipp. These books were not broadly available because of an active campaign by Ford to buy up available copies and destroy them.[119]

E.G. Pipp resigned from *The Dearborn Independent* in April, 1920, on the cusp of Ford's attack on the Jews. Taking over as chief editor and anti-Semitic coordinator was William John Cameron, a portly man adorned with wire-rimmed spectacles, who looked and sounded like W.C. Fields, who shared Fields' personal taste for the liquid product of fermented grain mash. Cameron belonged to a British religious sect that claimed that Anglo-Saxons,

115. Id.

116. Berlet, Chris and Lyons, Mathew, *Right Wing Populism in America: To Close for Comfort*. The Guilford Press, N.Y. & London. (2000), at 110.

117. Lewis, Supra at 189.

118. Pipp II, supra, at 347

119. Id.

one of the lost tribes of Israel, were granted special status and favored by God. Cameron served as the first President of the Anglo-Saxon Federation of America, which published the magazine *Destiny* with a heavily anti-Semitic focus.

Ford charged Cameron with the duty of conjuring up the shrapnel for his anti-Semitic fusillade. In describing Cameron, Pipp said, "He was never so strong on original thoughts as in molding over material furnished to him." "Cameron," he stated, "is ready to place his mind at the disposal of another, take the ideas of another and express them." An ideal match for Ford.

Assisting Cameron with his editorial duties and serving as business manager of the *Independent* was Fred L. Black. An engaging, extroverted showman, Black helped Ford find and acquire an 1890 printing press from *Franklin Press*, which Ford installed in his tractor factory at the River Rouge Plant to print *The Dearborn Independent*. Black reported directly to Ernest G. Liebold, who served as the overall manager of the paper. Liebold assigned Black to investigate and communicate with the various "Ford for President Clubs" that were springing up around the country. Henry Ford didn't finance these clubs, but he was acutely interested in knowing who his supporters were. While never officially campaigning for the Presidency, Ford did tell Black, "I'd like to be down there [in Washington, D.C.] about six weeks to throw monkey wrenches into the machinery."[120]

With his next media move, Ford threw a wrench of immense proportions into the spokes of his own wheels.

THE PROTOCOLS

Henry Ford "developed a kind of right-wing populist politics without a mass movement political organization."[121] He let "the

---

120. Byron, Ford R., *Henry's Lieutenants*, Wayne State University Press, Detroit (1993), p. 39.

121. Berlet and Lyons, supra, at 105.

news" be his rally point. The first round of his anti-Semitic onslaught involved printing a fake story: the alleged minutes of meetings held by an international Jewish conspiracy to achieve world domination and the enslavement of Gentiles. Ford published these "minutes" serially in the *Independent* as *The Protocols of the Elders of Zion.* Boris Brasol, an exiled Russian monarchist, who immigrated to the United States following the Russian Revolution, provided a Ford agent with a copy of the manuscript which Brasol had arranged to have translated into English. The *Protocols* were purported to have been stolen from a secret Jewish organization at the heart of the conspiracy.

Sergei Nilus, a Russian mystic and theologian, published the first full copy of the *Protocols* in 1905 as the last chapter of his book, *The Great Within the Small & Antichrist.* The *Protocol*s advance 24 rules that are supposedly embraced by the Jewish people and "their enslaved sycophants," the Freemasons, for world domination. The *Protocols* were widely distributed among Russian White Army Officers, who were battling Red Army Bolsheviks for control of the country, to provide propaganda to discredit Jewish-identified elements among the Bolsheviks. Leon Trotsky takes center stage as Jewish scapegoat for both the Russian loss in the Russo-Japanese war and the Russian Revolution of 1905.

In the spring of 1920, *The Dearborn Independent* began its campaign with the weekly publication of a series of Anti-Semitic articles that went on for ninety-one issues. Rural readers gobbled them up. Each chronicled a major story of alleged Jewish evil doing, including the *Protocols,* all under the rubric of *The International Jew: The World's Problem.* The Jewish invasion of American agriculture, argued the *Independent*, had been prophesied many years earlier in the *Protocols:*

> We shall soon begin to establish huge monopolies, colossal reservoirs of wealth, upon which even the big Gentile properties will be dependent.... that the true situation shall not be noticed by the Gentiles prematurely we will mask it by a pretended ef-

> fort to serve the working classes.[122]

The *Protocols* zeroed in on the control of the world's supply of money as the weapon of choice in obtaining world domination for the Jews.

> A government finding itself under the influence of internal upheavals, one that is at the mercy of external enemies, because of the disordered conditions of its own land, must undoubtedly be consigned to oblivion. The control of it is in our power. The dominance of money, over which we alone dispose, extends a straw to the government that it must grasp for good or ill if it wants to keep from sinking into the abyss.[123]

Henry Ford, as a rigid teetotaler and inveterate supporter of Prohibition, completely identified with the *Protocols* connection of Jews with the spread of alcohol and bootlegging.

> Observe the drunkards, befogged by alcohol. They believe themselves to possess the right to unlimited pleasure which they confuse with the concept of freedom. The non-Jewish peoples are befogged with alcohol; their youths are infatuated with humanism and premature vices. To these they have been led by our agents, administrators, teachers, servants and, governesses to the rich as well as by our women in pleasure resorts and public houses.[124]

The *Protocols* struck such a chord in the imaginations of the *Independent's* readers. Ernest G. Liebold arranged for their assembly into pamphlets, hoping to gain a much wider audience. He also reprinted them in a four-volume set. Volume I, entitled *The International Jew: The World's Foremost Problem,* plumbs Jewish ties to Bolshevism, Jewish imperialism, Jewish character, farms, the

---

122. The sixth protocol, quoted by Baldwin, supra, at 127.

123. Segel, Binjamin W., *A lie and A Libel: The History of the Protocols of the Elders of Zion,* The University of Nebraska Press, Lincoln & London, 1995; Levy, Richard, translator and editor, 1995 at 132.

124. Id at 135.

"Jewish question," and Jewish political power. Volume II, *Jewish Activities in the United States* (1921), details Jewish money and power, Jewish control of the theater and movie industries, and the clash of Jewish rights with American rights. Volume III, entitled *Jewish Influence in American Life* (1921), relates the Jewish degradation of baseball, Zionism and Armageddon, Jewish hotheads of Bolshevism in the United States, the rise of jazz as "Jewish music," and the high level of Jewish involvement in American monetary affairs. Volume IV, *Aspects of Jewish Power in the United States* (1922), purports to outline Jewish involvement in the "Liquor Trust" and in "bootlegging" and, ironically,[125] the involvement of Jewish associates of Benedict Arnold in the commission of treason against the United States.

The International Jew was never copyrighted and was widely republished around the world in many different languages. In Nazi Germany, it went through six editions, and in many circles, it was required reading. Jewish leaders in the United States were appalled by the publications but largely uncertain and divided as to how to respond to them or stop the onslaught.

In 1921, Philip Graves, the elder half-brother of the writer Robert Graves, set the record straight. While serving as the Constantinople correspondent for *The Times of London,* Graves thoroughly discredited the *Protocols* as a complete fabrication. He published a series of articles in the *Times,* from August 16 to August 18, identifying the *Protocol*s as a "clumsy plagiarism" going back to the reign of Napoleon III in France. The originator, lawyer Maurice Joly, wrote a politically inflammatory satire[126] about an imagined discussion between political philosophers Machiavelli and Montesquieu to criticize Napoleon's autocratic regime. Published anonymously in Brussels in 1865, the book was smuggled into France

---

125. Ford could only identify Benedict Arnold as a "writer" while on the witness stand in the *Ford v. Chicago Tribune* trial.

126. *Dialogue aux Enfers entre Machiavel et Montesquieu, ou la Politique de Machiavel au XIX.* Siecle.

and instantly seized by police, landing Joly in jail in short order.

Graves demonstrated that the dialogues correspond neatly with the protocols published by Nilus, the self-proclaimed Russian mystic. Fifty pages in, the *Protocols* are direct paraphrases of the passages in the *Dialogue*. The initial publication of the *Protocols* is said to have been sponsored by the Tsarist secret police, the Okhrona, for use as propaganda in the monarchist efforts to suppress the Russian Revolution of 1905 and were widely applauded by Russian conservatives seeking to resist constitutional demands by "red" revolutionaries. Said Graves,

> They *[Protocols]* have done harm, not so much, in the writer's opinion, by arousing anti-Jewish feeling, which is older than the protocols and will persist in all countries where there is a Jewish problem until that problem is solved, rather, they have done harm by persuading all sorts of mostly well-to-do people that every recent manifestation of discontent on the part of the poor is an unnatural phenomenon, a factitious agitation caused by a secret society of Jews.[127]

This debunking by the *Times* carried little weight. Copies of Nilus' book flooded Europe, spread by Russian expats, and then jumped the Atlantic to influence thought in the United States. Despite Graves' overwhelming evidence of plagiarism, Henry Ford and his personal secretary, Ernest G. Liebold, firmly backed the authenticity of the *Protocols*. Liebold responded to press inquiries regarding them:

> If the *Protocols* had not been authentic, we would never have published them. We took the *Protocols* at their face value of what the *Protocols* say is what happened. That's all we tried to do. In the various activities [the Jews] performed, we could show a definite trend or definite instance of the actual things as set forth in the *Protocols* and where they took place.[128]

---

127. "The Protocol Forgery," *The Times of London,* Aug. 18, 1921, at 9 and 10.

128. Baldwin, supra, at 141.

Henry Ford personally endorsed the legitimacy of the *Protocols*. "They fit with what is going on. They are sixteen years old, and they have fitted the world's situation up to this time. They fit it now."[129]

AARON SAPIRO AND THE CALIFORNIA COOPERATIVES

Emboldened by the positive rural public reaction to his anti-Semitic campaign, Ford directed the *Independent* to focus its fire on Jewish involvement in agriculture. Since the Middle Ages, Jews have been by statute, rule, or practice excluded from participation in the agricultural segment of economic life, primarily in Europe but also in the United States. They were not precluded from the buying and selling of agricultural products in the market place. Serving as "middlemen" and brokers in the sale and marketing of agricultural products, they did little to endear them to the vast majority of farmers, who felt ripped off by middlemen who made agricultural profits without actually turning a spade in the soil.

As we've seen, farmers were being squeezed hard by postwar recession a decade before the financial markets crashed. Farmers felt victimized by both the railroads, which they felt charged extortionate fees to move their crops, and by the Wall Street bankers and money lenders who held mortgages on their land and were ever-pressing for payment. Behind them all, thanks in no small part to the "secret plans" revealed in the *Protocols*, farmers saw worldwide Jewish interests pulling the strings and thriving off the sweat, toil and risks undertaken by American farmers and workers.

Henry Ford felt particular concern about the Jewish infiltration of agricultural and commodity markets. Farmers formed the core of his political base, and he knew how to push their buttons. Ford wanted to sharply focus attention on the involvement of a rising young Jewish lawyer from San Francisco, Aaron Sapiro, who made a name for himself developing the so-called "California" or "Sapiro" plan for using specific commodity-based coop-

129. Id at 160.

erative organizations to market agricultural products and reduce destructive competitive infighting among farmers. Sapiro's plan eliminated the role of brokers and middlemen in bringing product to market. The basic idea was to use modern business methods to maintain a fair price level for a given commodity–corn, wheat, rice, raisins, tobacco, sheep, avocados, soybeans, hogs, or what have you. This was to be accomplished, essentially, by creating an effective monopoly for each particular commodity.

Sapiro's plan was ingenious but rigid in its requirements. To maintain discipline, farmers had to sign a long-term, five-year contract to deliver all of their commodity to the cooperative, with strict penalties for non-compliance. They would receive partial payment upon delivery of their product, and the rest over time as the cooperative managed the resale of the commodity. Membership cooperatives would finance their purchase of the commodities through warehouse receipts provided to banks. The cooperatives would negotiate sales of the commodity directly to millers, manufactures, exporters, and retailers, with a minimal storage expense, and the ability to cut out the middle-guy brokers who could play one farmer against another in price negotiations.

The idea relied on sales being evened out and spread over a year or so—to avoid price plunges from seasonal spikes in supply and plunges in demand. Central to the "California Plan" was quality maintenance, fair grading, dumping prevention, and above all, discipline. It did not always go according to plan. Political infighting, corruption, and general farmer contrarianism and suspicion led to the collapse and failure of some of the cooperatives. Maintaining obedience among the troops was always a problem and the enforcement of sanctions often led to hostile pushback against the Sapiro concept.

Aaron Sapiro, the son of poor Jewish immigrants, had risen to prominence in the Bay Area by gaining a law degree and then a position on the California markets board staff. In the 1920s, Sapiro became an evangelist of cooperative agriculture, giving inspiring speeches with a revivalist fervor all across the country. An organizational firebrand, he helped found the National Council of Farmer's Cooperative Marketing Associations. Sapiro, at his peak, came to represent more than sixty cooperative commodity associations which generated yearly market revenues in excess of four hundred million dollars.[130] He developed a staff of lawyers working for him in major cities across the United States, New York, Washington, D.C., Dallas, Chicago, and San Francisco. Sapiro and his lawyers drafted many model state statutes, explicitly permitting and supporting the growth of agricultural cooperatives.[131] He and his colleagues successfully defended his cooperatives in state and federal courts, including his one-time appearance before the United States Supreme Court.[132]

In that case, Liberty Warehouse appealed the imposition of a fine of five hundred dollars issued under the State of Kentucky's *Bingham Cooperative Marketing Act* for soliciting one Mike Kielman to breach his agreement with Burley Tobacco Association by selling his tobacco product directly to Liberty and not through the cooperative. The Kentucky statute declared that farmer cooperative marketing was in the public interest and not an illegal conspiracy, combination or monopoly. The Supreme Court justices, noting that forty-two states had passed similar statutes and that the Congress of the United States confirmed the utility of agricultural cooperatives in the Clayton Antitrust Act and The Cooperative Marketing Act of 1926, found that the statute did not violate any federal interest of liberty. Aaron Sapiro and his partner, Robert S. Marx of Cincinnati, represented Burley.

Sapiro was an intense presence with dark brown eyes and a zealous, passionate demeanor. He presented a compelling story. His father had died in a train/wagon accident when he was young, and because his mother was unable to support him, Sapiro grew up in an orphanage in San Francisco. He was ambitious and

---

130. Baldwin, supra, at 206.

131. Also, to insulate cooperatives to concerns about antitrust law exposure.

132. *Liberty Warehouse Co. v. Burley Tobacco Association*, 276 U.S. 71 (1928).

smart. He trained early to become a rabbi at the Hebrew Union College in Cincinnati, Ohio. He graduated Phi Beta Kappa in 1908 and later gained a master's degree in history. Still later, he studied law at the University of California Hastings College of the Law, where he graduated at the top of his class in 1911. While giving his class's commencement address, he attracted the attention of progressive California Governor Hiram Johnson, who had an interest in agricultural reform. In 1915, the California legislature, with Johnson's support, created the California State Commission Market, a vehicle for organizing marketing cooperatives for California farmers. The Commission hired Sapiro and the law firm he formed to serve as the Commission's attorneys.

Sapiro excelled at this groundbreaking work. He developed the so-called "California Plan" to pursue farmer organization by commodity. Initially, Sapiro benefitted with a substantial income from an area of the practice of law which he had largely invented. But at the onset of World War I, the government froze food prices for the duration of the war, offsetting the need for the cooperatives. Sapiro then shifted his focus. Sensitive to the lack of patriotism frequently ascribed to Jews, he repeatedly attempted to enlist in the Army as an officer, but was rejected for color blindness. Sapiro finally enlisted as a private in a field artillery unit in June, 1918. He was discharged following the Armistice in November, 1918.

Returning to agricultural marketing, Sapiro rose in the cooperative movement by grim determination and grit. He pursued his goals aggressively and found it difficult to broach resistance and opposition. Psychologically, he found it hard to negotiate or compromise. He could be insecure, rigid and intense. Gutting it out, he became a highly connected and visible figure across the country.

Following the war, American farmers tended to continue to magnify production, a strategic mistake which hurt their own cause. They also grew weary of the contractual constraints imposed by the cooperatives. By 1924, Sapiro and his cooperatives were already feeling significant negative pressure, when Henry

Ford decided to hold the prominent lawyer up as a sort of Jewish piñata—to be broken by outrageous stories pointed at him in *The Dearborn Independent.*

"DUNNING" SAPIRO

Starting in late April, 1924, Henry Ford released a barrage of anti-Sapiro articles in the *Independent* designed to chasten Sapiro and to bring him to his knees. In focusing its attack on Sapiro, the *Independent* enlisted the support and contributions of Harry H. Dunn, a former semi-pro baseball player and marginal journalist from Berkeley, California, who was more than happy to cobble together a series of racially antagonistic and factually disturbing articles disparaging Sapiro. Dunn and the *Independent* decided to publish the articles under the *nom de guerre*, Robert Morgan, rather than Dunn's real name. The *Independent* commenced its campaign against Sapiro with an article headlined, "Exploiting Farm Organizations: Jewish Monopoly Traps Operate under Guise of Co-Operative Marketing Associations." Over the next twenty-five months, Dunn wrote nineteen additional articles personally attacking Aaron Sapiro's integrity. Dunn wove a picture of a Jewish conspiracy to capture and subdue American agriculture. He asserted that Sapiro baldly exploited the American farmer for his own economic ends and to reward prominent Jewish co-conspirators like Albert Lasker, the leader of the U.S. Shipping Board, Bernard Baruch, recently head of the War Industries Board, and Eugene Myer, from the War Finance Corporation.

Dunn stressed, in his series of articles, that Sapiro, as a Jew, had never engaged in farming, learned all he knew of it from books, and lined his pockets at the naïve farmers' expense for services they did not want or need. Dunn's lack of understanding of the complex factors affecting farm prices and the efforts of the government to help stabilize fair prices was profound. As an "Iago" figure of Shakespearean dimensions, Dunn was a journalistic assassin for hire, devoid of ethics, conscience or consistency—eager to fire his racist salvos in any direction suggested by Ford's lieutenants—Liebold and Cameron.

As early as the summer of 1924, Liebold and Cameron began to edit and focus Dunn's stories on Sapiro himself rather than on Jews generally. On July 26, 1924, the *Independent* published a Dunn story with the headline, "Potato Growers Beat Sapiro at his Own Game." The article claimed that Sapiro was channeling Colorado potato farmers' funds to a Jewish advertising company, Weyl and Zuckerman, and to Jewish bankers, while interdicting distribution of sales proceeds to the farmers. Liebold and Cameron then sent Dunn on a nationwide excursion to dig up or to manufacture as much dirt as possible on Sapiro and his colleagues.

A further thrust of Dunn's many articles was that Sapiro enforced his "iron clad" contracts against farmer organizations, and that he refused to respond to requests for legal assistance from farmer groups even while he was on retainer. Dunn insisted that Sapiro was engaged in exploiting rather than in assisting farmers. He was quick to connect Sapiro to farmer concerns about Russian and Eastern European immigration. He promoted a "three pin" theory that connected Sapiro with Bolsheviks and the I.W.W. Pointing to the rise of cooperatives in Idaho, Oregon and Washington, Dunn wrote that on a map of the Northwest states, if one placed a red pin where there had been an outbreak of communism, radicalism or I.W.W.-ism, and then placed a white pin where there was Jewish farm exploitation through implementation of the California or Sapiro plan, one would also find many blue pins indicating where one or more cooperatives had failed.

Dunn loudly blamed Sapiro for the collapse of various cooperatives, where Sapiro had no involvement at all. While many farmers were willing to accept the Ford team's publication of "alternative facts" concerning Sapiro and a Jewish conspiracy to control agriculture, there were also many farmers who were appalled by the *Independent's* gross misstatement of facts. A tobacco farmer, R. M. Barker, wrote to the *Independent,* "If you would be just as willing to publish the facts, as you are to publish a lot of lies, you would be doing a greater benefit to the farmers than you are by your knocking of the greatest cooperative association that has ever been formed, and . . . the fact that you don't like Sapiro is no reason that every cooperative should come under your blasphemous tongue."[133] L.A. Hunt, the manager of the Northwest Hay Association, wrote a sarcastic response to the *Independent* articles, which the *Yakima Valley Farm News* was pleased to publish.

> In the past, we have had our doubts as to our worthy Uncle's [Ford's] fitness for the United States Senate and confess, with much humility, the error of our judgment. A man of his proven sagacity, untiring energy, and such a keen sense of humor and fully able to hire a minimum corps of reporters with Mr. Morgan's fearless disregard for the truth, cannot fail to be a source of great entertainment in that august body, where facts are of little value anyway. Our uncle has won his spurs – we're for him! We move nominations be closed.[134]

A.C. Cherry, a lawyer for the Northwest Hay Association, which Dunn marked as a Sapiro victim, wrote to Henry Ford that the *Independent's* publication regarding Sapiro and the Hay Association "contains numerous false and untrue statements—statements known to be false by practically every person in this community." Cherry's denial asserted that neither Sapiro nor any other Jew had anything to do with the hay growers.[135] Cherry chastised Ford for allowing his anti-Semitism to reflect poorly on a cooperative organization attempting to perform a public service for farmers. He firmly denied any Bolshevik or I.W.W. involvement in the Hay Association's organization.[136]

When editor Cameron and business manager Black requested documentation from Dunn to respond to numerous complaints

---

133. Quoted in Woeste, supra, at 162.

134. Id 163.

135. File 7, Box 122, Acc. 1, BFRC.

136. Id.

they were receiving from agricultural cooperatives across the country, Dunn left them adrift. Actual sources were not his strong suit. So, they sought other confirming information from various Ford employees located in agricultural sections of the country, a sort of "make the news if you cannot report it" approach which we now call "fake news." Undeterred, the *Independent* published four more articles concerning Sapiro, in October and in December, 1924, and in April and May, 1925.

That's when Sapiro rose up to deter them.

After the December publication of a story regarding Sapiro's involvement with the Southern Rice Growers Association, Sapiro exploded with anger. He had had enough. On January 6, 1925, he sent a thirty-page demand for a retraction to Henry Ford, threatening to force him once again to the witness stand, referring to him as "a malicious bigot." He said that he had nothing whatever to do with the hop growers, the wool harvesters, and other organizations mentioned in the Dunn articles. He disputed allegations that he quit the Colorado Potato Grower's Exchange to collect his fee. Sapiro said that the Exchange had paid him a five-thousand-dollar organizational fee without complaint, and that he ceased representing the Exchange when they declined to follow his legal advice.

The Ford crew at the *Independent* saw no reason to dignify Sapiro's demand with a reply. In his personal reminiscences, collected at the Benson Ford Archives in Dearborn, Michigan, Ernest G. Liebold recounts a conversation that he had with Henry Ford regarding the Sapiro articles running in the *Independent*. Liebold told him, "You know that Cameron is going a little wild on this guy Sapiro?" Ford, confident that his immense wealth would insulate him from a libel action, replied, "That's just what I want. Don't you interfere with Cameron. If he can get me into a lawsuit with Sapiro, that's just what I want. I'd like to see the fellow start a suit against me."[137] Ford told Liebold that he had better get the

137. Liebold, supra at 483.

best lawyer in the country to represent the paper and suggested Frederic Coudert. Coudert, a star lawyer of the *Selden* patent case, was otherwise occupied with his maritime interests.[138] Liebold confided that Henry Ford, despite his bravado, would at this stage do everything to avoid the humiliation of being called again to the witness stand.[139]

Sapiro's aggressive action took many by surprise. His demand for a Ford retraction was largely out of step with prevailing opinion among the American Jewish leadership, and in particular, the American Jewish Committee. Although there was no truly unified Jewish community at the time, a plurality of Jewish leadership preferred to hunker down and hope that the whole Ford anti-Semitism business would just go away. The clear leader among Jewish advocacy groups in the United States was the American Jewish Committee, founded in 1906 in response to Russian pogroms against Jews. Louis B. Marshall, a prominent New York lawyer and principal in the law firm of Guggenheim, Untermeyer & Marshall, served as the Committee's president from 1912 to 1929. Anchored with Marshall's voice, the AJC became a leading advocate against growing postwar anti-immigrant restrictions surfacing in the U.S.

Marshall had not watched idly as the *Protocols* circulated and stirred up unrest. In 1921, he approved the AJC's publication of *A History of a Lie,* by journalist Herman Bernstein, which attacked the authenticity and reliability of the *Protocols.* Ford cruelly and falsely identified Bernstein, in the *Independent*, as the source for much of the negative information contained about Jews in *The International Jew.* Bernstein was one of the journalists who had accompanied Ford on his Peace Ship, the Oscar II, Ford's unsuccessful attempted to bring an end to the World War. Outraged at the negative claims, Bernstein sued Ford for libel in 1922 in New York. He hired Samuel Untermeyer, Marshall's partner, as

---

138. Id.

139. Ibid at 495.

his counsel, over Marshall's objections. Marshall, himself, doubted that Bernstein had suffered legal damage from Ford and was concerned about jury bias in favor of Ford. His insights proved prophetic. Bernstein was never able to secure service on Ford in New York and the case languished in a New York court. Henry Ford would just stay in the cocoon he built around himself and nobody could touch him. Harry H. Bennett, Ford's chief of security, once remarked that it was easier to reach the President or the Pope on the telephone than Henry Ford.[140]

Sapiro's fiery response surprised Ford. Sapiro made two important strategic decisions that Ford did not expect. First, Sapiro chose to file suit against the *Independent* and Henry Ford in Detroit, which was a little like suing the Pope in the Vatican. Second, he retained an Irish Catholic lawyer from Detroit to represent him rather than "a Jew lawyer from New York" as expected by Ford. Still Ford didn't have much respect for Catholics either, frequently referring to them as "tools of the Jews." Ford was pretty well convinced that his phalanx of thuggish body guards, personal secretaries, and assistants would render him impervious to service of process, either as a party or a witness.

BRINGING IT TO FORD

Unlike today, service on a company alone would not require the company to produce certain employees or officers as witnesses without being individually and separately served with a subpoena. Thus, Henry Ford felt secure in the belief that he could run Sapiro and his attorneys dry and ragged through delay, obfuscation, and dialing up expensive depositions of witnesses all over the United States, many at overlapping times. A relatively mild form of the tactic had successfully placed the Bernstein suit against Ford in New York on "high center" for years. Ford also had all of the resources of the entire national corps of the Ford Motor

140. Baldwin, supra, at 158.

Company at his command, employees who could be engaged as private investigators to root out facts and witnesses averse to Sapiro in far flung parts of the country. Ford believed that he could keep Sapiro's lawyers chasing their tails for years.

Henry Ford was, quite simply, inviting Aaron Sapiro to "bring it on," never suspecting that Sapiro might be up to the challenge or that the protective compartments that he'd built around himself could be penetrated. Sapiro advanced on Ford with a sixty-nine-page "Declaration" or complaint with one hundred forty-one specific counts of libel:

> The Declaration seeks to recover on the grounds that the various articles complained of charge that the Plaintiff Mr. Aaron Sapiro, was one of a number of Jews and others who had entered a conspiracy to gain control over farmer's organizations and thereby create a monopoly of the produce of said farms for the members of said conspiracy and not for the benefit of the farmers.

Aaron Sapiro was not a Jew to turn the other cheek. He had climbed high from the beginnings of a hardscrabble life and he was not ready to surrender his accomplishments to the whims of a benighted bigot, regardless of how wealthy or influential. He stood alone without endorsement or support from major Jewish organizations, many of which felt that more harm than good would likely emerge from a direct confrontation with Henry Ford.

Chapter 16

Lawering Up

Clifford Boles Longley assumed the duties of Ford Motor Company's General Counsel in 1921. Longley's star rose as Alfred Lucking's descended from the fallout of the *Chicago Tribune* lawsuit. Ford biographers, Nevins and Hill, wrote, "It was during *The Dearborn Independent's* first year that the *Chicago Tribune* suit inflicted upon Ford perhaps the cruelest mortification of his career."[141] Born in Chicago, Longley obtained a law degree from the University of Michigan in 1913. Starting out as an associate in the Detroit law firm Choate, Robertson and Lehman, Longley moved to the Ford Motor Company in 1919. Longley, handsome, patrician, elegant, square jawed and competent, offered an abrupt change from Alfred Lucking's voluble intensity, which had lost favor with Henry Ford in the confrontation in Mount Clemens.

Longley became involved in every aspect of the business of the Ford Motor Company and in the private legal affairs of its owners, Henry and Edsel Ford. Ford's legal department dealt with provider and dealer contracts, trademarks and patents, labor disputes, personal injuries, federal and state tax and regulatory issues, the acquisition and disposal of companies and real estate holdings, capitalization and bank loans and mortgages. After long ser-

141. Nevins, Allan and Hill, Frank Ernest, *Ford: Expansion and Challenge, 1915-1933*, Charles Scribner's Sons, N.Y., 1957 at 129. Ford never fully recovered from the humiliation he felt as a result of Elliott Stevenson's cross examination of him in Mt. Clemens.

vice, Longley left the Ford Motor Company in 1929 to start his own law firm, Longley, Boyle and Middeton. Henry Ford ushered him out of the Company and significantly downsized the Ford Motor Company legal staff, largely due to a concern that Longley was getting too close to his son Edsel. When he left the Company, Longley took much of Ford's internal legal business and all of Edsel Ford's private legal business with him. He became intimately involved in Edsel Ford's banking ventures, the Guardian companies and their successor, the Manufacturer's National Bank.

In the critical years 1925–1927, Longley served as Secretary to *The Dearborn Independent* and was responsible for organizing the legal defense of the *Independent* against claims of defamation. In a search for outside legal defense counsel for the *Independent,* Longley first favorably considered Delancey Nicoll, a principal in Nicoll, Anable, Tuller and Sullivan in New York. The Nicoll firm had represented the Ford Motor Company in a number of lawsuits in New York. Famously, Nicoll had obtained a dismissal form Judge Hough in New York against the publishers of the *New York World,* who were charged with criminal libel by the Justice Department under the 1825 *Story Act.*[142] The *World* published articles intimating that Theodore Roosevelt and William Howard Taft were involved in a scheme to profit from monies paid by the U.S. Government to French contractors involved in building the Panama Canal. Only the U.S. Government was a plaintiff in the action, and Nicoll convinced the court that the federal criminalization of domestic defamation law was beyond the scope, intent and power of the *Story Act.*

Henry Ford personally rejected Nicoll largely because of his known appetite for alcohol and tobacco, a distinction that would disqualify much of the litigation bar at the time.

When Aaron Sapiro selected local Irish Catholic lawyer Wil-

142. The Crimes Act of 1825 was drafted by Supreme Court justice Joseph Story to expand federal criminal jurisdiction over certain actions involving federal officials. This was an attempt to criminalize the law of defamation where federal officials were victimized.

liam Gallagher to represent him, Longley knew that Ford would have to dig deep for counsel whose own reputation would present Ford in a favorable light. He focused his attention on Senator James A. Reed, a colorful and mellifluous former prosecutor and current lion of the United States Senate, representing the State of Missouri. Reed himself had been a potential Presidential candidate in 1924 and still had his eye on a possible 1928 campaign. As a young prosecutor, Reed had once unsuccessfully prosecuted Jesse James, Jr., the son of the infamous bank robber, for the robbery of a Missouri Pacific train. He dismissed the case against James, in disgust, when a Missouri jury chose to acquit one of James' fellow gang members, who was clearly guilty.[143]

Reed was an unlikely choice. In fact, he was about the last person who would come to mind as a match to represent Henry Ford as a client. Reed had a fondness for alcohol, cigars and chewing tobacco, and he was not a fan of Ford's antipathy toward Jews and his religious and racial bigotry. The ever-present E.G. Pipp quoted Reed chastising Ford's stand on anti-Semitism.

> The poorest American is one who will condemn his fellow American on account of his race or religion. The most contemptible character in public life today is Henry Ford. I don't care how much he has given to charity or to what extent he has increased wages. I don't care how much he talks of his Americanism. Any man who can deny the right of religious freedom to a race is a disgrace to this republic, an enemy of the Country.[144]

Ironies abound in legal life. Perhaps it was the irony of Sapiro's selection of an Irish Catholic plaintiff's lawyer that led Henry Ford to approve Langley's recommendation to hire Reed, a highly prominent defender of religious liberty. In any event, comedian and social critic Will Rogers thought it was a brilliant move. "But when a man goes out and hires Jim Reed for his lawyer–that is in-

143. James later became a lawyer and opened a law practice in California.

144. Pipp II, supra at 352.

spired genius. The other side needs Moses to compete with him."[145]

Longley later described his efforts to persuade Reed to take Ford's case to Reed's biographer, Lee Merriwether. Longley made an offer that would have been difficult to refuse.

> I knew he was the man to do it, Longley said, "and I simply took the train to Washington, went to the Senate office building and sent my card to Senator Reed. I was ushered into his private office at once; no cooling the heels in the Senatorial ante-chamber."
>
> "What can I do for you?" Reed inquired.
>
> "Senator, a man named Aaron Sapiro has sued Mr. Ford for a million dollars."
>
> "That's a lot of money."
>
> "It certainly is," Longley agreed. "He claims that he has been damaged in that amount by an article published in Mr. Ford's magazine, *The Dearborn Independent*."
>
> "What did the article say?"
>
> "Sapiro says that it intimates that Jewish bankers have entered into a conspiracy to control the food markets of the world and that this will cause mass suffering, perhaps starvation."
>
> "How does this damage Mr. Sapiro?"
>
> "Well Sapiro has spent a great deal of money organizing farmer cooperating groups."
>
> "Why do you tell me this?"
>
> "I have come to you because Mr. Ford wants you to defend him; he authorized me to offer you a retainer of $100,000 and a thousand dollars a day for each day you are engaged on the case."[146]

Merriwether was given to exaggeration and hyperbole in his bi-

---

145. *The New York Times*, 24 March, 1927, at 16.

146. Meriwether, Lee, *Jim Reed, Senatorial Immortal: A Biography*, The International Mark Twain Society, Webster Groves, MO, 1944 at 128-129;

ography of Reed. The daily rate agreed upon was two hundred dollars, not one thousand dollars but still the monetary offer rang loud.[147] For a sense of perspective, Reed's Senatorial salary was ten thousand dollars a year. During the 1920s, many politicians accepted money-making assignments outside of their governmental positions. Reed took the job and also continued to maintain his Kansas City, Missouri, law practice.

Apparently, both Henry Ford and James Reed put aside their personal scruples to advance their respective self-interests. Reed took over as lead counsel for the Ford defense in December, 1926, some twenty months after Sapiro filed his suit. Longley managed nine in-house lawyers in Ford's headquarters as well as a number of lawyers on retainer for Ford around the country to gather facts, interview witnesses and obtain depositions. He retained his grizzled former senior partner, Ward N. Choate, to help with discovery, and retained former prosecutor and Wayne County Probate Judge Stewart Hanley for pre-trial motions and other courtroom appearances. Reed brought with him his Kansas City law partner, Richard Higgins.

On Sapiro's side, the self-confident Gallagher was a force to be reckoned with. "William Henry Gallagher, attorney for Aaron Sapiro, is a rather youthful and decidedly personable and adroit practitioner of this town, not widely known in Detroit, and seeing him in action, one wonders why."[148] Gallagher was the son of an Irish immigrant who died in his early thirties. Gallagher's mother, Clementine, ran a boarding house to support her family for over thirty years. Her son earned a master's degree in arts and later an LL'B from the Detroit College of Law in 1906. During the 1920s, Gallagher stewarded over fifty cases through the Michigan Supreme Court. Youthful, intelligent, and quick on his feet,

---

147. Longley had already earlier approached Reed about defending the *Independent* and Ford through Ford's Washington, D.C. Counsel, F. Hunter Creech.

148. Parton, "Thongs Jam Quiet Ford Courtroom," *Oakland Tribune,* March 23, 1927 at 2.

he was a more than adequate successor to Elliot G. Stevenson, as a potential thorn in the side of Henry Ford.

Gallagher obtained the assistance of lawyers in the various Sapiro law firms, including Sapiro's brother Milton, and Chicago lawyer William S. Lynch. Of all the help Gallagher obtained, no one was more committed or intense than Robert S. Marx, a Sapiro partner and former judge in Cincinnati. Marx, while a captain in the U.S. Army in France, was severely wounded on the last day of World War I. He was awarded the Distinguished Service Cross, the Verdun Medal and the Purple Heart. Years later, he personally founded the Disabled Veterans of America. Marx brought his fighting spirit to the case; he was extremely aggressive and difficult when dealing with the Ford counsel.

Marx once utilized emotional theatrics in a courtroom when faced with blatant anti-Semitism. In an earlier case involving a Jewish client, the opposing counsel had made an anti-Semitic remark to the jury. Marx responded by taking off his shirt in the courtroom and disclosing the scars from his war injuries. Marx told the jury that no one asked whether he was a Jew or Gentile when called to sacrifice for his country.

In the course of his career, Marx befriended and advised Franklin Roosevelt, before he became President. Marx served as Gallagher's second chair during the course of the trial, playing a low-key support role to Gallagher.

SCORCHED EARTH FOREPLAY

The economics of a plaintiff's law firm are such that it is generally important to get to trial as soon as possible. Plaintiff lawyers are generally not paid, if at all, until the end of legal proceedings, and it is frequently to a well-heeled defendant's economic and strategic advantage to delay and obstruct proceedings as much as possible, to grind the plaintiff into submission. The proliferation of discovery and procedural motions not only tend to delay the process of a case but also obstruct it by emotionally grinding down and consuming the resources of the opposite party.

This routine practice in big value litigation—repeated motions for the continuance of proceedings in order to allow for additional fact discovery—suited Ford's lawyers to a "T." In the Sapiro case, they sought to wear down and impoverish this California upstart financially and emotionally by demanding depositions of marginal witnesses all over the nation. The effect did indeed debilitate Sapiro and his lawyers, who complained bitterly to Chief Judge Alfred Tuttle in the U.S. District Court for the Eastern District of Michigan.

Just after Ford secured the representation of Reed as Chief Defense Counsel, Judge Tuttle tried to shut the door on Ford's repeated requests for continuances and delays in the proceedings. Tuttle felt sympathetic to the argument that Henry Ford's immense wealth was working to his advantage in the case. He first set a trial start date for January, 1926. Ford's requests to delay the trial were not well received, but Tuttle granted a continuance of the trial date to March, 1926 in light of Ford's recent retention of Reed.

Lawyers on both sides viewed the testimony of Harry Dunn, alias Robert Morgan, the publicity-shy author of most of the anti-Sapiro articles, as critical to their cases. Sapiro served Dunn with a subpoena to appear for his deposition in San Francisco on January 25, 1926. Longley had concerns about the credibility and reliability of Dunn as a witness. He engineered an indefinite postponement of Dunn's deposition until the summer, after obtaining one further continuance of the trial date from Judge Tuttle. The trial was now set for September, 1926.

Ford investigators fanned out over the country in search of witnesses who could and would testify to the venality of Aaron Sapiro. Ironically, in the highly contentious and competitive world of "cooperative marketing," they found little more than bupkis. They spoke with many who disliked Sapiro and many whom he had rubbed the wrong way or had offended but found it a stretch to get actual evidence of misconduct or breach of fiduciary duty on his part, despite their strong beliefs that such evidence was there and available if only it could be found.

The Ford defense team settled on two principal prongs of defense, each with its own ethical constraints. The first prong was to keep Henry Ford, himself, as far away as possible from the center of the action at the *Independent*. They would paint Ford as a "hands off" owner and innocent bystander, perhaps naively unaware of the actions and directions undertaken by his surrogates at the newspaper who pursued their own personal agendas in the Sapiro articles. They would paint a picture of Ford as aloof and personally pre-occupied with much more important matters than the editorial direction of the *Independent*.

The second prong would be to demonize Sapiro as a crooked, unethical lawyer, driven by concern for his own pocketbook rather than the needs or concerns of the American farmer. In pushing the first prong they knew they were presenting a wholly false gleam on the known facts. In pulling the second prong, they were developing a theme they, perhaps in their hearts of hearts, truly believed, but the legal team failed to see the warping of their own vision—perhaps caused by the poison of their own unacknowledged racism and the irony contained in Reed's own "Faustian" fee bargain with Henry Ford. As strategists, they gave few value points to Sapiro for his legal expertise developed in a field of law that he had practically invented on his own, while fully valuing Senator Reed's services as a litigation strategist and point man in the courtroom.

Sapiro and Ford differed not so much in their passion for their work as in their methods of succeeding. There were, no doubt, times when Sapiro engaged in the rough and tumble of agricultural politics, playing a hard hand for the attention and approbation of competing groups in any particularized commodity segment, but he did so largely through the use of rhetoric and passion rather than deviant maneuvering. Sapiro could muster intense powers of persuasion. In a mid-century study of Aaron Sapiro, persons seeing him in action stated that Sapiro could "make the marketing of a barrel of apples more exciting than a tale from Boccaccio, and the signing of a cooperative agreement seem as vital to social justice and progress as the Magna Carta."[149]

Sapiro made a practice of permitting each cooperative he represented to set its own fee schedule with him after he was retained. While it is highly probable that he communicated at some level his expectation regarding fees, Sapiro had in fact relatively few disputes over his fees. Most of the disputes Ford's minions managed to uncover arose from political and strategic rather than economic issues.

In order to smear Sapiro's reputation, the defense ultimately developed three main live witnesses, all of whom had previously worked with Sapiro. Their testimonies, it was hoped, would anchor Sapiro to a crusade of unrelenting greed. The first witness, Joseph Passeneau, had been a former ally in organizing tobacco cooperatives in Kentucky. He later became Colorado's state Director of Markets, after a falling out with Sapiro. Passeneau accused Sapiro of obtaining approval of a thirty-thousand-dollar legal fee by falsifying the minutes of the Board of Directors of the Dark Tobacco Growers Association in Kentucky and hiring unqualified personnel for the association at exorbitant salaries. Their heated encounter had Passenau and Sapiro parting ways with Sapiro calling Passeneau a liar, and Passenau punching Sapiro in the face with his fist. Several days after their blowup, Robert W. Bingham, a Barley Grower and Kentucky newspaper owner, allied with Sapiro and fired Passeneau.

As witnesses go, Passeneau had his merits and his faults. The Ford lawyers wrangled with Passeneau to get what they wanted in their deposition. Despite his disdain for Sapiro, Passeneau was a true believer in the cause of cooperative commodity marketing. He disputed many of the more colorful allegations about the movement and challenged "alternative facts" manufactured by Mr. Dunn. In the end, the defense lawyers were happy to accept Passeneau's assertion that Sapiro was in the movement for his

149. Larsen, Grace H. & Erdman, Henry E., "Aaron Sapiro: Genius of Farm Cooperative Promotion," *The Missouri Valley Historical Review*, September, 1962, 49:250.

own gain, while overlooking Passeneau's many and frequent indications of racial prejudice against Jews.

The second defense witness, Charles E. Bassett, one-time chief of the Office of Markets at the U.S. Department of Agriculture, volunteered his services as a witness when he learned of Sapiro's demand for a retraction from Henry Ford. Bassett recounted how Sapiro foisted Jewish advertising colleagues, Weyle and Zuckerman, on the Colorado and Idaho potato cooperatives. Basset did not flinch from using direct terms in his dislike for Sapiro and the so-called "Christ Killers." In one of his letters to the defense team, Bassett wrote, "I have often wondered why Jews refuse to eat hog meat, but it must be the fear of being considered cannibals.[150]

The third witness, Sidney Rubinaw, was a cooperative organizer in Maine and Minnesota who served as one of Sapiro's principal lieutenants. Rubinaw was unable to provide any evidence of the "Jewish conspiracy" in the farm cooperative movement. But he had helpful information about the failures of some of Sapiro's cooperatives. Rubinaw seemed eager to "sell" his information to the Ford side in exchange for favorable promotion of himself in the pages of *The Dearborn Independent*. Reed, to his credit, expressed a distaste for purchasing evidence, and the Rubinaw evidence was not pursued.

STAINS IN THE CARPET

Meanwhile, the Ford lawyers were desperate to complete their unfinished depositions and to put off the trial for as long as possible, and the Sapiro lawyers were anxious to stop the incessant grind of the Defendant's discovery depositions. In an affidavit

---

150. Quoted in Woeste, supra, at 206. Accession 48, BFRC in Dearborn, Michigan, contains many transcripts, briefs, letters and communications regarding the Sapiro/Ford litigation. It is rife with letters from Ford supporters all over the country and contains what Ford author, Reynold M. Wik, describes as the "most bigoted expressions of opinion in American letters." *Henry Ford and Grass Roots America*, at 138.

filed with the court on July 24, 1926, Aaron Sapiro complained that he, as a party, was being ground down by Ford's scorched earth discovery onslaught:

> [R]ather than that Plaintiff be compelled to engage attorneys to wander all over the United States and Canada for month after month in what appears to be an effort to prevent a proper presentation of the case by the Plaintiff by compelling him to carry on litigation in a manner available only to men of extraordinary wealth and far beyond the means now or ever in the possession of this Defendant.[151]

In late July, 1926, Senator Reed appeared at a pre-trial conference before Judge Alfred J. Tuttle. Judge Tuttle, as Chief Judge, sat in what is argued to be the most magisterial and beautiful courtroom in the United States. It was located on the third floor of the U.S. Post Office, Courthouse and Custom House in downtown Detroit. The brutal Renaissance Revival structure, built with massive rough ashlar stone, upheld a two-hundred-forty-three-foot clock tower that hovered over its main entrance on Fort Street. The building struck similar dark notes to the aesthetic of Boston architect Henry Hobson Richardson. The Tuttle courtroom was and is a magisterial yet oddly comfortable work of art.[152]

The courtroom, surprisingly small and intimate for its extravagance, contains thirty different types of marble laid out in classic Renaissance formats and arches. The Judge's bench was carved out of East Indian Mahogany. Whatever is not marble in the courtroom is beautiful, dark, carved mahogany, including the lawyers' tables and podium and a number of large arched doorways leading from the side of the courtroom to the central hallways. On either side of the Judge's bench are stationed

151. Accession 48, Box 40, BFRC.

152. The courtroom, at Judge Tuttle's request, was taken apart, piece by piece and reinstalled in the 1931 replacement U.S. District Court, where it stands today.

a sentry-like, translucent onyx marble column, capped with four lions holding a globe. Behind the bench, a marble frieze of ten female figures represents the purity of justice. Another frieze of one hundred unique lions' heads, just below the ceiling, feels like an apt representation of the force of the law. The courtroom contains only three rows of public visitors' pews. It seems the sort of place where one would expect the Pope to appear to say a private mass, without public attendance. The massive clock in the Post Office tower never really kept very good time, to many public complaints, perhaps because of the short-fall of available cash to invest in a mechanical device, given the diversion of resources to the "million-dollar courtroom." The clock can now be seen in the Henry Ford Museum in Dearborn, Michigan, where it has been retired from its horological duties.

Judge Tuttle, who was rightfully proud and protective of the grandeur of his courtroom, quickly clashed with Senator Reed who had much less respect for the splendor and sanctity of public spaces. Reed spit onto the carpet quite carelessly to dispose of his chocks of chewing tobacco. His expectorations frequently failed to hit the intended spittoon or were, in the absence of a target, directed to alternative repositories. Reed's insensitivity to decorum enraged Tuttle, and when Reed requested yet another continuance of the trial date, Tuttle agreed but gave strict conditions, that 1) the trial would commence no later than March 14, 1927, following the Congressional recess; 2) that no further requests for a continuance would be entertained; 3) that Henry Ford would accept a witness subpoena by September 14, 1926, and; 4) that Ford would pay Sapiro's attorneys one hundred dollars per day for each additional deposition set to be taken by the Ford team, even if cancelled. Tuttle fully bought into Gallagher's equitable argument that the Ford lawyers were running up the costs on Sapiro.

Longley also met with Judge Tuttle. The lawyer struggled mightily to find a way to keep his principal client, Henry Ford, out of the courthouse. He offered to post a bond for the payment of any damage award against the *Independent*, in the event of Sapiro obtaining a verdict, in lieu of Ford being required to appear in the courtroom, but Gallagher wanted to question Ford. Longley also tried to limit, in advance, the scope of any testimony Ford might give. The prosecutors knew, in no uncertain terms, that they had to get Ford on the witness stand—Ford himself was the single biggest piece of leverage that Sapiro had in the case. With a serious demeanor and suitable respect, Longley advised the court that he could not agree to Ford's acceptance of a subpoena without consultation with his client. Just as Longley opened the door to leave, Judge Tuttle told him that if Ford testified, he would not permit a repeat of the *Chicago Tribune* spectacle where Ford was held up to ridicule.

Little impressed with the majesty of federal judges or their courtrooms, Senator Reed asked Longley to prepare and arrange to have Henry Ford sign an affidavit that accused Judge Tuttle of bias because of Ford's immense wealth. Reed included this in a Motion for Recusal. A federal judge is required by law to remove himself from a case and transfer it to another judge after the filing of a "timely and sufficient" motion for recusal. Failure to do so raises an appealable issue. Tuttle disqualified himself and could not participate further in the case. On August 3, 1926, Reed filed a renewed *Motion for a Continuance,* which Tuttle had to refer to another judge because of his own recusal. Judge Benson W. Hough of Columbus, Ohio, answered the call and presided over a turbulent seven-hour hearing on August 9, where Reed and Gallagher accused each other of delay and abuse of process. Exasperated, Hough finally dropped everything on the lawyers. He told them that either they find a way to agree on the continuance and the particulars of further discovery by the following morning, or he would himself unilaterally set the dates, times, and places of further proceedings, without regard to the convenience of the parties. The lawyers worked through the night to meet the Judge's deadline, and they agreed on another continuance until March 7, 1927, with a discovery schedule from September through January.

DUKE OF HAZZARDS

Henry Ford had the largest private police force in the United States, which was managed by the ruthless, crypto-criminal, Harry H. Bennett. Bennett, a former prize fighter with wide underground connections, who wore a bow tie to avoid his tie being used as a hand hold in a scuffle. Bennett encased Henry Ford in a tight protective shield of thugs and former athletes with large physiques, not unlike the character and image of those protecting Al Capone in Chicago. Ford shared with Bennett an interest in firearms and gangsters. He would sometimes show up in Bennett's office for target practice on an indoor range Bennett had set up. Bennett once granted an exclusive fruit concession in Ford plants to Chet LaMare, the Al Capone of Detroit, even though, as Bennett remarked, "Chet didn't know a banana from an orange." During prohibition, LaMare controlled Michigan's second largest industry, "bootlegging," on the Detroit waterfront, as well as an assortment of other unsavory activities. He was happy to lend his years of expertise as an informal consultant to Bennett on a range of "security" issues.

Obtaining service of process on Henry Ford, then, was not an activity engaged in by the faint of heart. Following eight months of failed attempts at serving Ford, an adventurous young lawyer, J. Frances Fitzgerald, found a way. On August 7, 1927, the Ford Motor Company opened Ford Airfield in Dearborn, Michigan, to the public for the National Reliability Air Tour. This annual event showcased the reliability and safety of commercial aircraft by commencing a multi-state tour of the Midwest from Ford Field,[153] with multiple, multi-state stops, and a loop-like return to Dearborn. Ford's entry in the competition was its Stout 2A-AT Pullman Trimotor, referred to by Ford as the "tin goose." Best in show, each year, earned the Edsel B. Ford trophy.

---

153. Ford Airfield had one of the first air passenger terminals in the United States designed by Albert Kahn.

Twenty-five contesting airplanes lined up on the runways for the competition. Ford Aviation also used the occasion to introduce its "sky flivver," a small-single seat, open cockpit, low single-wing plane, thought by some to presage the "flying car." Henry Ford's personal pilot, Harry J. Brooke, put the diminutive aircraft through its paces before the departure of the assembled pilots. A carnival atmosphere prevailed at the airfield, with the crowd sometimes growing unruly. The wily young Fitzgerald found Ford sitting in his Lincoln automobile, staring intently at the sky right along with his security team. When Ford complained about tobacco smokers crushing in near his car, Fitzgerald joined a group of volunteers charged with moving the crowd away from the Ford car. By dint of the deafening sound of aircraft engines poised for takeoff and the distracted guards, Fitzgerald dropped the subpoena into Ford's lap through the window and was immediately assaulted by a group of very large men in very ill-fitting suits.

Seeing the document in his lap, Ford recoiled, yelling, "No. No. Take it away." He then, in a rage, tore it up. Ford's security team commenced pummeling Fitzgerald. Ray Dahlinger,[154] Ford's chauffeur and one of his security assistants, approached Fitzgerald and said, "You think you are pretty smart, don't you? Well you didn't serve a subpoena on Mr. Ford at all. You served it on Mr. Ford's brother, John Ford." Fitzgerald responded with a smile. "Then what is all the fuss about?" The presence of other reporters and the public at the scene provided significant protection for Fitzgerald, who was later released relatively unharmed.

NEW JUDGE

Henry Ford, through Ernest G. Liebold, advised the court that he had not been served with a subpoena. But right along with a

---

154. Ray Dahlinger also served as an apparent "beard" for a former Ford Motor Company transcriptionist, Evangeline Dahlinger, who was alleged to have given birth to a son by Henry Ford. Gelderman, Carol, *Henry Ford: The Wayward Capitalist,* St. Martin's Press, N.Y. 1981 at 286-288.

clerk's notice of the Court's order of a continuance came a notification to Henry Ford that his subpoena had been continued to March, 1927. Henry Ford's lawyers had neither the evidence nor the credibility to keep asserting that Ford had not been served. Both sides, with some tension, awaited the identity of the new judge to replace Judge Tuttle. The short straw went to Judge Fred S. Raymond, newly appointed to the U.S. District Court for the Western District of Michigan by Calvin Coolidge. Raymond, from Grand Rapids, Michigan, would try the case in Judge Tuttle's courtroom in Detroit.

Judge Raymond once described himself as an "astonished and non-political lawyer, who neither sought to be nor strongly desired to be a federal judge, but was appointed due to the untimely passing of the President of the United States, the daytime doze of a Vice President during a vote on a tie vote on confirmation of an Attorney General and a sudden fatal illness of the leading aspirant." Prior to his appointment, Raymond practiced law in Grand Rapids. He was a Rotarian and a 33rd Degree Scottish Rite Mason. A western Michigan, conservative Republican, Raymond never developed a reputation for intellectual brilliance, but he maintained a steady hand on the workings of his courtroom, and was somewhat wary of legal firebrands like William H. Gallagher. Reed, through the forced recusal of Judge Tuttle, had markedly improved his client's position by acquiring a judge in the case, who would be much more likely to be receptive to his view of the case.

In January, 1927, Reed and Longley filed a two-hundred-seven-page Amended Answer, which was difficult if not impossible to fully grasp because it didn't synch up or line up with the Plaintiff's Declaration. On February 28, 1927, at a pre-trial conference regarding the Amended Answer, Gallagher and Stewart Hanley squared off on whether Ford would be required to prove the existence of a "Jewish conspiracy" of which Sapiro was a participant, rather than focus exclusively on whether or not Sapiro was an ethical and competent lawyer.

Gallagher strongly resisted,

> That is the very gravamen of the complaint, Henry Ford has spent millions of dollars trying to convince the American people that such a conspiracy exists. It is about the only purpose to which *The Dearborn Independent* has been put during its entire existence, just to attack the Jewish people and show there is such a conspiracy of international Jews trying to dominate this country. . . and now his lawyers have to stand here and say to your Honor the charge is false and they do not plead the truth of it.

Judge Raymond demurred for the time being on addressing the "Jewish Conspiracy question" and ruled that the Defendants' Amended Answer was defective and gave the Ford side a week to revise it and submit a procedurally conforming response. The revised Answer was not a significant improvement on the prior one, but Raymond was anxious to get the trial underway and accepted the revised pleading, with the understanding that its defects would be modified during the course of the trial.

Gallagher and Sapiro raised an open issue, about whether the term "Jew," if used in a pejorative context, could be defamation itself. Raymond rejected the concept as unduly widening the reach of the accepted law of defamation.

Gallagher produced in court the affidavit of J. Frances Fitzgerald, concerning his service of process on Henry Ford, with a question as to whether it would be necessary for him to file contempt proceedings to enforce the subpoena. The Ford lawyers were not prepared to challenge the affidavit, and did a "soft shoe" retreat, suggesting that Ford would testify if the court required him to attend.

Meanwhile the jury selection process was already underway. The Court provided the parties with the names and addresses of some two hundred potential jurors on February 15, 1927, and Ford investigators were dispatched to provide short assessments of each potential juror. The yellowing juror assessment forms, filled out by the investigators, are still available to be read in the Benson Ford Research Center in Dearborn. In addition to providing basic family and employment information and description of religious affiliation, if any, subjective information such as "works for Jews," "hates Jews," or has "favorable views toward Henry Ford" is documented in the forms. One interesting form that would have greater implications in the case was the review of Juror Cora M. Hoffman of 14th Street, in Detroit. Her husband was in the plumbing business, it said, and she was "not very well liked among neighbors." The fifty Ford detectives shadowing jurors, litigants, attorneys and witnesses before and during the trial took note.

Mrs. Cora Hoffman was among the six women and six men selected for the Sapiro/Ford jury. She was a "Pleasant faced woman in her thirties,"[155] a housewife who would have a large role to play in the events that followed. Group photos of the tight-lipped jury flew through the wire services, published by newspapers all over the country. The one-million-dollar libel suit rolled forward. Yet another "trial of the century" was about to begin. The new judge, like the old judge, had some surprises ahead of him.

155. Quoted in Woeste, supra, at 253.

Chapter 17

The Wheels of Justice[156]

WEEK ONE
MARCH 15, 1927 - MARCH 18, 1927

The trial began, at long last, on the afternoon of Tuesday, March 15, following the impaneling of the jury.[157] William Henry Gallagher led the charge with his opening statement on behalf of Aaron Sapiro, giving his overview of the case. The boyish-looking Gallagher stood nervously at the mahogany podium, a lock of his reddish hair drifting casually over his forehead. His earnest and intense blue-green eyes peered through round wire-rimmed glasses as he gathered his thoughts. The room pulsed with excitement. The press table vibrated especially hard, crammed with twenty-five national wire service and local reporters. Spectators filled each of the eighty public seats available in the back. All of them had hoped to get a peek at the famed outspoken industrialist. All were disappointed. A courtroom was the last place in the world that Henry Ford would voluntarily consent to make an appearance. The slight buzz from the hallway outside came from thwarted seat seekers moving on to other venues. Yet many

156. The Wheels of Justice turn slowly, but grind exceedingly fine – proverb.

157. *The Trial Transcript of Aaron Sapiro v. Henry Ford et al.*, is located at the Benson Ford Research Center, Dearborn, Michigan, Accession 48, Box 43, File 4.

people remained, just to be close to the event. A good number of those lurking outside the handsome carved double doors were Ford security agents and detectives watching the comings and goings with bright interest.

The Plaintiff, Aaron Sapiro, sat alone at the Plaintiff's table, leaning forward expectantly to catch every one of Gallagher's words. Now in his forties, with black hair and dark penetrating eyes, Sapiro had long awaited this day. He had earlier been sworn in as counsel to be able to participate in his own action. The phalanx of seven Ford lawyers, with legal pads at the ready, were determined to remain expressionless throughout Gallagher's address. In first chair sat the august, silver-haired and silver-tongued lion of the United States Senate, James A. Reed, Henry Ford's Chief Counsel for the proceedings. There was, of course, no Ford sitting beside him.

Gallagher provided a short discourse on the elements of a libel case, and the legal recourse provided to one who has been wrongly brought into disrepute by a written publication. He advised the jury that it would be their duty to determine whether *The Dearborn Independent* crossed the line of "fair comment" and reasonable criticism to bring harm to Mr. Sapiro, and whether the newspaper's actions and allegations were untrue and inspired by malice. Gallagher then differentiated between *First Amendment* rights and a narrower focus on connecting specific individuals with unsavory acts or conduct.

> Henry Ford has a perfect right, so far as the law is concerned, to make an attack on the Jewish people and to continue it as long as he wishes; but just as soon as an attack against a race is centered upon an individual of that race and made the butt of another attack, then that individual has the right to come into court and ask for a determination of the justice of that attack.

Gallagher focused on the individual as a muted response to a ruling by Judge Raymond earlier, that Sapiro could not amend his Declaration to assert that the use of the word "Jew," in and of itself, used in scorn, could be actionable in a defamation action.

Senator Reed, on behalf of the *Independent*, had argued,

> If Mr. Gallagher's motion is granted we would have to ask for a long continuance to study the matter. We admit we said Mr. Sapiro was a Jew, but we contend it was no reflection on him to call him a Jew. We are not attacking the Jewish race.

Gallagher moved the Court to dismiss the Defendant's five-hundred-seventy-one-paragraph answer which he claimed was deficient in that it failed to respond to the charge made by Sapiro that the *Independent* referred to Sapiro as a member of "organized international Jewry, seeking control of various farm marketing organizations" and that it charged international Jewry with teaching and advocating Bolshevism and Communism.

Overriding the proceedings was also the issue of whether Henry Ford would eventually appear in person, as a witness in the case. Ford's lawyers continued to waffle on whether Henry Ford had actually been served with a subpoena, while Gallagher waved the spectacle of bringing contempt proceedings against Ford. Gallagher and Sapiro persisted in their right and intent to call Ford to the witness stand, even though, under then existing and arcane federal court rules, if they called Ford as their witness, they could not impeach his testimony through cross examination, because he was being called as their witness.[158] Judge Raymond, in denying Gallagher's Motion to dismiss the *Independent's* answer, was anxious to weigh anchor and get the cumbrous proceedings under way. He said that he would deal with defects in the Defendant's pleadings as issues of evidence arose downstream.

Gallagher, continuing with his argument to the jury, painted *The Dearborn Independent* as the alter ego of Henry Ford. He described the paper as "merely a means of expression for Henry Ford. It conveys his message and conveys his thoughts, and so he,

158. The Modern Rule allows for a party to call an adverse party or a "hostile" witness for cross examination, without being bound by the witness's testimony. This was the rule in place in the Michigan state court proceedings during the *Chicago Tribune* trial.

standing behind it, controlling its policies, giving his thoughts to it, is himself, personally responsible for the thoughts that his *Independent* spreads throughout the country."

Several hours into Gallagher's opening statement, Judge Raymond, pointing to the clock, intervened to adjourn the proceedings for the day.

On Wednesday, March 16, Gallagher continued with his opening remarks, following an hour-long conference in chambers with the Judge and opposing counsel. He introduced his client to the jury, describing Sapiro's ascendance from the debilitating experiences in an orphanage to his education and his dedication to assisting farmers. Judge Raymond sustained an objection by Senator Reed to Gallagher's attempt to describe Sapiro's patriotic attempt to enlist in the Army during the Great War. Marshalling as much scorn as he could project, Gallagher derided claims by the *Independent* that a Jewish conspiracy sought to control American agriculture. He refuted their assertions that Sapiro dominated farmer's co-operative marketing organizations, and the very idea of co-operative organizations having originated with the Jews. He acknowledged the right of Ford to attack the concept of farmer co-operatives, "But he went further than that. He said Mr. Sapiro was a member of a Jewish combine conspiring to gain control of agriculture.... He claimed that Sapiro dominated agriculture, but also that he was a tool of the international conspiracy of Jews."[159] Gallagher exclaimed that both Henry Ford and Fred L. Black, the *Independent's* business manager, knew at the time of the printing of the Sapiro articles that they were false. He said that he would prove that Sapiro, although not a farmer, was a verifiable expert in the area of farmer marketing organizations.

He advised the jury that the question it must consider is whether there was a libel against Mr. Sapiro. "Was Mr. Sapiro injured when it was said he was a member of an international conspiracy to spread communism and exploit farmers? If it is true

---

159. The *Times Herald* (Port Huron, Michigan), March 16, 1927 at 1.

then there was no libel." "But," he continued, "in this case the publication stepped aside from fairness to make a personal assault on the character and motives of the individuals involved in the efficacy of the plan with which it disagreed. When one does that one is amenable to the law, if the assault is groundlessly made."

Senator Reed objected to Gallagher's remarks, and the Judge asked Gallagher to confine himself to statements of what he and his client intend to prove. Turning to the jury, Raymond then explained that printed attacks may be made on races, religions, and classes without fear of retribution, but that when individuals were singled out, the law could intervene. In effect, the Judge said that one cannot libel a race.

Gallagher continued with a repudiation of the idea that Sapiro had in mind the promotion of a communist system at variance with the policies of the United States, noting that over forty states had passed co-operative enabling statutes along the lines of Sapiro's suggestions. He chided the concept of a sinister "Jewish Ring." "We will prove it a figment of a not altogether good imagination . . . the product of venom, the creation of a prejudiced mind. We will prove that these articles contained error after error, that these errors were called to Mr. Ford's attention by men of standing in farm circles, and never was correction given."

Gallagher spent most of the day sloughing through the one hundred forty-one various libels recorded in Sapiro's Declaration, with Reed popping up and down like a "whack-a-mole" to make incessant objections. Gallagher promised that he would show that in a majority of cases, farmers sought his client's advice and that his client did not impose himself on them. He ridiculed the efforts of Ford investigators who "fished" the states of Washington, Oregon, and Idaho, attempting to connect Sapiro's activities there with the I.W.W. labor disruptions and Bolshevik activities without landing a legal-sized trout of connection. "Sapiro was trying to do good for the American farmer. The rest we will disprove when the time comes. We will prove that Mr. Sapiro never utterly controlled any of these organizations, that he was always subject to their wishes and not them to his. We will prove there was never any 'looting'; there never was a farmer terrified by a Jew master."

Following the adjournment and the completion of his day-long opening statement, Gallagher slumped briefly in his chair, his light gray Donegal tweed three-piece suit and trademark wing collar and bow tie none the worse for wear; a Gaelic lawyer, exhausted from the tension and scars of the day's skirmish.

On March 17, Senator Reed took his turn at the podium. Pulling off his tortoise shell glasses and forging a kindly, avuncular manner, Reed introduced himself to the jury. "I of course have the disadvantage of being a stranger to you all, and I hope that you will bear with me if I make the same mistakes which strangers are sometimes prone to make." Reed then made a quick pivot to Aaron Sapiro. "[T]he Hebrew race is not here bringing this suit and . . . Mr. Sapiro has no right to come here and recover damages for the Jewish race, and put the money in his own pocket as damages done to himself." Reed intentionally stumbled over the pronunciation of Sapiro's name, to emphasize its "foreignness." He proclaimed Henry Ford's innocence. "Henry Ford never saw these articles [and] has never read them to this blessed hour." He insisted that "[I]t is no libel to say truthfully of a man who is a Jew that he is a Jew. The law puts no bridle in the mouth of truth. And so we claim here . . . that what has been printed of Mr. Sapiro in all of its real essence was the truth."

Reed offered a host of generalizations in his clients' defense, which were long on mockery and short on specifics. Late Thursday afternoon, Gallagher requested an in-chambers meeting of counsel and the Judge to complain about the lack of factual specificity in Reed's opening statement as to facts which would be proven by Reed in the trial. During the rest of the afternoon, Reed churned out a number of slightly more particularized claims of Sapiro's greed and professional deviance, while sometimes misidentifying named third parties as "Jews," who were not, and repeating himself several times, to the controlled amusement of Sapiro, who would frequently shake his head at Reed's statements and pass notes to Gallagher.

Reed continually complained that it was Sapiro's practice to downplay his interest in obtaining fees, while manipulating farmer organizations into overpaying him. He asserted that Sapiro represented organizations generally failed while Sapiro's pockets bulged with their largess. Said Reed, "Sapiro pictured himself as Moses come to lead the farmers from the wilderness of bankruptcy into a promised land of prosperity, professing to want no money for aiding and organizing co-operatives and get from one cotton association alone, $142,000." He asserted that Sapiro plundered farmers for exorbitant fees while farmers were starving and contemplating bankruptcy, describing co-operative after co-operative where Sapiro prospered at farmers' expenses until the court's clock mercifully struck five and the Judge excused the jury for the evening.

On the following morning, March 18, Reed plunged in where he left off, maligning Sapiro's competency and his ethics. He droned, "All of Sapiro's claims that these associations could control prices turned out to be false, to be failures and the whole plan and scheme of his organization was unsound and in many respects, unworkable." Over Gallagher's strident objections, Reed intoned a litany of Sapiro's professional shortcomings.

> To hold out false promises to clients is unprofessional. To agree to allow clients to fix fees, and then to breach that agreement is unprofessional. To work for two or more clients having opposing interests is unprofessional. To connive with a lawyer to get business partly in his name and partly in the name of another lawyer and then to split the fees by previous agreement is unprofessional. To induce the organizers of an association, without authority, to secretly pay a large fee is unprofessional.

Completing his recitation, Reed said, "Finally we will show that these *[Independent]* articles were printed in good faith for the purpose of protecting the farmers and growers of the United States against these schemes of the Sapiro. And, having shown all of this, we will ask that you find that Aaron Sapiro was an exploiter of the American farmer."

Following the noon break, Gallagher called his first witness, William J. Cameron, the roly poly editor of *The Dearborn Independent,* to the stand. It became apparent from the start of his testimony that Cameron would play the role of Henry Ford's "beard," or scapegoat, accepting all responsibility for the *Independent's* publications. Cameron insisted that Henry Ford neither imposed his ideas on the editorial staff of the *Independent,* nor actively monitored what the paper was publishing. Giving an example of the differences between Ford and the paper, Cameron related that although Ford was more tolerant of the Russian Soviet experiment than the paper's editors, Ford never asked them to accept his views.

Gallagher snapped, "Do you mean that he is pro-Soviet?"

Cameron replied, "I didn't say that. I said he was more tolerant of the Soviet experiment than the *Independent.*"

Gallagher seemed to increase in stature with each slowly passing hour. He requested that the Court order all of the books and records of the *Independent* be brought into court on Monday. Ford lawyer, Stewart Hanley, asked him what he meant by "all the records." Gallagher answered, "I mean all of the records covering the period since Mr. Ford bought the paper and put the stock in the name of his wife, son and himself."

Hanley objected angrily to Gallagher's statement, identifying Ford's connection with the *Independent* before the jury. The judge then excused the jury for the weekend and took the lawyers into his chambers to squabble over the scope of the evidence to be presented to the jury in the coming days. With the glacial pace of the trial, it was apparent that Gallagher's request for Ford's appearance would not be honored any time soon.

WEEK TWO
MARCH 21, 1927 - MARCH 26, 1927

William J. Cameron sat in the witness box on March 21, as the files of *The Dearborn Independent* from 1919 until 1925 were admitted by the Court as evidence. Cameron testified that the *In-*

dependent began receiving letters from farmers for almost a year before the publication of the Sapiro articles. He stated that he had not discussed Sapiro's alleged involvement with a "Jewish Ring" with anyone including Henry Ford.

Gallagher inquired,

> Q. Did Mr. Ford talk them over with anyone else in your presence?
>
> A. I never heard him.
>
> Q. Did you never discuss with Ford, Mr. Sapiro's alleged connection with an international band of Jews or hear him discuss that subject with someone else?
>
> A. I didn't.

Gallagher did not shilly-shally. He pushed Cameron on the opening statement in the first Sapiro article that claimed Sapiro was part of a "band of Jews" on the "back of the American farmer." Cameron stated his belief that the *Independent* and its special agent and writer, Harry H. Dunn, a.k.a. "Robert Morgan," had made a sufficient investigation to verify the allegations.

Gallagher asked him, "When did you first discuss with anybody the publication by *The Dearborn Independent* of allegations that charge Aaron Sapiro with being allied with an international gang of Jews?" Reed objected. Judge Raymond sustained Reed's objection, and Gallagher adjusted his thrust.

"Who contemplated placing the farmers of this country under the domination of an international banking ring?"

Reed again objected but was overruled.

Cameron replied, "When the storm of the complaint began to be strong enough to register itself on my mind."

Gallagher tried to draw out the nature and character of the relationship between Cameron and the Teutonic Ford secretary, Ernest G. Liebold, concerning editorial policy Judge Raymond apparently drew a blank, sustaining defense objections.

Gallagher then began chipping away at Cameron's credibility. The witness could not identify any specific bankers allied with

Sapiro nor identify any farmers' co-operatives that borrowed money from Jewish bankers. Cameron said he didn't know that only two associations ever engaged a Jewish produce company as a selling agency.

> Q. Where did you understand the headquarters of the alleged ring to be?
>
> A. It wasn't a question of where but who.
>
> Q. Were the articles printed in the *Independent* as the views of the *Independent* or the views of Morgan or Dunn?

On objection, Raymond refused to allow the answer and also prevented Cameron from defining the "Jewish Movement" as it was referenced in the paper. Then Gallagher asked a simple question which threw the trial off the tracks.

"What is your best recollection of your original plans? Was it for a series of articles against the Jews or a set of stories about Sapiro?"

Following a firestorm of objections, the Court excused the jury and entertained a five-hour argument by counsel as to the scope of the admissibility of evidence or testimony on "the Jewish question." A reporter described the debate among the lawyers as the "placement of legal tacks in the other's chairs" and the creation of "legal trip wires" for the unaware.[160]

Gallagher wanted to place into evidence a copy of *The International Jew,* the anti-Semitic diatribe published earlier by the *Independent* under Ford's direction. To endorse the admission of this book into court, Gallagher relied principally on *Watson v. Detroit Journal,*[161] which held that there was no harm caused to the plaintiff in a defamatory publication about trading stamp companies, where no individual was identified by name. Gallagher wanted to tie the anti-Sapiro articles to the bile and bias pervading the loathsome pages of *The International Jew*. Both sides argued that

---

160. The *Detroit Free Press,* March 22, 1921 at 1.

161. 143 Mich. 430 (1906).

the case supported their particular argument in issue, Sapiro saying that the fact that he, unlike *Watson*, was specifically identified in the publication, gained him the right to complain.

Clearly frustrated, Gallagher argued, "These articles were started against the Jewish people. They had no intent of attacking Sapiro when they started. The vicious and dangerous thing is that Sapiro was charged with only being a cog in the machine, a band organized for unlawful purposes and sharp practices, wholly contrary to American ideals. They charged him and this band with working for the subjugation of American farmers. When the articles were started, *The Dearborn Independent* didn't even know that Sapiro existed. We have the right to know just what they mean when they call Sapiro a member of an international band of Jews."

Ford lawyer, Stewart Hanley, quickly responded that no proof had been introduced to show that the term *Jew* carried any derogatory implications and that there was no reason for the introduction of articles [*The International Jew*] printed years before the alleged libels.

Gallagher charged that the anti-Jewish articles were begun at the direction of Henry Ford and suspended at the direction of Ford to show Ford's involvement in directing the content in the *Independent*.

Hanley again, "It is our position that opprobrious articles toward a race or class are not competent evidence to prove malice toward a member of that race or class." He described the earlier publications as being exclusively aspersions on the whole Jewish race and not on individuals.

Judge Raymond sustained the Defendants' objections, later advising the press that "[I]n this trial, Mr. Ford's ideas of the Jews and his attitude toward them as people will be barred."

Tuesday, March 22, was a largely frustrating day for Gallagher in his attempts to link Henry Ford with the *Independent's* editorial policies. Cameron repeated his mantra that he was the editor and made all the calls. He said that Henry Ford told him, "You are the editor" and "get the facts right." He avoided all of Gallagher's inquiries as to the specific grants of authority to Cameron and their source. Cameron related his personal ignorance as to the workings of the farmer co-operatives. The Judge refused to allow Gallagher the right to examine Cameron on the content of letters written to the *Independent* or to Henry Ford about misstatements of facts, without the testimony of the authors of the letters. Certain letters from the *Independent's* files that Gallagher did manage to place before jury found *Independent* correspondent Harry H. Dunn opining to the *Independent* staff that there was nearly "unanimous opinion [among farmers] that the associations are good things, quite the best marketing the fruit growers and vegetable men ever had." That was not an avenue the *Independent* wanted Dunn to travel on in his articles. An August, 1923, letter from an *Independent* editor to Dunn led off with the injunction, "Do not snicker when I tell you that the Jewish boys are putting their work on the farmers."[162]

Ford's lawyers successfully blocked Cameron from testifying as to how he became the sole arbiter of the *Independent's* editorial policies. He did say, "If I am running a paper, I am going to run it and not be responsible for anyone else's ideas." Gallagher retorted, "Well, is the paper's attitude toward prohibition your personal attitude?" Cameron's red nose reddened. The predictable objection was sustained by the Judge.

A press observer[163] described the day's events.

> The suit wheezed and panted on the steep roadbed of technicality, and at times one wondered if a wheel was moving. There was the pretension of progress . . . solemn words . . . profundity. . . the rustling of legal leaves. But once a lawyer turned upon the witness Cameron and sought illumination, a nimble legal hand interposed and stopped any intention he might have had to throw a light into the darker corners of the controversy.

---

162. The *Detroit Free Press*, March 23, 1927 at 14.

163. William C. Richards, *Detroit Free Press*, March 23, 1927.

On the chilly morning of Wednesday, March 23, Aaron Sapiro arrived in court with his wife who was tastefully outfitted in a spring green suit. Sapiro, acting as his own counsel, read to the jury a number of the articles about him published in the *Independent*. He read selected *Independent* articles aloud in a suave and controlled voice.

> Whenever the Jew appears promoting associations for the benefit of the American farmer, these appear as henchmen for the radicals, the agents of the I.W.Ws., even open adherents of communism and bolshevism as the strong-arm men to put the work on the hesitant farmers.
>
> ...
>
> The story of the history of the wheat crop is going to be told, but first this is the outstanding example of the combination of the Jew and radicalism, a clear exposition of the hand to hand workings of the notorious Sapiro plan of marketing and principles of bolshevism which must be told.
>
> ...
>
> This is the effort of Aaron Sapiro to seize control of the American farm Bureau Federation, take it completely away from the American farmers, clear it of American direction and operation and use it by which Jewry could come into power over all of the farmers and farms of the United States.
>
> ...
>
> It is a story also for those who believe that this group is working honestly or dishonestly merely to fill their own pockets. It is a story last of all for those who are beginning to see the truth behind the Jewish exploitation of the American farmer...

Sapiro read the *Independent's* calumnies clearly with a voice that caught the edge and cadence of the hate they communicated. The courtroom was quiet as he resumed his seat with dignity and Gallagher gathered his notes to continue his interrogation of Cameron.

Continuing with his examination of Cameron, Gallagher tried

to admit a letter to the *Independent* from the general counsel of the Northwest Hay Association in Yakima, Washington, taking extreme exception to many of the factual claims made by Harry Dunn and the *Independent* about the association. Gallagher wanted to demonstrate that the *Independent* was on notice that Dunn's reporting was unreliable and reckless and yet continued nevertheless to stand by his stories. Judge Raymond excluded the letter on the basis that Dunn's unreliability could only be shown by evidence of his general reputation and not through specific instances of unreliable behavior.

Gallagher found himself hamstrung through most of the day by objections to nearly every question he chose to ask, primarily by the arcane federal rule prohibiting him from cross examining his own witness, no matter how hostile. Tension between Reed and Gallagher escalated. Once, Gallagher walked over to Reed's table and thumped it, while accusing Reed of making suggestions of facts as to things that were not in evidence. Reed half rose from his chair, growled, and sat down. Echoing the chill among the lawyers, the courtroom itself was drafty and cold, with most of the public in attendance clinging to their overcoats.

Thursday, March 24, began with the windows closed and the courtroom warm for the first time. The day opened with a procedural move by Sapiro to connect Ford's anti-Semitism to the anti-Sapiro articles. Sapiro sought permission to amend his Declaration to define the term "Jew" as one of "reproach, hatred, contumely and scorn." The proposed amended Declaration also cut the original one hundred forty-one allegations of libel to fifty-four. While the Sapiro side was unable to get *The International Jew* series admitted into evidence, the Judge indicated that it might be used as the basis for some "preliminary questions." He reiterated his ruling that one cannot libel a race. The Judge then released the jury for the day while the Ford lawyers reviewed Sapiro's revised Declaration.

Cameron returned to his seat on the witness stand for the start of the proceedings on Friday, March 25. His testimony remained vague and evasive, and Gallagher's questions were constantly interdicted by Stewart Hanley's and James Reed's constant sniping with objections. Cameron recounted ambiguous discussions with Henry Ford about Ford's "philosophy." Gallagher asked him, "Have you sought his opinion as to the policy of the *Independent*?" Cameron skated, quite practiced at it for a man of his girth. "The attitude of the *Independent* is usually expressed first, and Mr. Ford might comment afterwards." He admitted that he and Ford on occasion discussed the "international banking ring" but not the attitude of the *Independent*.

Reed asked the Judge to excuse the jury and then objected to the whole line of Gallagher's questions, because the only way Ford would have personal liability would be if he directly instigated the attacks on Sapiro. Gallagher, for his part, argued that it would not be necessary to show that Ford picked out Sapiro individually, only that he communicated to the staff of the paper that he hated Jews and that he wanted the paper to attack all or any of them.

Judge Raymond upbraided both sets of lawyers.

> I think both sides are getting far off the issue. We'll never get to the meat of this case. If I am wrong there is a remedy in the Circuit Court of Appeals. What we need is a little more light and perhaps less heat. Recall the jury and take the answer to the question.

Cameron, his face flushed, confirmed under questioning that he did not direct an investigation of the facts contained in the Sapiro articles, after the paper began receiving complaints of factual errors. He said that he believed that the *Independent's* business manager, Fred L. Black, may have undertaken an investigation of sorts, after a complaint by Walton Peteet, National Secretary of the Council of Farmer's Co-operative Associations. Cameron reiterated that his only discussion with Henry Ford about Sapiro occurred after Sapiro's demand for a retraction. He said the discussion was largely one-sided with Cameron doing most of the talking and Ford being generally uninterested. The Judge, at a point, cut to the chase and asked Cameron if he could remember the substance, if not the exact words, of his conversations with Ford. Cameron answered, "No."

Gallagher probed Cameron's editorial processes on the Dunn articles and Cameron admitted he was trying to narrow the scope of the attack to a "few of the financial group," but Raymond prevented Gallagher from forcing him to name particular alternative targets because the articles themselves were the "best evidence." In anticipation of Cameron producing other documents that had been request by the Sapiro side, Gallagher deferred further examination of Cameron until the documents would be available. The Ford lawyers, in turn, deferred their cross examination of Cameron as well.

Then, in a surprise move, Gallagher left the courtroom briefly and returned with his next witness, James Martin Miller in tow. Miller was a writer and former reporter with the *New York World,* who worked for Ford earlier and wrote an obsequiously flattering "authorized" book about him, modestly entitled, *The Amazing Story of Henry Ford: The Ideal American And the World's Most Famous Private Citizen.*[164] Miller testified that in the early 1920s, Ford had asked Miller if he knew Aaron Sapiro. Ford told him that Sapiro was "organizing farmers with that bunch of Jews down there, and trying to bilk them." Further, Ford told him, "We are going to expose him, and I think *The Dearborn Independent* has a good circulation among the farmers, and we will upset the apple cart." Reed's only cross examination of Miller was to ask him what happened when Miller sued Ford for the non-payment of his fees. "I lost," he said. Reed turned his back to Miller and

---

164. The S.A. Mullikin Co., Cincinnati, 1922. Miller, in his book, sought to soften the hard edges of Ford's anti-Semitism. "He [Henry Ford] saw from the beginning that the Jews themselves would be the greatest beneficiaries of this work. He felt that if even one man was fearless enough, and fair enough and well-informed enough to show a certain type of Jew what figure he cut in American opinion, it would open up the way for those Jews' self-correction," at 139.

waved him off the stand. Miller with a glare at Reed that could have melted rocks, slowly gathered himself and stepped down from the witness stand, but he had made the crucial evidential connection between Henry Ford and the Sapiro articles.

Late in the day, with a rough wind rattling the windows, Gallagher called Fred L. Black, the *Independent*'s affable business manager, to the stand. Black admitted taking part in the publication of *The International Jew.* Gallagher asked him to recount his memory of his September, 1924, meeting between the *Independent's* staff and Walton Peteet from the Council of Farmer's Co-operative Associations—the President of the co-op who had registered complaints written in letters to Henry Ford about false assertions in articles bashing Sapiro and the co-operative movement.

But before Black could open his mouth, Raymond abruptly adjourned the proceedings for the weekend, happy to be headed back home to Grand Rapids.

Chapter 18

Fruits, Vegetables and "Dough"

WEEK THREE
MARCH 28, 1927 - APRIL 2, 1927

A FEW CHEEKY NEWSPAPER reporters dubbed this "Fruit and Vegetable Week," in growing anticipation of the appearance of Aaron Sapiro as a witness to discuss his history with farmer co-operatives. Journalists had spent much of the weekend speculating as to when Henry Ford would appear, likely, they said, on Tuesday or Wednesday. On that chill March morning, following legal arguments, Judge Raymond accepted Sapiro's amendments to his Declaration over Senator Reed's objections. Reed then made a motion for a mistrial, which Raymond rejected.

Fred L. Black returned as a witness to complete his testimony as the *Independent's* business manager. Black testified that all mail received at the *Independent* and addressed to Henry Ford, marked "personal" or otherwise, went to the paper's sorting office. He admitted that the *Independent* was not a money-making proposition (thereby dependent upon regular Ford subsidies to stay afloat). Black told the jury that he sent a copy of Sapiro's demand for retraction addressed to Henry Ford to Ford's general secretary, Ernest G. Liebold, not Ford, "because I did not take things like that up with Mr. Ford." The chain of command thus established, Judge Raymond found that there was sufficient nexus between Ford and Liebold to allow the entry of sections of the Peteet letter, identified by Black as also having been sent to Liebold, into evidence. Reed objected, saying there was no evidence that Ford, himself, actually read the letter.

Peteet wrote, in part:

> Of my personal knowledge, I tell you that many of the statements about it in the Dearborn Independent [*sic*] are untrue and the philosophy and aim of the movement has been grotesquely misrepresented. It is strange indeed that your employees should, in your name, seek to destroy a movement which seeks to do for agriculture what you are trying to do for industry. It seems to be another case of paid writers writing what they think will please and twisting the facts to that end and keeping you away from men who know the real facts: but the co-operative movement can take care of itself.

The Peteet letter established that Henry Ford, or at least his personal secretary, Ernest G. Liebold, had reason to know that facts reported by the *Independent* concerning the co-operative marketing movement were being misrepresented. It was a small crack in the personal armor of alleged ignorance in which Ford's lawyers wrapped their client. Black, smiling amiably, nodded to the Judge as he left the stand.

Shortly before 4:00 in the afternoon, Aaron Sapiro, slim, confident, and impeccably dressed, strode to the witness stand with a curled document in his left hand, a closed fist in his right. In a firm, melodic voice, he introduced the jury to his remarkable rise from a San Francisco orphanage to his education at the Hebrew Union College in Cincinnati and the Hastings School of Law at the University of California in San Francisco. He described his early interest in the marketing problems of farms and his absorption of books on farm economics from the "great library" of his mentor, Col. Harris Weinstock, the first State Marketing Commissioner of California. He traced the development of his so-called "Sapiro plan" for co-operative marketing of single commodity farm products up until the War. Over the objections of

Senator Reed, the Judge allowed him to testify concerning his multiple attempts to join the U.S. Army during the War and his ultimate success in enlisting as an artillery private after being turned down in his application for officer's candidate school.

Sapiro described the growing interest in his plan from California to Canada across all product lines, from peanuts, pears, prunes, potatoes and beyond. Sapiro and Gallagher developed a smooth, seamless, call and response delivery of Sapiro's testimony, prompting Reed to complain that Sapiro answered Gallagher's questions so quickly that he was unable to get his objections in on time. Gallagher ended the day anticipating that Sapiro's direct testimony would only take a few hours on Tuesday and that Henry Ford would be called soon thereafter. But Gallagher had not counted on the intransigence of Senator Reed nor the cunning of Henry Ford.

A new sense of energy crackled in the courtroom on Tuesday morning in anticipation of the completion of the Sapiro presentation and the arrival of Henry Ford. Gallagher and Sapiro continued their easy duet, punctuated by the Ford team objections. Sapiro would smile at Gallagher and tell him to "try it another way." Sapiro described the development of his plan by his analysis of what worked in the past and what hadn't. He described the inspiration that he received from the Denmark agricultural distribution system. He recounted his merger and incorporation of both new and old ideas for co-operative marketing. He related his experience in drafting co-operative marketing statutes in many states and defending them in state supreme courts. Judge Raymond, on motion from Gallagher, accepted Sapiro as a qualified expert witness in the technical field of co-operative marketing. Clearly, the press corps in attendance did too, but what they really wanted was not dry professional expertise, but the unexploded bomb of Henry Ford being sworn in to testify.

Sapiro held the stand. He described the innovation of organizing by single commodity and the insertion of strict enforcement provisions in the grower contracts that bound them to the co-operative and prevented farmers from self-marketing or from "dumping" agricultural product on the market. In particular, Sapiro described the travails of the California tomato growers with federal price controls during the War, and in passing, mentioned that his clients were unsuccessful in obtaining any federal relief until Senator Reed, himself, came to their aid. Gallagher then asked, with a grin, "Was he one of those 'Gentile fronts' referred to in *The Dearborn Independent?*"

Reed broke in ahead of Sapiro, "I didn't know at the time who I was representing." Raymond pounded his gavel with annoyance to disperse the laughter in the courtroom.

Sapiro completed his direct testimony with a description of his yearly earnings from co-operative marketing ranging from a low of ten thousand dollars in 1916 to a high of sixty-one thousand five hundred thirty-one dollars in 1922. He testified that both his reputation and income dropped precipitously following the commencement of the *Independent* attacks on his character. With only two new farm groups retaining his services after the articles, his income dropped into the low forties. Gallagher, with a quick look at the clock, turned from Sapiro to Reed and with an open hand gesture, offered, "You may take the witness."

Reed, with a snort, pulled up a large, battered briefcase onto his table and ruffled through a bunch of notes on crumpled yellow paper. One newspaper described Reed as the "Missourian champion goat getter" and a master of "finesse of a poisonous attack."[165] With a snarl and a sneer, in a dangerously low voice, Reed soon wiped the smile from Sapiro's face as he bored in with his weapon of choice—Sapiro's pursuit of money. Reed focused his queries on Sapiro's law partnerships—the splitting of fees, the breakups, the hard feelings. He demanded precise fee earnings and their distribution among Sapiro's staff. He pushed Sapiro on the whereabouts of his legal firm's account journals going back for decades and the reasons that they had not been produced earlier as requested.

---

165. *Detroit Free Press,* March 30, 1927 at 2.

During a brief recess, the most exciting event of the afternoon buzzed the courtroom. A Henry Ford look-a-like, James E. Goodrich, appeared. A nonplussed bailiff ushered the man to a seat directly behind the Ford counsel table—as privately directed by several newsmen—before the lawyers returned to their seats. Goodrich asked about all the special attention he was getting, when he was just a curious spectator. With his everyman identity revealed, Goodrich became a ripple in the courtroom and a Ford twin's picture in the papers.

While his "double" was playing identity games in the courtroom, Henry Ford played a game of deceit himself. He faked an automobile accident and injury, which he hoped would prevent or at least delay him from being called to testify in the near term. Ford's "accident" had all the finger prints of a charade by his security chief, Harry H. Bennett. Bennett has been described as a man who thinks with his muscles. Sapiro's lawyers, observing Bennett skulking around the courtroom during the second week of the trial, assessing the jury, talking to the press and conferring privately with Ford's lawyers, were on the alert that something unusual was in play. It was. A formal statement written by Cameron and issued by Ford's lawyers stated:

> At 8:30 P.M., Sunday, March 27, a Ford Coupe driven by Henry Ford and occupied alone by him, was forced off the south drive of Michigan Avenue a few feet east of the River Rouge bridge and plunged down a steep embankment into a tree. Mr. Ford states that he was forced over the embankment by a car which came upon him from behind as he emerged from the driveway of the Ford laboratories at Dearborn.
>
> . . .
>
> Dr. R.D. McClure, Chief surgeon of the Henry Ford Hospital, was immediately called and remained with the injured man until Tuesday night, when he was removed in an ambulance to Henry Ford Hospital where he is now undergoing treatment. There has been a minor operation. *Because of the law suit now in progress,*

> *and the unavoidable and unfounded inferences, that may be drawn, t*he facts were withheld from the public although communicated to the court Monday morning.
>
> . . .
>
> Mr. Ford strongly depreciates the suggestion that the accident was the result of intent on anyone's part. At present, Mr. Ford is resting easily and no serious complications are expected. (emphasis supplied.)[166]

Was the car accident an accident? Alan Nevins and Frank Hill, in their epic Ford series, claimed "that Ford's injuries were real is shown by the statements of the doctors who were of too high a character at deception."[167] With all due respect to Nevins and Hill, their conclusion seems remarkably naïve. Dr. McClure was the Chief Surgeon at a hospital owned outright by Henry Ford. McClure reputedly spent two full days, around the clock, "caring" for Henry Ford at his home before sending him to the hospital for injuries never specifically documented elsewhere.

Bennett indicated to the press that the vehicle alleged to have forced Ford's car off of the road was a Studebaker, the manufacturers of which were Jewish. Bennet made every effort to downplay the incident as an accident. He and his subordinates, who requested and received no assistance from federal investigative agencies, undertook the investigation themselves. Years later, Bennett disclosed one aspect of the contrivance. In his memoir, he describes a conversation with Henry Ford where Ford told him, "Well Harry, I wasn't in that car when it went down in the river. I don't know how it got down there. But now, we've got a good chance to settle this thing."[168] The accident served as a de-

166. *Minneapolis Star*, March 30, 1927 at 1.

167. Nevins, Allan and Hill, Frank, *Ford: Expansion and Challenge: 1915-1933*, Charles Scribner's Sons, N.Y. 1957 at 320.

168. Bennett, Harry, *We never called him Henry*, (Greenwich: Fawcett, 1951. at 93.

laying tactic, but it was not, in and of itself, enough to derail the trial. Bennett and his cohorts had more work to do, and they were up to the task.

Wednesday, March 30, delivered the surprising news of Ford's accident. Gallagher responded to the news "leak," saying, "Naturally, we regret that such a thing has happened, and our regret is possibly more keen because it happened during this suit." He and his client suggested that there was nothing apparent in the information released that Ford would be unable to take the stand before the completion of the case, and that an independent, court ordered, physical examination of Mr. Ford might be necessary on the horizon.

This dramatic blip gave way to the long, dry, technical slog of cross examination. Reed continued to pound Sapiro repeatedly about the amount of money he collected in fees and the failure of many of the co-operative associations, relentlessly impugning that Sapiro's alleged loss of income might likely have derived from other events than the *Independent* publications. Reed detailed the dissolution of several of Sapiro's law firms and the failure of a large number of the co-operatives that he represented. Judge Raymond permitted Reed to read from a letter Sapiro wrote in which he related the failure of the California Tomato Growers Association. The letter graphically described, in Sapiro's own hand, the economic collapse of one of Sapiro's principal clients, but the letter had "two hands," that softened the thrust Reed was trying to make. On the other hand, the letter contained Sapiro's note that the "fatal blunders" which wrecked the association occurred while he was in the army and could not be held accountable for those events. Gallagher, smilingly, requested the court order Reed to read that counterpoint to the jury himself.

The *Detroit Free Press* described the Reed/Sapiro confrontation:

> The cruel eraser of cynicism rubbed off that look of sociability [from Sapiro], Wednesday. He and Reed fenced without any buttons of sham joviality on their faces. Sapiro was cold as Reed was cold, but temperament saddled him with a certain disadvantage. He riled easier than the imperturbable Senator. Always

> to Reed there was the Mississippi drawl, thrumming on Sapiro's nerves. Reed was no slugger, he was a boxer, beating flesh to rawness by jabbing constantly at the same spot.[169]

Reed's cross examination of Aaron Sapiro continued on Tuesday, April 1, as newspapers all over the country sought news of Henry Ford and his condition. The acrimonious give and take in the courtroom again centered on fees and failures, with Sapiro carefully parsing answers to Reed's questions. Reed, while reading from a letter that Sapiro wrote about organizing a group of wheat growers, misread the letter.

> Q. (While reading) ". . . mailing plan for central agency followed by Rio Grande Grower's Exchange which will best suit the needs of Northwest Group. Also, please go over this with Garrick and Adopt."
>
> A. And "adapt."
>
> A. I am going to ask you to read it correctly, Mr. Reed.
>
> Q. I what?
>
> A. I am going to ask you to read it correctly. It says "and adapt."
>
> Q. That is true, it is "adapt." What did I say, "adopt?"
>
> A. "Adopt."
>
> Q. Very well, you distinguish between "adapt" and "adopt."
>
> A. Any man does.

Meanwhile, Harry Bennett worked at feeding stories and inside information with a negative bent on Sapiro to William K. Hutcheson, a wire service reporter affiliated with the Hearst syndicate,[170] via the *Detroit Times*. The *Times* published a report in the morning

---

169. *Detroit Free Press,* March 21, 1927 at 4.

170. Henry Ford had a close, personal relationship with Arthur Brisbane, Chief Editor of the Hearst Syndicate, and later consulted with him and Bennett privately about settling the Sapiro case.

edition on April 1, that an agent of the federal court was investigating the Ford accident to determine if there was a relationship with the libel case, the inference being that Sapiro's "friends" might have attacked Ford in an attempted assassination. The courtroom humming with the news, the assembled reporters pressed Raymond for confirmation of the report. Judge Raymond announced to the press that the story was without foundation and cautioned the jury against reading newspapers about the case. The speculation of an assassination attempt on Henry Ford preoccupied the press focus on the trial. The murder plot story died hard.[171]

Friday, April 2, continued in the same pattern: Reed examining Sapiro's work in many and diverse product co-operative organizations. Reed would ask Sapiro if he formed the organization to which Sapiro would respond, "Yes." Reed would ask, "Didn't you make speeches to the growers?" "I explained the contracts and urged them to join," Sapiro would answer. Reed would ask, "What did you get paid for it?" and Sapiro would dig out his ledgers and list his fees. Reed particularly underscored cases in which Sapiro had difficulty collecting his fees, and would ask how those controversies squared with Sapiro's espoused policy of letting the client set the fees. Reed continued to plug away on his insistence, as one paper put it, that Sapiro engaged in billing policies designed to "feather the nest of his altruism."[172]

Reed hammered away like a Southern Paul Bunyan. He found it necessary, from time to time, to vent his frustration with Sapiro's rapid fire and particularized responses to questions where he hoped to elicit a "yes" or "no" response. The Judge, impatient with the lagging examination, more often than not, would tell Reed to move on to another question. Reed, becoming physically fatigued with the burden of extended cross examination, asked for and received permission from the Court to continue his examination while sitting down.

The Ford team decided to back away from any assassination

---

171. *News Journal,* (Wilmington, Del.), April 2, 1927.

172. *Detroit Free Press,* April 2, 1927 at 1.

attempt suggestion. Outside of the courtroom, Harry Bennett reported to the press the results of his weeklong "investigation" of the Ford "accident." The burly Bennett foreclosed further inquiry by local government officials, announcing that he had provided a full investigative report to Robert M. Toms, the Wayne County prosecutor. Newsmen took note. The report concluded that the incident had been an unavoidable accident. Toms closed his file on the matter. Ford's physicians reported that Ford was resting comfortably at his Fairlane estate. The *Detroit Free Press* later reported that, "Despite the fact that Ford himself appears to have originated the charge or suspicion that the sideswiping was deliberate, Ford, Saturday deplored the circulation of this report and ordered that the incident thereafter must officially be called an accident, at least by his own employees."[173]

WEEK FOUR
APRIL 4, 1927 - APRIL 8, 1927

On Monday, April 4, Sapiro's brother, Milton, arrived from California with additional financial ledgers requested by Reed. Milton Sapiro, also a lawyer, was sworn in as a counsel in the case for Aaron Sapiro. Reed devoted six hours of the day to further cross examination, attempting to establish that if a farmer organization was unresponsive to Sapiro's direction, he would vent his spleen in an attempt to wreck that group in favor of another; and that Sapiro's main, overarching interest was the collection of large fees. Over Sapiro's passionate denials, Reed attempted to show that Sapiro participated in political and jurisdictional disputes between grain grower organizations, which he suggested were motivated by a quest for fees. Gallagher objected stridently and repeatedly. Reed asked that the jury be excused while he explained his line of questioning to the Judge.

One of our contentions is that Sapiro was not practicing law in

---

173. April 2, 1927 at 1.

> the ordinary way. He was promoting various organizations in an endeavor to gain control over them or obtain employment with them, and when he could not gain control, he undertook to wreck them. All of this was improper work for an attorney, and it naturally would destroy his reputation as an attorney or even as an organizer. His income would be adversely affected by it.[174]

The Judge, hesitantly, with limitations, permitted Reed to continue with his general line of questions of Sapiro, with an advisement to the jury that the interrogation was limited to the issue as to the existence of an alternative source of Sapiro's alleged damages.

Whether through fatigue or intention, Reed continued to mispronounce Sapiro's name throughout the day and was forced to apologize for his mistake when Sapiro complained.

On Tuesday, the ongoing drone of relentless cross examination continued, with audience seats available for the taking. No Henry Ford in court. More fees, more explanations. More descriptions of the Sapiro plan.[175]

Wednesday, April 6, proceeded with much more of the same, until the exasperated Judge reprimanded Reed and Sapiro, complaining that the record contained too much drivel and the examination was taking up too much time. Gallagher advised the Court that he would not call Henry Ford to testify until near the end of the following week, because his redirect examination of his client would require him to cover much of the same ground to clean up misperceptions left by Senator Reed. Rolling his eyes, Judge Raymond pounded his gavel and adjourned the court for the day.

On Thursday, Reed focused on a letter written by Aaron Sapiro after a Ford attack on him in 1924. Sapiro wrote, "While some people think these Ford articles have crippled us, we ask favors from no

---

174. *Detroit Free Press,* April 6, 1927 at 2.

175. Rather than tie himself to preparation for the next day, Reed gave a little talk to the University of Michigan Grid Iron Club that evening in Ann Arbor, where he was presented with an inscribed brass spittoon. Reed, oddly, spoke to a number of groups in the midst of the trial, when most lawyers would be consumed with their preparation.

one." He wrote this in correspondence with the Minnesota Potato Growers Exchange, during a dispute over fees. Reed intimated that the letter showed Sapiro's real problem with his income was not the articles, but his poor relationships with the co-operatives. Reed then spent a good part of the day fingering Sapiro's relationship with a West Coast agricultural brokerage and marketing venture, Weyl and Zuckerman, referred to by Reed as "speculators," while also representing growers doing business with that firm. Reed had a point, but lost it in the mass of examination details.

The strain showed on all participants, Reed chief among them. On Friday, April 8, Reed attempted to chase his younger and far more energetic opponent. He tried to show that Sapiro was involved in negotiating a sale of warehouses to tobacco farmers for two million dollars over their market price, and persisted in the effort—even though the warehouses did not exist at the time. The deeply deceptive Dunn, in one of his articles, had said that they were sold, and Reed bought Dunn's "fake news" story. The court, under Judge Raymond's guidance, did not.

Mercifully, Reed slid into a weekend of rest, with his cross examination scheduled to continue on Monday. Both sides were emotionally spent, knowing that the examination of Aaron Sapiro would likely continue through the coming week.

WEEK FIVE
APRIL 11, 1927 - APRIL 16, 1927

Week five started with a bang. Following a confrontation with Judge Raymond, on Monday, April 11, Gallagher moved for a mistrial, arguing that the Judge's language and demeanor "unjustly prejudiced" Sapiro. In response to one of Sapiro's own arguments to Reed, the Judge snapped, "I must insist that you confine yourself to answering the questions—and I shall have to be more insistent in the future than I have been in the past because of your apparent willingness to disobey the injunction of the court." He went on, "The difficulty has been that there has been too much controversial matter which led us nowhere. There seems no way to end any discussion. Even the final statement of the court does not seem sufficient. I am not familiar with that particular type of procedure in federal court. It will be necessary to end it summarily in the future."

William Gallagher, his cheeks red as a beet, replied caustically, "I feel that you have unjustly prejudiced us by this comment. We have endeavored to facilitate this case in every way and bring out everything germane to it. To put us in the light of obstructing this case is certainly, it seems to us, absolutely unfair to the witness and myself."

The Judge denied his motion and took a moment to cool down. Turning to the jury, he remarked,

> I think the difficulty we are now in is due to the fact that the witness is a lawyer himself and it is difficult for any lawyer to avoid controversy and argument. I do not think it is due to any unwillingness of this witness to refuse to obey the order of the court, but is a natural and obvious consequence of a lawyer being also a witness.[176]

The day continued on in the potato fields of Idaho and Colorado.

Tuesday, April 12, the 11th day of the Sapiro cross examination, brought a milder day in the courtroom. The name of famed Jewish-American financier, investor, philanthropist and consultant to President Woodrow Wilson, Bernard Baruch, surfaced. During World War I, Wilson put Baruch in charge of the War Industries Board, which successfully managed America's economic mobilization during the War. Baruch was one of the "All little pals together," that Harry Dunn, sarcastically accused of being part of the Jewish "conspiracy" to gain control of American agriculture.[177] Bernard M. Baruch entered the record when Sapiro testified that he met

---

176. *Chicago Daily Tribune*, April 12, 1927 at 23.

177. Morgan, Robert (Harry Dunn), "Jewish Exploitation of Farmer's Organizations, II. The story of the Sapiro Boys," *The Dearborn Independent,* April 19, 1924 at 4.

for the first time with Robert W. Bingham, a tobacco farmer and publisher of the *Louisville Courier Journal* newspaper, in Baruch's office. The audience sat up in attention as Reed explored the meeting. Perhaps evidence of the conspiracy was at hand.

Q. What were you doing in Baruch's office?

A. Meeting Mr. Bingham.

Q. What was Mr. Bingham doing in Mr. Baruch's office?

A. Meeting me.

Q. What were you both doing there?

A. We were discussing the tobacco problem.[178]

While Bernard Baruch was an enthusiastic supporter of the concept of co-operative marketing to assist farmers, Reed was unable to establish any kind of nefarious connection between Sapiro and Baruch, other than Baruch let him use his office, in Washington, to meet with a prominent Gentile tobacco grower. Sapiro went on to discuss a conference there in which sixty Kentuckians, including growers, warehouse owners, and bankers were present, and where Spiro outlined the co-operative marketing concept. Reed spun his wheels looking through account ledgers trying to elicit evidence of the amount the Kentuckians paid Sapiro for his services, dates and other references.

It was a day of starts and stops due to Sapiro's lack of knowledge of events at which he was not present and the Court's refusal to allow Reed to press beyond the penumbra of Sapiro's personal knowledge in his examination. Reed, looking for gold, found mostly lead.

Out-of-court proceedings far outshone in-court proceedings for sheer drama. Mid-day, Gallagher announced that his process server, Thomas S. Warsham, had successfully served Ford's personal secretary Liebold with a subpoena. Just that morning,

178. *Detroit Free Press*, April 13, 1927 at 7.

Warsham eluded the Ford bodyguards of Ernest G. Liebold, the Vice-President and Treasurer of the Dearborn Publishing Company, the corporate entity of the *Independent.* After an automobile chase and a two-block sprint on foot, Warsham served the hefty, panting Liebold with a subpoena to appear as a witness. Though the subpoena was returnable on Wednesday, the next day, Ford's lawyers agreed that Liebold would henceforth appear when asked.

Two of Ford's attorneys, Stewart Hanley and Richard J. Higgins, chewed up most of the day on Wednesday, April 13, by reading into the record a long speech given by Aaron Sapiro when he crossed into Bluegrass Country and turned his attention to the tobacco growers of Kentucky on March 25, 1921, which was also Derby Day. Sapiro spoke of their problems and potential solutions. He explained what he had accomplished with purple prunes, processed eggs, and red Walla Walla wheat. He said, "You have not half realized your opportunities in China for instance. You should see how the Chinese in California have taken to the cigarette. If they find it to their liking, what is wrong with extending commerce to China itself? It might even ween the Chinese from opium in time."[179]

The Ford lawyers had intended to read only four paragraphs of the speech into the record, but one of the jurors, Amor Duart, an accountant, had requested that the entire speech be read. Barely audible groans seeped through the courtroom. The Judge steadied his elbows on his desk. The reading of the twenty-four-thousand-word speech went on and on, the attorneys, unfamiliar with the content and lacking personal enthusiasm for the task, sucking all vitality and interest out of Sapiro's address. All this, hours and hours of this, to establish that Sapiro had received a fee of ninety thousand dollars for his services, and his vivid description of a coming "tobacco millennium."

On the 13th day of the Sapiro cross examination, birds took center stage. Excitement in the courtroom arose with the pres-

---

179. *Detroit Free Press,* April 14, 1927 at 2.

ence of two pigeons who encamped on top of one of the Italian marble pillars next to Judge Raymond's bench. According to *The New York Times,* the pigeons seemed to sympathize with Sapiro, as they began cooing loudly whenever Reed raised his voice to ask a question.[180] Reed's split focus for the day was avoiding droppings and challenging the farmer bona fides of Sapiro's Kentucky tobacco audience. "Isn't it true that 75% of the men who attended your organization meeting in Louisville, March 25-26 of 1921, were owners of warehouses or financially interested in them?"

> Sapiro: "As far as I know that is not the fact."
>
> Reed: "Well how far do you know?"
>
> Sapiro: "I don't believe any large number of them were warehouse men. Some may have been interested in farmer's warehouses."

Around and around went the Reed blame wheel, rarely finding purchase.

The court released the jury, the lawyers and the pigeons in the early afternoon, over Good Friday. Reed's "crucifixion" proceedings of Sapiro paused for the weekend. Aaron Sapiro traveled to New York and Senator Reed grabbed a train to Washington, D.C.

WEEK SIX
APRIL 18, 1927 – APRIL 27, 1927

Senator Reed failed to appear in court on Monday, April 18. He sent word that he was confined to his hotel room because of illness. Judge Raymond granted the Ford lawyer's request for a continuance until the following Thursday. Gallagher did not oppose the continuance but raised the hackles of his opponents by saying before the jury, "Our attitude is this. We do not want the defense to have any pretense or claim that they were injured in the defense of the case through the untimely illness of Senator Reed. We pre-

180. April 15, 1927 at 9.

fer to have the case stand over until the man in charge of the matter, himself, be upon the ground, so there will be no alibi or excuse for the collapse of the defense, just because the man in charge could not carry on." Crimson with anger, Clifford Longley, normally silent before the jury, demanded that Gallagher's remarks be stricken. Gallagher, pulsing a smile, responded, "Perhaps the defense cannot collapse, when it never has been maintained."[181]

The scuttlebutt around the courthouse said that Henry Ford was expected to appear the following week. In the meantime, a Kansas City rabbi, Harry H. Mayer, asked Jews not to condemn Senator Reed for defending Ford.

> It was a matter of regret to me that our senior senator has combined himself with the greatest enemy, if an ignorant enemy, that the Jew ever had. I plead with you, however, to remember, before passing judgment, that Senator Reed always has shown a magnificent freedom in religious and racial matters.[182]

But a far greater hum arose from the underground workings of Ford's henchmen. Since the Ford "accident," Harry Bennett and his detectives and security men had been very busy. One of the Ford lawyers, Stewart Hanley, late on Monday, advised the Judge that the defense would be filing a motion for a mistrial based upon juror misconduct. A deputy U.S. Marshal, George H. Boermer, escorted one of the jurors, Mrs. Cora Hoffman, into the Judge's chambers for a forty-five-minute interview. A relative of Hoffman's, employed by Ford, had claimed that Mrs. Hoffman before the trial expressed a deep-rooted prejudice against Mr. Ford, and that she was disposed to enter a verdict in favor of Sapiro, were she to be impaneled on the jury. In chambers, it was reported, Mrs. Hoffman denied the charges.

Gallagher, for his part, contained his fury at the unfolding events but not his legal acumen. In conference in the Judge's

---

181. *The New York Times*, April 20, 1927 at 4.

182. Quoted in the *Lansing State Journal*, April 18, 1927 at 5.

chambers, with all attorneys present, he requested the Judge to rein in the Ford detectives from any contact with the jury. When Clifford Longley, the Ford Motor Company's General Counsel suggested, in Reed's absence, that Stewart Hanley take over the cross examination, Gallagher objected. He believed he had Reed on the ropes and preferred to wait for Reed's return. Letting a stronger, younger attorney step into the ring at this late date endangered the outcome. Gallagher's objection was sustained.

Reporter William K. Hutchinson, covering the investigation and mistrial motion for the Hearst syndicate, kept in close contact with Harry Bennett. Bennett gave Hutchinson the address of Mrs. Hoffman on 14th Street in Detroit. Hutchinson hunted her down overnight. Pressed for information, Hoffman angrily defended herself. She denied having expressed prejudice against Ford, but in the context of her personal self-defense, she stated, "It looks to me as if certain people were trying to get a hold of something to have the case thrown out of court." Hutchinson published his interview with Hoffman in the late edition of the *Detroit Times*. This was just the key to a mistrial which Harry Bennett sought. When the defense lawyers took a copy of the article to the Judge, he declared that the *Times* was in contempt and that sanctions would follow.

And then the dice house tumbled.

On the morning of Wednesday, April 20, Clifford Longley filed fifteen affidavits with the Court executed by Ford detectives, a Ford lawyer and a Ford employee (Mrs. Hoffman's relative). The affidavits essentially set forth four grounds for a mistrial. First, Mrs. Hoffman on voir dire claimed that her husband was a plumbing contractor, but neglected to state that he also ran a "blind pig"[183] drinking establishment. Second, Mrs. Hoffman claimed on voir dire to have no personal interest in the case, but before being selected to sit on the jury she told a relative that if

183. There were an estimated twenty thousand "blind Pigs" in Detroit during prohibition. The term derived from entrepreneurs selling tickets to see a "blind pig" in a joint and being served an illegal libation once inside.

she were selected "it would not be healthy for Mr. Ford." Third, Mrs. Hoffman expressed partisan views in her interview with the *Detroit Times.* Fourth, Mrs. Hoffman was overheard talking with a man referred to as "Kid" (from his boxing days) Miller, a "gentleman with a Jewish cast of countenance," concerning a proposition that would bring her money, and who during a break provided her with a five-pound box of candy.[184]

Could a suspect car "accident," a timely Reed health crisis, a harmless box of chocolates, and a passing chat with a real estate broker euchre Henry Ford out of the potential humiliation of another visit to the witness stand?

The move blindsided Gallagher and his team. He complained bitterly that the defense had been discussing these issues with the Judge for some time; he wasn't made timely aware of the claims. "I learned of it on the way to the courtroom after it was in flaming headlines in the press." Gallagher and Sapiro described the defense motion for a mistrial as a "perfect frame-up," and in view of Ford's refusal to proceed with eleven jurors, rather than twelve, a "desperate attempt to postpone Ford's appearance in court."

---

184. Miller was apparently a realtor and the box candy actually came from a male juror as a prize for a winning bridge game. Mrs. Hoffman shared the candy with all the jurors.

CHAPTER 19

Denouement

JUDGE RAYMOND REQUESTED FEDERAL investigators to look into the matters raised by the Ford affidavits, and after interviewing Mrs. Hoffman and Mr. Miller himself, and receiving the investigators' reports, he concluded that there was no basis for any allegation of jury tampering on the part of Sapiro or his lawyers. Gallagher had told the court, "We knew these detectives [estimated at around 50] were hanging around outside of the doors of the courtroom and everywhere, and what they were there for was to get evidence upon which some sort of a charge or insinuation might be based." The prosecutor said that he had never known of a case where "justice was not merely blind but apparently manacled and chained and gagged." Gallagher harkened back to the Defense's hardball efforts to disqualify Judge Tuttle.

> What I had to say about Justice being "gagged" and "manacled" refers to the conduct of Ford counsel in this case. If I shall make it specific, I will refer to the fact that when Judge Tuttle had told them they would not have an adjournment and that this case must go on, they tied his hands so that he could not sign an order; they gagged his lips so that he could not issue one, by filing this affidavit of prejudice against this man who has the righteous respect and confidence of this community throughout a long period of public life.[185]

185. *Detroit Free Press*, April 22, 1927 at 8.

Though Judge Raymond found that no jury tampering had occurred, he granted the motion for mistrial. Gallagher conceded that Raymond had no choice. The irony was lost on no one: Mrs. Hoffman was just defending herself, and her statement to the effect that she believed (correctly) that the attack on her was precipitated by the Ford team's perception that they were losing the trial, established the very bias that led to her disqualification. The Judge issued a statement to the press exonerating Mrs. Hoffman and Aaron Sapiro from any hint of jury tampering, while striking out angrily at the *Detroit Times*. He said, "This case fails to a large extent because justice has been crucified upon the cross of unethical and depraved journalism."[186] He ordered that contempt of court proceedings be commenced against the newspaper, but that action was eventually dropped. Raymond was either unaware of or reluctant to pursue any connection between Ford and the *Detroit Times*, or both, but it is difficult to imagine that he didn't have some clue as to what was going on. This was a door he really didn't want to open. In his heart of hearts, he was just happy to return to Grand Rapids. He set April 30 as the date to reconvene and set a new trial date.

Mr. Hutchinson, whose name did not appear in the *Detroit Times* interview with Mrs. Hoffman, never once mentioned his role in creating the mistrial proceedings. That would have landed him a personal contempt citation.[187] On the 30th of April, Judge Raymond continued the trial setting date until July 1, largely due to the failure of the federal government to refill the jury payment coffers of the court.

In May, 1927, the Arbitration Committee of the Detroit Board

---

186. Id.

187. Hutchinson, who was a lawyer, also covered the famous Scopes "Monkey Trial," where John Scopes was prosecuted for teaching the theory of evolution. Hutchinson, at Scopes' request, suppressed information that he received from John Scopes, who admitted he never actually taught evolution in the classroom—which would have blown up Clarence Darrow's show trial.

of Commerce offered to arbitrate the whole dispute, but the Ford interests rejected the offer, even though Henry Ford's son Edsel was a member of the Arbitration Committee. Aaron Sapiro put forth a proposal to pay half of the costs of the jury fees himself to speed up a retrial, but the Ford side refused to pony up the other half.

The million-dollar "trial of the century" bumped like a deflated balloon to rest.

A Separate Peace

> "Ford has to his debit, more erratic interviews on public questions, more dubious quotations, more blindly boasted ignorance of American history and American experience, more political nonsense, more dangerous propaganda, than any other dependable citizen that we have ever known."[188]

So said Arthur Vandenburg,[189] publisher of the *Grand Rapids Herald*. He, like many others, believed the country had dodged a bullet when Ford withdrew from the presidential election. That had occurred in December of 1923, when Henry Ford (who never had announced his candidacy anyway) conceded the territory to Calvin Coolidge. Ford tended to back a horse until that horse showed signs of losing. He was not good at losing.[190] In the late spring of 1927, under mounting evidence that his bloated and unruly libel trial would require that he actually stand as a witness, with news accounts claiming the jury felt the whole trial was already tipping to Sapiro's favor, Ford set his minions onto the task of dismantling it.

---

188. Sward, supra at 127.

189. Vandenburg, an internationalist, later served as a Republican U.S. Senator from the State of Michigan.

190. Ford's prospects for the Presidency diminished when the unpopular Warren G. Harding died in office. Ford, sensing a change in the playing field, endorsed Harding's successor, Calvin Coolidge, in exchange for Coolidge's support for Ford's efforts to purchase, on short sale, the Government's water power and fertilizer plants at Muscle Shoals, Alabama. Coolidge, to Ford's regret, was unable to deliver.

Ford had many reasons for bailing. Principal among them, his wife Clara and son Edsel's plainspoken opposition to his anti-Semitic fervors. They disliked the hounding trial publicity and cringed under the onus of reading yet another national article on Henry's amped-up hate campaign. Hate was fine, in private, but Henry had balled up his fists and bared his wrists in the most public of rings. Secondly, the Ford Motor Company had begun losing money on its out-of-date Model T and was about to introduce its new Model A, with a V-8 engine. As New York Ford dealer Gaston Plantiff reminded Ford, even Jews buy cars.

The members of the jury expressed disappointment when they learned of their dismissal. A general public perception prevailed that Ford was on his way to losing the case. *The New York Times* ran a story, after the mistrial, that the jury, at the time of the mistrial, believed the Ford defense had collapsed. The paper quoted juror Amor H. Duart, an accountant, that Sapiro "was in a fair way to get a verdict."[191] Duart said, "The jury almost unanimously believed that the defense had collapsed and that the plaintiff was justified in bringing the suit." Post-trial interviews[192] with the witnesses suggested that it was a closer case than *The Times* suggested. Mrs. Hoffman was not particularly liked by a number of the jurors. Nor was Mr. Duart, who allegedly arrived at the courthouse with a scent of alcohol on his breath. One of the jurors, Grace A. Jewell, stated to Ford investigators that she "always looked up to Mr. Ford as a second Lincoln." Juror Grace Stiles was not a fan of Sapiro, but Juror Emma Clarkson liked Gallagher and felt Reed was a "dottering old man." Others suggested they had not made up their minds. When the grueling task of following circuitous court arguments for six straight weeks came to nothing, they all trooped out into the humdrum April sunshine of a busy Detroit day.

So, Henry Ford, who nearly ran for president, who feared public speaking more than he hated Jews, decided to make peace and

---

191. April 22, 1927 at 2.

192. Box 40, Accession 48, BFRC.

thus bury the libel trial in a deep, dark hole of public forgetfulness.

Harry H. Bennett, "the little man in Henry Ford's cellar," orchestrated Ford's armistice with the Jews. Consulting with newsman Arthur Brisbane, from the Hearst syndicate, Bennett learned the pathway to resolution led through the American Jewish Committee. He chose as emissaries two men, outside of the legal team, who had considerable leverage in Washington. The first, Joseph Palma, was a member of the New York Field Office of the U.S. Secret Service who, like Bennett, had significant underworld connections.[193] The second was Earl J. Davis, a former assistant U.S. Attorney General and the U.S. Attorney for the Eastern District of Michigan, known for his aggressive pursuit of bootleggers during prohibition. Making the rounds in Washington, D.C., the men easily linked up with Nathan D. Perlman, a former U.S. Congressman and Vice-President of the American Jewish Committee. Perlman sent Ford's envoys to Louis Marshall, then the President of the Committee, to discuss terms of a rapprochement.

Once his astonishment had cleared, Marshall told the Ford emissaries that they would need to obtain an official disclaimer of the anti-Semitic publications and a formal apology for the harm inflicted by Ford and company. Ford passed on to Marshall his intent to settle both the Bernstein and Sapiro lawsuits as part of the process. The formal "apology," drafted by Marshall, not Ford, was long on regret and short on responsibility. Marshall was more of a mediator than a litigator.[194] His goal, clearly, was to obtain a repudiation by Ford of his anti-Semitic diatribes, while providing Ford the personal cover of business distraction to explain the malfeasance of his subordinates. Marshall wanted peace with

---

193. Palma later became the first Ford dealer on Staten Island. His home on Staten island was the location for the Corleone compound in the filming of The Godfather.

194. In 1910, Marshall, along with later U.S. Supreme Court Justice, Louis Brandeis, acted as mediators in a strike by seventy thousand cloak workers in New York. He was also part of the legal team that represented Leo Frank.

Ford and Ford's expression of regret was enough to satisfy him. Ford directed that Arthur Brisbane, from the Hearst Syndicate of newspapers, would have the exclusive right to publish the text of the apology after it was signed. The apology, in part, said:

> Although both publications [*The International Jew* and *The Dearborn Independent*] are my property, it goes without saying that in the multitude of my activities it has been impossible for me to devote personal attention to their management or to keep informed as to their contents. It has therefore inevitably followed that the conduct and policy of these publications had to be delegated to men whom I placed in charge of them and upon whom I relied implicitly.
>
> . . .
>
> This has led to my direct personal attention to this subject, in order to ascertain the exact nature of these articles.
>
> . . .
>
> Had I appreciated even the general nature, to say nothing of the details, of these utterances, I would have forbidden their circulation without a moment's hesitation, because I am fully aware of the virtues of the Jewish people as a whole, of what they and their ancestors have done for civilization and for mankind and toward the development of commerce and industry, of their sobriety and diligence, their benevolence and their unselfish interest in the public welfare.
>
> . . .
>
> Those who know me can bear witness that it is not my nature to inflict insult upon or to occasion pain to anybody. . . . I deem it my duty as an honorable man to make amends . . . by asking for forgiveness for the harm I have unintentionally committed . . . and by giving them the unqualified assurance that henceforth they may look to me for friendship and good will.

After Ford deputy, Harry Bennett, read the apology and expressed strong concerns about it to Ford, Ford told him to sign Ford's name to it, without change, without himself reading it, which Bennett did on June 30, 1927. The apology appeared in the Hearst newspapers on July 8, 1927.

Ford paid Bernstein and his lawyers seventy-five thousand dollars in settlement, half of the net going to his lawyers. Marshall, as partner to Untermeyer, Bernstein's lawyer, received half of the legal fee, indicating that he was going to save it for the refunding of a reprint of Bernstein's book that had discredited the *Protocols*. Marshall died in 1929 before the republication. He left no provision for Bernstein.

In the Sapiro settlement, Aaron Sapiro netted twenty-eight thousand eight hundred dollars, after payment of expenses. He adopted the mantel of a white knight, who had successfully defended his race. He even praised his adversary, Henry Ford, as having done "the square and manly thing, and I believe he meant every word of the public apology. He is now doing his utmost to wipe out the harm he caused to the Jewish people." We have no idea how sincere Sapiro's claim may be.

Gallagher accepted fifty-seven thousand seven hundred fifty dollars in fees after initially stalling for one hundred thousand dollars, the amount of Reed's retainer. Shortly after being retained by Sapiro, Ford had apparently offered Gallagher a piece of Ford Motor Company business, which Gallagher declined. Gallagher later stated, "I thought that the prosecution of Mr. Sapiro's claim was little short of a public duty."[195]

Ford worked every one of these settlements in back channels, outside the knowledge or input of his staff or his attorneys. Henry Ford left them all twisting in the winds of ignorance—embarrassed and angry. Said Chief Attorney Reed, "All I want to say about that case is that, whatever the amount of the fee, it was not big enough to pay me for a client lying down after I had won my case." Later in a letter to Clifford Longley, to settle up his fees, Reed said, perhaps posturing, "In view of the miserable outcome of the case, I would like to get the matter [of my fees], settled and

---

195. Woeste, supra, at 388, n. 70.

off my mind, and as far behind as possible. I hardly need to say to you that If [*sic*] I had dreamed before entering the case of any such denouement, I would not have gone into it for any kind of a fee."[196] Reed continued to serve in Congress, and when he lost the Presidential race, in 1928, he returned to private practice, living out his life in high color and contrast.

After these settlements were made public, E. G. Pipp wrote:

> Henry Ford loves money, he loves power, he loves leadership. He likes to be first in everything. Ford for years encouraged Cameron in the work of vengeance. Now that he sees the effect of it on himself as well as others, he repudiates Cameron and his works, works molded after Ford patterns. I will not say the spirit is not contrite. I will not say that he has not been overpowered by the awfulness of that which had been done in his name. I will not say that he is sorry for business reasons alone. You will have to judge that for yourself.[197]

In answer to the question of Ford's contrition, Ernest G. Liebold said, "I don't know as Mr. Ford ever apologized for anything. Of course, he was supposed to have apologized to the Jews, but I think everyone knows about that. He never even read that or never even knew what it contained. He simply told them to go ahead and fix it up."[198]

The New York Times heaped praise on Sapiro for pursuing his cause, Sapiro now a David standing up to Henry Ford's fallen Goliath.

> Whatever else may be said or thought of Mr. Sapiro, he certainly showed courage in bringing suit against a man whose great wealth enabled him to avail of every legal recourse in defense. No one knows what would have happened if the second trial had come and the case gone to the jury. It is far better, that Mr.

---

196. Reed to Longley, September 27, 1927, Box 1, Accession 1740, BFRC.

197. E.G.Pipp, "Ford's Recantation Analyzed," *The American Hebrew,* July 15, 1927 at 347.

198. Liebold, Reminiscences, supra, at 1384

> Ford should have become convinced of the baselessness of the accusations made in his name against Mr. Sapiro and should have completely withdrawn them. This fact does not in the least diminish the credit due Mr. Sapiro for standing up for his personal rights against a powerful adversary.[199]

TENUOUS TRUCE

During his settlement negotiations, Henry Ford agreed to make amends to the Jewish race by gathering up and destroying his anti-Semitic publications and prohibiting their republication. He agreed to close down the *Independent* and to terminate Messrs. Cameron and Liebold. He shuttered the *Independent* in December 1927, and merely moved his two "editors" to other positions in the Ford Motor Company. Ford enjoyed about six years of balmy relations with the Jewish community. His apology[200] was accepted and well received by Jews and the Ford Motor Company passed out its advertising largess to Jewish publications. On May 23, 1929, Henry Ford attended a testimonial dinner with about two thousand Jews in New York City celebrating the appointment of philanthropist David J. Brown, of Detroit, as chairman of the board of the Broadway National Bank. Ford did not speak, but issued a glowing statement likely written by Cameron.

> I am happy to come here tonight to pay tribute to my old friend David J. Brown and through him the great race which is proud and fortunate to count him among its own. David A. Brown is a shining example of the great benevolence of the Jewish people, their philanthropy, their eagerness to make this world better, to educate the untutored, to heal the sick, to care for the orphans; their intense and intelligent participation in all that makes for civic righteousness and social justice stamps them a great people – and David A. Brown is one of their finest sons.

---

199. *The New York Times,* July 18, 1927 at 16.

200. Ford made a point privately to colleagues that he never really apologized because Harry Bennett forged his name to the document.

The truce began to fray when, in the early 1930s, copies of *The International Jew* began sprouting up in Europe and South America. Liebold had, carefully, never bothered to obtain a copyright for the publication and had quietly encouraged its metastasis abroad. *The International Jew* was translated into sixteen different languages. A half-million copies circulated in the United States alone. Henry Ford's popularity and renown as an industrial genius and the "Great Simplifier" propelled a rapid and resilient worldwide interest in the most virulent and damaging anti-Semitic propaganda to ever rise out of the United States—with a sickening impact in Europe where it was used to incite the Holocaust. Some twenty-nine editions of the book were printed in Germany alone where, in some circles, it became mandatory reading. Ford, in the end, in the greater scheme of history, had his say.

Adolph Hitler admired Henry Ford greatly; Ford was the only American mentioned by Hitler in his book, *Mein Kampf*.[201] As early as 1923, Hitler had expressed his esteem for Henry Ford. When Hitler learned that Ford might run for President, he was quoted to say, "I wish I could send some of my shock troops to Chicago and other big American cities to help in the elections. . . . We look to Heinrich Ford as the leader of the growing fascist movement in America." A former Nazi, who later turned against the movement, relayed a conversation that he had with Hitler concerning *The Protocols of the Elders of Zion* as quoted in *The International Jew:*

> In those [early days] [of our movement] I read the *Protocols of the Elders of Zion* – I was really shocked. [said Hitler] The perilous stealth of the enemy, and his omnipresence. I saw at once that we would have to imitate this – in our own way of course.
>
> Don't you think, I objected, that you are overestimating the Jews?
>
> No, no, no! Hitler screamed. It is not possible to exaggerate the Jew as an enemy.

201. Houghton Mifflin & Co., Boston, 1943 at 639.

> But, [I said], the *Protocols* are an obvious forgery. I learned about them in 1920 from Muller von Hausen. And it was immediately evident to me that they could not possibly be genuine.
>
> Why not, [Hitler said, getting angry. Whether they were genuine in a historical sense was not the issue for him. Their inner truth was what made them so convincing.]
>
> We must strike at the Jews with their own weapons. That was clear to me as soon as I read the book.
>
> [I asked], Were you inspired by the *Protocols* in your [political] struggle?
>
> Yes, indeed, and in detail. I learned enormously from these *Protocols*.[202]

Baldus von Schirach, a leader of the Hitler Youth movement, testified as to the impact on him as a Nazi, when he first read *The International Jew*. "You have no idea what a great influence this book had on the thinking of German youth. The younger generation looked with envy to the symbols of success and prosperity like Henry Ford, and if he said the Jews were to blame, we naturally believed him."[203]

Efforts to pound a stake in the heart of *The International Jew* and the *Protocols* have been largely unsuccessful as copies are still generally available and there is always a surge in interest in them with every rise of populist fascism. Like the feather story in Alfred Lucking's closing argument in the *Chicago Tribune* trial—that libelous claims are like thousands of feathers cast to the wind, and it is impossible to recover them all—Henry Ford's lies and his libel of the Jewish race was outrageous, unprecedented and irredeemable.

Fawning flattery remained the one sure path to Henry Ford's

---

202. Levy, Richard S, Translator and Editor, Segel, Binjamin W., *A Lie and a Libel: The History of the Protocols of the Elders of Zion*, University of Nebraska Press, Lincoln and London, 1995 at 29-30.

203. Pool, James and Pool, Susan, *Who Financed Hitler: The Secret Funding of Hitler's Rise To Power*, Dial Press, 1978 at 90.

heart and attention. In 1938, on his seventy-fifth birthday, Ford happily accepted the Grand Cross of the German Eagle, an award created by Adolf Hitler and celebrated as the highest honor Nazi Germany could bestow upon a foreigner.[204] Jews and concerned Gentiles were aghast at pictures showing Ford in a white suit and sash receiving the medal from German Consuls Fritz Heiler and Karl Kapp. Liebold, several months later, also accepted a medal, The Order of Merit of the German Eagle, First Class. He dismissed public criticisms with his usual deaf ear: "For a nation of 70,000,000 to recognize the achievements of a man in another land seems to be an honor which cannot be disregarded or ignored. We have interests, physical, financial, and moral, which have taken many years to establish, and consequently such foundations cannot be uprooted overnight to comply with propaganda intended to arouse American sympathy."[205]

Ford's friend and former neighbor, Rabbi Leo M. Franklin, sought to quell the uproar in the Jewish community and thought he had obtained Ford's approval to issue a statement that read, "My acceptance of a medal from the German people does not, as some seem to think, involve any sympathy on my part with Nazism. Those who have known me for years realize that anything that breeds hate repulses me."[206]

Harry H. Bennett then cut the legs out from under Franklin's efforts by allowing Charles E. Coughlin, the demagogic, neo-fascist, radio priest in Detroit, to issue a sermon that disclosed that Franklin wrote the statement, not Ford, and that "Rabbi Franklin came to Ford to ask him if his factory would assimilate Jewish refugees, the result of Nazi persecution. Ford said that he believed there was little or no persecution in Germany; if any it was due not to the German Government but to the war mongers, the international bankers. Moreover, while Mr. Ford expressed his hu-

---

204. Benito Mussolini and Charles Lindbergh were two other recipients.

205. Lewis, supra, 150.

206. Ibid at 151.

manitarianism for people, yet he believed that Jews wouldn't be content to work in factories."[207]

Bennett, himself, described the reasons for Ford's acceptance of and refusal to return the award as "mulishness, ignorance and failure to understand." He also claimed that Ford thought the acceptance would annoy Franklin D. Roosevelt, whom Ford despised.[208] Ford's unapologetic behavior led to a widespread and costly boycott of Ford products by Jews and concerned Gentiles.

The start of World War II gave the opportunity for Edsel Ford to maneuver the Company into a better light. He set up a meeting between his father and Richard E. Gustadt, National Director of the B'nai B'rith Anti-Defamation League, whereafter Henry Ford issued a signed letter deploring "hate-mongering against the Jews."[209] Ford's signature was likely motivated more by practical necessity than heartfelt sincerity.

In May of 1945, while watching an unedited Russian film of the liberation of the Majdanek Death Camp near Lublin, Poland, seated at his own River Rouge Plant Auditorium, Henry Ford suffered a major stroke. The Majdenak extermination camp has been described, by its liberators, as the "most ghastly place on earth." The quickly advancing Russian Army reached Majdanek before the Nazis could destroy the evidence and the camp was perfectly preserved. On the day before the Russians arrived, July 16, 1944, the German's executed four hundred fifty people by close-range gunshots to the head. Their bodies were still lying around or partially cremated in the completely intact crematorium ovens. These gas chambers were fully preserved, where seventy-eight thousand victims, fifty-nine thousand of them Jews, were gassed to death using Zyklon B, a cyanide-based pesticide, and carbon monoxide. In one single day alone, November 3, 1943, eighteen thousand four hundred Jews died in the camp. Their

---

207. Id.

208. Bennett, supra, at 210.

209. Lewis, supra, at 153.

ashes were used to fertilize cabbage fields next to the dormitories.

Ford never fully recovered from the effects and disorientation of his stroke. His condition was a carefully guarded family secret, hidden from the public for the two remaining years of his life. In his confusion, he was said to have repeatedly asked, "Where is Harry? Hasn't he been here today. Why doesn't Harry come?"[210] He died on April 7, 1947, of a cerebral hemorrhage.

Henry Ford's family and the Ford Motor Company have been making amends ever since to the Jewish race and the Nation of Israel. The Ford Motor Company and the Ford Foundation arguably have done more for Jewish interests around the world and in Israel than any other private American enterprise. Henry Ford II, Ford's grandson, served as chairman of the National Conference of Christians and Jews, and the Ford Motor Company provided a million dollars toward the creation of its headquarters. Gifts to Yeshiva University, Hebrew University, Weizemann Institute of Science, and Albert Einstein Medical Center have been generous and potent. Henry Ford II, shouldering extreme criticism by countries of the Arab League and a heavy loss of their business, invested significant Ford assets in manufacturing facilities in Israel.

Yet the antipathy toward his grandfather by Jews remains strong. Said one,

> You ask me about my attitude toward Ford. I did have an unlimited hatred toward Henry Ford – that old ignorant hating bastard, who in my mind, was a vastly overrated genius, who cheated some of his early associates and by his conduct must have helped drive some of them to untimely graves, including his own son. But, certainly the grandsons have given every indication of making every effort to atone for the sins of that contemptible old bastard ignoramus. You may have gathered that I didn't like him.[211]

In the Bible it is said, "Who is this that darkeneth counsel by

---

210. Harry Bennett.

211. Lewis, supra, 159.

words without knowledge?"[212] Knowledge and empathy in our public life matter more today than ever, where lies and projections of "otherness" and hate toward our fellow humans seem to have become an accepted, even expedient routine, a customary way of doing business in a world where facts are dismissed as meaningless. Let us not forget Henry Ford and his legacy. Let us assist the long-lasting effects of acceptance, tolerance, and truth telling.

These are our armaments against hate and the dark fruits of narcissism.

---

212. Job, xxxvii, 2.

Epilogue

"Time Wounds All Heels"[213]

DESPITE HIS EXTRAORDINARY INDUSTRIAL success and his astronomic personal wealth, there was something missing at the core of Henry Ford's being. There was an itch he could not scratch, a fear he could not quell, a ring he could not reach. The void left him incomplete, with an epic lifelong struggle to gratify his need for constant, unalloyed public admiration and reverence. Even though he rose to become one of the most admired men on the planet and had his name stamped on hundreds of buildings, thousands of airplanes, and millions of automobiles, he harbored an unrequited longing for public recognition of the brilliance of his mind and the cunning of his thinking. All this, from a man who left school at age fourteen and could not read a blueprint.

Ford's lack of formal schooling, and the narrow focus of his self-education on the inorganic and mechanical, left him woefully inarticulate and insecure. Machines he could read and interpret with ease. People confounded him. Isolation and protection from unwarranted intrusion, by those who could solve the riddle of his vulnerability, became paramount to Ford's grab at happiness. Thus, he chose to channel his communications with the world through a small group of myrmidons. These "interpreters" of his thoughts followed Ford's orders and inclinations and sculpted and shaped his meandering musings into comprehensible and publishable missives.

213. John Lennon.

Ford's eloquence was not his own. Ford's ideas rose from a "25-track mind," most of them hashed and borrowed. Brutishness fueled his ascent and descent. Whether striving for world peace, the Presidency of the United States, or a faster assembly line speed, he sought salve to the wound at the center of his soul. He was a narcissist, plain and simple. Which led him to freeze out the quality of empathy from his being.

How many times will humankind be led into the future by a bully? Why do bullies draw us in so effectively? A prominent psychotherapist and expert on the condition of narcissism wrote, "The narcissist lives in a world populated by two classes of people, the winners and the losers. His constant aim in life is to prove he is a winner and to trump the losers."[214] For Henry Ford, the legal system offered the perfect win/lose arena.

Bullies with great wealth are primed to use the legal system and the courts as weapons with which to beat the losers. Justitia, the blindfolded woman who symbolizes justice, holds a set of scales in one hand and a two-edged sword in the other. The blindfold and the scales represent the unbiased and equal treatment of litigants before the law. The sword symbolizes power, protection, authority and reasoning under the law. In reality, a heavy hand of superior resources can tip one of the scales to skew the results and it takes an opponent of extreme courage to resist. Henry Ford first called upon the law to protect him and his company from the greedy and opportunistic wrath of the powerful ALAM Syndicate. He then endeavored to use the law as a shield to help him unfairly manipulate the assets, earnings and interests of the minority shareholders of the Ford Motor Company, all for his personal benefit. The Dodge Brothers penetrated the guise of his preposterous, altruistic cover. He then tried to use the law as a sword to punish the *Chicago Tribune*, a newspaper that affronted his personal dignity by calling him an "ignorant idealist" and

214. Burgo, Joseph, "All Bullies are Narcissists," *The Atlantic*, November 14, 2013.

an "anarchist." After spending a grotesque amount of money to shame a defendant who happily could and did defend itself, Ford damaged his reputation and humiliated himself in newspapers around the world. Finally, after spending over a million dollars to prove that his false anti-Semitic attacks on a Jewish lawyer were justifiable, he grew weak in the knees when he realized that his wealth and resources could not keep his vulnerability from being exposed again in court on the witness stand.

Give a narcissist myrmidons, money and power, and watch as the arrows fly backward into his camp. Ford's own newspaper, as much as his legal battles, served to do him in. His "America First" isolationism and xenophobic anti-immigrant Nativism are remarkably similar to a currency in vogue today. Spitting his own personal venom on those he wished to debase, Ford tried, as a sort of amoral outlaw, to fan the flames of division and sectarianism against an ancient and noble people, who at the time were ill-equipped to deflect the impact. Distrust and prejudice had followed all of their migrations. Thanks, in part, to Henry Ford's wide dissemination of bogus anti-Semitic plotting, their fate drove forward into terrible hands.

In the end, Henry Ford lacked the courage and resolve to stand by the appalling words he cast like goose feathers into the wind, allowing his phalanx of attorneys to present a fiction to the jury: that he was not personally aware of what his newspaper was printing, that he permitted subordinates to speak for him (and absorb all of the legal blame). Ford and his misanthropic cronies, Liebold and Cameron, failed to grasp the enormity of the harm they were unleashing when they unshackled fear and hate in that tinder box world of Biblical resentments.

The Holocaust had many supports; *The Protocols of the Elders of Zion,* published in Ford's *International Jew,* was one of them. One day in 1945, in the auditorium of the Rouge River Plant, the full effect of Ford's words finally landed on him. Facing the unadulterated black-and-white film horror of the forces he helped release in Germany, Henry Ford's brain stroked out. Josephine

Fellows Gomon was with him that day, and she marked the impact of the visual reality those pictures had on Ford,

If it is true, as the bitter enemies of Mr. Ford have said, that he was responsible for the racial hatred that brought Hitler to power, then Mr. Ford, himself, was killed by what he himself had created. The circle was complete.[215]

John Paul Sartre, the great French existentialist philosopher, reminds us that "Every word has consequences. Every silence too." It is certainly possible for a wealthy, narcissistic, demagogue to evade the personal consequences of imagined conspiracies, hate speech, and a misguided catalogue of lies, but there does seem to be some cosmic hand at play, some counterforce in the universe that quietly and unobtrusively arises to effect retributive justice for the world's bullies in the long run.

The problem is always how much damage can they do in the interim.

---

215. Gomon, Josephine Fellows, *Poor Mr. Ford,* (an unpublished manuscript) (undated), Bentley Historical Library, University of Michigan at 122. Gomon served as the Director of Woman's Policies at the Ford Willow Run bomber plant during World War II. Ms. Gomon's manuscript was originally discovered by Carol Gelderman and mentioned in her book *Henry Ford: The Wayword Capitalist*, supra, at xi-xii.

Acknowledgements

I WOULD LIKE TO express my appreciation for the love, support and encouragement of my wife, Tamara K. Vincelette, in my pursuit of the legal adventures of Henry Ford. My sister, Renee Van Assche and brother, Gordon Piché, read early drafts of the work and provided important comments and suggestions. My editor, novelist Barbara K. Richardson, was crucial to helping me to move the narrative of this story through the dusty bins of legal history and in supporting its merit.

I owe a great deal of thanks for their competence and assistance to the staffs of the Benson Ford Research Center in Dearborn, Michigan; the Burton Historical Collection and the National Automotive History Collection at the Detroit Public Library; the McCormick Archives of the First Division Museum in Wheaton, Illinois; the Bentley Historical Library of the University of Michigan in Ann Arbor, Michigan; and, the Meadowbrook Hall Archives, Oakland University, Rochester, Michigan.

Finally, I would like to thank my late grandfather, George W. Hergenroether, for his long – ago inside stories of the Dodge Brothers' adventures.

Bibliography

RESOURCES:

Benson Ford Research Center, Dearborn, Michigan.

Burton Historical Collection, Detroit Public Library, Detroit, Michigan.

National Automotive History Collection, Detroit Public Library (Skillman Library), Detroit, Michigan.

Bentley Historical Library, University of Michigan, Ann Arbor, Michigan.

Meadowbrook Hall Archives, Oakland, University, Rochester, Michigan.

The Detroit Jewish News Archives, University of Michigan, Ann Arbor, Michigan.

The McCormick Archives, "The Papers of Col. Robert R. McCormick," First Division Museum at Cantigny Park, Wheaton, Illinois.

Walter P. Reuther Library, Archives of Labor and Urban Affairs, Detroit, Michigan.

Library of Congress, Washington, D.C.

Hathitrust Digital Library.

AACA Library and Research Center, Hershey, PA.

BOOKS:

Avrich, Paul, *The Haymarket Tragedy*, Princeton University Press, Princeton, N.J., 1984.

Baime, A.J. *The Arsenal of Democracy: FDR, Detroit and an Epic Questto Arm America at War,* Houghton – Mifflin 2014.

Bak, Richard, *Henry and Edsel: The creation of the Ford empire, John Wiley and Sons, N.J. 2003.*

Baldwin, Neil, *Henry Ford and the Jews: The Mass Production of Hate,* Public Affairs, New York, *2003.*

Barendt, Eric, *Freedom of Speech*, Clarendon Paperbacks, Oxford University Press, Oxford. 1985.

Barnard, Harry, *Independent Man: The Life of Senator James Couzens*, Charles Scribners Sons, N.Y., 1958.

Bennett, Harry, *We never called him Henry*, (Greenwich: Fawcett, 1951.

Berlet, Chip and Lyons, Mathew N., *Right-Wing Populism in America: Too Close for Comfort.* The Guilford Press, New York & London. 2000.

Bernstein, Herman, *The History of a Lie: A Literary Forgery,* J.S. Olgivie, London, 1921.

Billstein, et al., *Working for the Enemy, Ford, General Motors and Force Labor in Germany During the Second World War*, Berghahn Books, N.Y., 2000.

Brexel, Bernadette, *The Knights of Labor and the Haymarket riot: The Fight for an Eight-Hour* Workday, The Rosen Publishing Company, N.Y., 2004.

Brinkley, Douglas. *Wheels for The World: Henry Ford, His Company, and a Century of Progress, 1903-2003.* Viking, N.Y. 2003.

Bryan, Ford R., *Clara: Mrs. Henry Ford,* (Ford Books, Dearborn, Michigan 2001.

Bryan, Ford r., *Henry's Lieutenants,* Wayne State University Press, 1993.

Bryan, Ford R., *The Fords of Dearborn*, Harlo Press, Detroit, 1989.

Bucci, Federico, *Albert Kahn: Architect of Ford,* Princeton Architectural Press, 2001.

Burton,(ed.), Clarence M.,: *The City of Detroit Michigan: 1701 – 1922,* The S.J. Clark Publishing Company, Chicago-Detroit, vols.1-5, 1922.

Carpenter, Rolla C., *Internal Combustion Engines, Their History Construction and Operation,* D.Van Norstand Company, N.Y. 1909.

Cohn, Norman, *Warrant for Genocide: The Myth of the World Conspiracy and the Protocols of the Elders of Zion,* Harper & Row, N.Y. 1969.

Collier, Peter and Horowitz, David, *The Fords: An American Dynasty*, Summit Books, N.Y., 1987.

Crabb Richard, *Birth of a Giant: The Men and Incidents that Gave America the Motorcar,* Chilton Book Company, Philadelphia, N.Y. and London, 1969.

Dinnerstein, *Anti-Semitism in America*, Oxford University Press, New York and Oxford, 1994.

Donovan Frank, *Wheels for a Nation,* Thomas Y. Crowell Company, 1965.

Editors of Automobile Quarterly, *The American Car Since 1775*, L. Scott Bailey, 1971.

Ervin, Spencer, *Henry Ford and Truman Newberry: The Famous Senate Election Contest: A Study in American Politics, Legislation and Justice*, R.R. Smith, N.Y. 1935.

Fireside, Byrna J., *The Haymarket Square Riot Trial: A Headline*

Court Case, Enslow Publishers, Inc., Berkley Heights, N.J and Aldershot, U.K. 200.

Fish, Frederick P., *Letters Patent: article from the Scientific American of September 27 and October 4, 1913, Read before the American Bar Association at Montreal, Canada, entitled " Letters Patent in relation to modern industrial conditions*, (Making of Modern Law, 1913).

Flink, James J., *The Automobile Age*, The MIT Press, Cambridge, MA 1988.

Ford, Henry, *The International Jew*, Dearborn Publishing Company, Dearborn, Michigan, 1920.

Ford, Henry, (with Samuel Crowther), *My Life and Work*, Doubleday Page & Co, N.Y., 1922.

Fox, Craig, *Everyday Klansfolk: White Protestant Life and the KKK in 1920s Michigan*, Michigan State University Press, East Lansing. 2011.

Galbraith, John Kenneth, *The Liberal Hour*, Houghton Mifflin, Boston, 1960.

Gelderman, Carol, *Henry Ford: The Wayward Capitalist*, St. Martin's Press, N.Y. 1981.

Gies, Joseph, *The Colonel of Chicago: A Biograph of the Chicago Tribune's Legendary Publisher, Colonel Robert McCormick*, E.P. Dutton, N.Y. 1979.

Goldstone, Lawrence, Birdmen, *The Wright Brothers, Glenn Curtiss, and the Battle to Control the Skies*, Ballantine Books, N.Y. 2014.

Goldstone, *Lawrence, Drive: Henry Ford, George Selden, and the Race to Invent the Auto Age*, Ballantine Books, N.Y., 2016.

Gomon, Josephine Fellows, *Poor Mr. Ford* (unpublished manusript) (undated), Bentley Historical Library, University of Michigan, Ann Arbor.

Graves, Phillip, *The Truth About the Protocols*, The Times Pub. Co., London, 1921.

Greenleaf, William, *Monopoly on Wheels: Henry Ford and the Selden Automobile Patent*, Wayne State University Press, Detroit, 2001.

Gunther, John, *Inside U.S.A.*, The New Press 1997.

Hill, Frank and Wilkins, Mira, *American Business Abroad: Ford on Six Continents*, Wayne State University Press, Detroit, 1964.

Hitler, Adolph, *Mein Kampf*, Houghton & Mifflin Co., Chicago,1943.

Hyde, Charles K., *Riding the Roller Coaster: A History of the Chrysler Corporation*, Wayne State University Press, Detroit, 2003.

Hyde, Charles K., *The Dodge Brothers, The Men, The Motor Cars, and the Legacy*, Wayne State University Press, Detroit, 2005.

Jardim, Anne, *A Study in Personality and Business Leadership: The First Henry Ford*; *A Study Business Leadership*, The Colonial Press, 1970.

Lacy, Robert, *Ford: The Men and the Machine*, Little Brown & Co., Boston and Toronto, 1986.

Lathem, Caroline and Agresta, David, *Dodge Dynasty*, Hart Brace and Janovich, N.Y. 1989.

Lee, Albert, *Henry Ford and the Jews*, Stein and Day, N.Y. 1980.

Leeland, Mrs. Wifred C. and Millbrook, Minnie Dubbs, Master of Precision: Henry M. Leland Wayne State University Press, 1966).

Leonard, Jonathan Norton, *The Tragedy of Henry Ford* G.P. Putnam's Sons, N.Y & London, 1932.

Lewis, David L., *The Public Image of Henry Ford: An American Folk Hero and His Company*, Wayne State University Press, Detroit, 1976.

Liebling, A.J., C*hicago the Second City*, University of Nebraska Press, Lincoln and London, 1952

Jonathon Norton Leonard, *The Tragedy of Henry Ford*, G.P. Putnam & Sons, NY & London 1932.

Madden, Jean and Elwart, Jean Potter, *The Dodges: The Auto Family Fortune and Misfortune,* Icarus Press, South Bend, Ind. 1981.

Marquis, Samuel S., *Henry Ford: An Interpretation,* (Wayne State University Press, Detroit, 1927).

Marx, Robert S., *Round the World with Stella: The story of a Journey over Seven Seas and Four Continents*, Johnson & Hardin, Cincinnati.

Maxim, Hiram Percy, *Horseless Carriage Days*, Dover, N.Y., 1962.

McManus, Theodore and Beasley, Norman, *Men, Money & Motors*, Harpers, N.Y. 1937.

Mecklin, John Moffat, *The Klu Klux Klan: A Study of the American Mind*, Harcourt Brace and Company, N.Y. 1924.

Merriwether, Lee, *Jim Reed, Senatorial Immortal: A Biography*, The International Mark Twain Society, Webster Groves, Mo 1944.

Miller, James Martin, *The Amazing Story of Henry Ford: The Ideal American And the Worlds's*

Most Famous Private Citizen, S.A. Mulliken Co., Cincinnati, Ohio, 1922.

Morgan, Gwen and Veysey, Arthur, *Poor Little Rich Boy (and how he made good): The Life and Times of Co. Robert R. McCormick*, Crossroads Communications, 1985.

Nevins, Allan, (with Hill, Frank E.) *Ford: The Times, The Man, The Company*, Scribners, N.Y. 1954.

Nevins, Allan and Hill, Frank Ernest, *Ford: Expansion and Challenge: 1915-1933*, Scribners, N.Y. 1957.

Nye, David E., *America's Assembly Line*, The MIT Press, Cambridge and London, 2013.

Pipp, Edwin Gustav, *The Real Henry Ford – Primary Source Edition*, Pipp's Weekly, Detroit, 1922.

Pomerantz, Gary M., The Devil's Tickets: A Vengeful Wife, A Fatal Hand, and a New American Age, Broadway Paperbacks, N.Y., 2009.

Pool, James & Pool, Susan, *Who Financed Hitler: The Secret Funding to Hitler's Rise to Power*, Dial Press, N.Y. 1978.

Pujo, Arsene, *Report of the Committee Appointed Pursuant to House Regulations 429 and 504 to Investigate the Concentration of Control of Money and Credit*, Government Printing Office, Washington, D.C. February 28, 1913.

Purdy, Ken W., *The Kings of the Road*, Little, Brown & CO., Boston, 1952.

Quaife, Milo M., The Life of John Wendell Anderson, Privately Printed, Detroit, 1950.

Rae, John Bell, ed., *Henry Ford*. Prentice Hall, Englewood Coffs, N.J., 1969.

Richards, William C., *The Last Billionaire Henry Ford*, Charles Scribner & Sons, N.Y., 1976.

Roosevelt, Theodore, *Autobiography*, Charles Scribner's & Sons, N.Y. 1927.

Seabrook, John, *Flash of Genius and other true stories of Invention*, St. Martin's –Griffin, N.Y.

Segel, Binjamin W., *A Lie and a Libel: The History of the Protocols of the Elders of Zion*, University of Nebraska Press, Lincoln and London, 1995, trans. Richard W. Levy.

Sinclair, Upton, *Flivver King: A Story of Ford America*, (Station A, Pasadena, 1937.

Smith, Richard Norton, T*he Colonel; The Life and Legend of Robert R. McCormick*, Houghton Mifflin Co., Boston and New York, 1997.

Snow, Richard, *I Invented the Modern Age: The Rise of Henry Ford*, Scribner, N.Y. and London, 2013.

Sorensen, Charles E., *My Forty Years with Ford*, Collier Books, N.Y., 1962.

Stevenson, *Elliot G., John F. Dodge and Horace E. Dodge, Plaintiffs and Appellees, vs. Ford Motor Company, Et. Al., Defendants and Appellants*, Making of Modern

Law, Plaintiff's Reply Brief, 1918.

Sward, Keith, *The Legend of Henry Ford*, Rinehart & Co, 1948.

The McCormick Tribune Foundation, *Robert R. McCormick: A Celebration of His Life and Legacy*, McCormick Tribune Foundation, 2005.

Tuchman, Barbara w., *The Zimmerman Telegram: American Enters the War, 1917-1918*. Random House Trade Paperbacks, N.Y. 2014.

Veenswijk, Virginia Kays, *Coudert Brothers: A Legacy in Law*, Truman Talley Books/Dutton, N.Y. 1994.

Waldrop, Frank C., McCormick of Chicago: An Unconventional Portrait of a Controversial Figure. Prentice-Hall, Englewood, N.J., 1966.

Wallace, Max, *The American Axis: Henry Ford, Charles Lindbergh and the Rise of the Third Reich.* St. Martins Press, N.Y., 2003.

Watts, Steven, *The People's Tycoon: Henry Ford and The American Century*, Vintage Books, N.Y. 2006.

Wendt, Loyd, *Chicago Tribune: The Rise of Great American Newspaper*, Rand McNalley and Company, Chicago, New York and San Francisco. 1979.

Wik, Reynold M., *Henry Ford and Grass Roots America*, The University of Michigan Press, Ann Arbor. 1972.

Woeste, Victoria Saker, *Henry Ford's War on Jews: and the Legal Battle Against Hate Speech.* Stanford University Press, Stanford, California, 2012.

PERIODICALS:

Bosworth, David. "Idiot Savant: Henry Ford as Proto-Post Modern Man, *Georgia Review*, 54 no.1 (Spring 2000: 11-39).

Burgo, Joseph, "All Bullies are Narcisscists," *The Atlantic,* November 14, 2013.

Couzens, James, "What Learned About Business from Ford," *System: The Magazine of Business,* September, 21, 1921.

Hough, Charles Merrill, "Concerning Lawyers," The Ohio State University Law Journal1, 6-7, December, 1938.

Larsen, Grace & Erdman, Henry E., "Aaron Sapiro: Genius of Farn Cooperative Promotion, The Missouri Valley Historical Review, September, 1962.

PIPP, E. G. "Ford's Recantation Analyzed," *The American Hebrew, (Vol. 121, Issue 10,* 347, July 15, 1927.

Pipp, E. G. "About Ford and Benedict Arnold," (*Pipp's Weekly,* Vol. II –No. 26, 1-5 October 15, 1921).

Rae, John Bell, "The Electric Vehicle Company: A Monopoly that Missed," *Business History Review 29*, no. 4 (December, 1955):298-311.

Reed, John, "What About Mexico" *Masses,* June, 1914.

Ribuffo, Leo R., "Henry Ford and The International Jew," (*American Jewish History,* Vol. 69, No. 4, June, 1980, 437-477).

Rockaway, Robert, "Anti-Semitism in an American City: Detroit 1850 – 1914," *American Jewish Historical Quarterly*, Vol. 64,

No. 1, Sept., 1967, 43-54).

The American Hebrew, Michigan Jewish History.

OTHER:

Barthel, Oliver E, *Reminescences* (oral history) Benson Ford Research Center, Dearborn, Michigan.

Black, Fred L., *Reminescences* (oral history) Benson Ford Research Center, Dearborn, Michigan.

Klann, W.C., *Reminescences* (oral history) Benson Ford Research Center, Dearborn, Michigan.

Liebold, Ernest G., *Reminescences* (oral history) Benson Ford Research Center, Dearborn, Michigan.

Waddell, W.H., *Reminescences* (oral history) Benson Ford Research Center, Dearborn, Michigan.

Wollering, Max F., *Reminescences* (oral history) Benson Ford Research Center, Dearborn, Michigan.